Anti-Colonial Theory
and Decolonial Praxis

This book is part of the Peter Lang Education list.
Every volume is peer reviewed and meets
the highest quality standards for content and production.

PETER LANG
New York • Bern • Frankfurt • Berlin
Brussels • Vienna • Oxford • Warsaw

Anti-Colonial Theory and Decolonial Praxis

Edited by George J. Sefa Dei
and Meredith Lordan

PETER LANG
New York • Bern • Frankfurt • Berlin
Brussels • Vienna • Oxford • Warsaw

Library of Congress Cataloging-in-Publication Data
Names: Dei, George J. Sefa (George Jerry Sefa), editor.
Title: Anti-colonial theory and decolonial praxis /
edited by George J. Sefa Dei, Meredith Lordan.
Description: New York: Peter Lang, 2016.
Includes bibliographical references.
Identifiers: LCCN 2016014962 | ISBN 978-1-4331-3388-6 (hardcover: alk. paper)
ISBN 978-1-4331-3387-9 (paperback: alk. paper) | ISBN 978-1-4539-1857-9 (ebook pdf)
ISBN 978-1-4331-3554-5 (epub) | ISBN 978-1-4331-3555-2 (mobi)
Subjects: LCSH: Decolonization—Cross-cultural studies.
Anti-imperialist movements—Cross-cultural studies.
Classification: LCC JV51 .A67 2016 | DDC 325/.301—dc23
LC record available at https://lccn.loc.gov/2016014962

Bibliographic information published by **Die Deutsche Nationalbibliothek**.
Die Deutsche Nationalbibliothek lists this publication in the "Deutsche
Nationalbibliografie"; detailed bibliographic data are available
on the Internet at http://dnb.d-nb.de/.

The paper in this book meets the guidelines for permanence and durability
of the Committee on Production Guidelines for Book Longevity
of the Council of Library Resources.

© 2016 Peter Lang Publishing, Inc., New York
29 Broadway, 18th floor, New York, NY 10006
www.peterlang.com

Printed in the United States of America

Table of Contents

Introduction

Envisioning New Meanings, Memories and Actions for Anti-Colonial Theory and Decolonial Praxis

GEORGE J. SEFA DEI AND MEREDITH LORDAN

Anti-colonialism is often taken up in the same breath with post-colonialism. There has been an unfortunate tendency to conflate the two frameworks. However, these frameworks are not the same. This book begins with the understanding of anti-colonialism as a continuous process of challenging colonial and neo-colonial legacies, relations and power dynamics, taking up the subject of anti-colonial praxis and its specific implications—the larger questions of schooling and education in global and, particularly, diasporic contexts. Even though we live in an era characterized by the "independence" of Lands once held by the most influential (largely European) colonial powers, this book takes the position that this era is still perpetuating colonial vestiges. From the promotion of the continued occupation of Indigenous Lands, English as a second language to the marginalization of Indigenous knowledges, topics considered in this collection, colonization endures. The goal is to re-theorize the *anti-colonial* for the *decolonial* projects of transforming schooling and education, defined broadly. Anti-colonial praxis is deeply implanted in the ways we transform our political, economic, cultural and school systems. In rethinking these systems in an era remarkably different in its celebration of difference and diversity, it is important for critical scholarship to broach some key questions: How do we theorize education within the context of the colonial, colonized relations and the aftermath? How are the experiences of Indigeneity, migration, post-migration, agency, resistance and the reclamation of multiple identities and representations informing our understandings of the colonized subject? How do our differences, multiplicities, ambivalences and contingencies shape educational practice? Answers are not easily forthcoming. Resisting the monolithic construction of the (white) settler and settled Lands, anti-colonial theory invites us, as social agents, to inhabit these multiple ways of being *and* being seen. Contesting long-standing power hierarchies and definitions of identity, race and culture, this collection asks readers to enter a wide range of anti-colonial contexts, from Somalia to Canada, and, in so doing, to consider their own identities and complicities.

This edited collection re-theorizes and reframes both anti-colonial and decolonial theories from the multiple perspectives of contributors currently engaged in anti-colonial education. In pointing to the possibilities of critical education for contemporary learners, the book considers how these learners can simultaneously embrace and challenge their—and our, we are learners as well—colonial investments through anti-colonial educational praxis. The anti-colonial stance is about our praxis as learners seeking to transform our subjectivities, creating ourselves from history, culture and Indigeneity. While we must acknowledge the fluid nature of identity, we need anti-colonial perspectives that also complicate the shiftiness of the interstitial in-between spaces. Being a "universal learner" is not the same as being without roots or culture. Without a firm cultural rootedness, some type of epistemological anchorage, colonial modernity would only ensure that all learners simply embrace Western culture with an inferiority complex. The hegemonic production of Western epistemologies, evidenced by the dominance of Eurocentric curricula in colonies around the world, the ubiquitous use of the English language and the systematic silencing and erasure of many Indigenous cultures and knowledges perpetuate this sense of inferiority today.

The book highlights some key questions:

- How do we theorize anti-colonial and decolonial perspectives as lenses through which to interpret and understand the history of colonized, racialized, immigrant and Indigenous peoples' narratives, myths, spirituality and cosmogonies?
- How do we understand the anti-colonial moment?
- How and where does the anti-colonial moment locate within the epistemological, cosmological, ontological, ethical and aesthetical?
- With colonial and colonizing attempts to define what it is to be Indigenous/black/racialized, as bodies traveling over borders and continents, what does it mean to be Indigenous/black/racialized in a white dominant society?
- How do we account for the disruption and silencing of Indigenous identities as forms of knowing what it means to be human?
- How does the anti-colonial perspective allow us to challenge the existence of the Indigenous as a product of European invention?

- What are the consequences of the colonial and colonized subjects negotiating their ways into "Western modernity" through a refashioning or even shunning of their pasts?

Beyond serving as broad meditations on power imbalances, these questions offer structural frames through which to consider the replication of Western colonization, the impact of this dominance and its implications for racialized communities.

Dei (2016, in press) notes that many have mimicked Western intellectual traditions when theorizing about our identities and subjectivities in the vein of social theory. Homi Bhabha's (1994) conceptions of hybridity, particularly its exploration of in-between-ness and liminal spaces, are key aspects of textuality theory. The theory is relevant but only to a point when it comes to understanding colonized experience in white contexts. Bhabha's post-colonial theorizing is useful, but limited, as it relates to the question of "elite culture and power" and, particularly, the dynamics of the oppressed social and political ecologies when read across time and history. Identity and subjectivity cannot be discursively engaged or seen simply as part of a "cultural discourse." For example, there is a materiality to blackness, brownness, Indigeneity, mixed-race identities and racial 'Otherness' in the white-dominated global society, one with real social, economic, political and educational consequences. The anti-essentialist character of post-colonial theorizing ends up being equally essentialist, unable to escape from what one sets out to critique. The powerful "discourses of language" and "cultural identity" do not fully capture the relations between the experiences of colonized and Indigenous bodies in Euro-American contexts.

The self-other binary invites us as critical anti-colonial theorists to inhabit the hybrid spaces, the ones that defy the simple settler-colonizer analyses. These are the *spaces of praxis* wherein the "otherness of hybridity" is used as an instrument of identity and political mobilization. Marginalized and silenced knowledges and cultures may reclaim their agency, with otherness as a central catalyst for mobilization. Lordan (2013) observes that theory and politics, as sites of political engagement within a global change era characterized by multilateral agreements, ranging from climate change to sustainability measures, require praxis. All too often, however, there is a denial of the *deep recognition* of marginalized communities within these quantitative measurements and the accompanying international agreements. It is a false separation to claim an existential opposition between them. We must understand that there is a conjunction of theory and practice that manifests itself in the everyday material lives of colonized and oppressed peoples around the globe.

In complicating the long-standing perspectives of the imposed and dominating, this book attempts to move the narrative from one of control and power to a conversation about resistance and the rupturing of established colonial and colonizing practices. This book examines the nature of Indigeneity in its own terms through discreet, yet thematically connected, chapters that speak to the uniqueness of resistance in various global contexts. There are many takes on anti-colonial, with the concept of anti-colonial itself being contested. In fact, some seek to conflate anti-colonial and decolonial theory and practice, while others make distinctions. 'Anti-colonial' brings an action-oriented stance, one that is beyond theorizing. Dei (2013) points to the understanding of the anti-colonial as being tied to questions of Land, Indigeneity, local cultures, knowledge and spiritual ontology. These important markers distinguish the 'anti-colonial' from the colonial. The anti-colonial manifests itself as staunchly opposed to 'colonial'—which is anything that is "imposed and/or dominating" and not simply "foreign and alien" (Dei, 2000; Dei & Asgharzadeh, 2001). The processes and histories of Euro-coloniality raise some important questions for anti-colonial practice.

Colonialism has its roots in European expansionism and imperial conquest, and these are by no means concluded. Colonialism today manifests itself in variegated forms, from the dominance of the English language to the rise of the (often Western) transnational state and global capitalism. While we acknowledge the multiple forms and varied contexts of colonialism and colonial practices, we also maintain a historical genesis that roots colonialism in Euro-coloniality and racism. Notwithstanding our multiple implications in colonial projects and the fact that we all have colonial investments that we protect, the colonial dominant is intertwined with whiteness. Discourses of plurality, wherein we equally share in the blames and atrocities of colonial histories, ignore how all of us may be implicated to varying degrees in the genocides of Indigenous peoples globally, European imperial conquest and Land dispossession, cultural annihilation and enslavement.

Colonial practices and colonial relations have international reach. A genuine anti-colonial practice seeks to subvert the colonial and colonizing tendencies of the dominant and marginalized when they take on the tropes of colonizer. Emerging understandings and theorizing must reconfigure coloniality in order to bring international perspectives and dimensions to both decolonial and anti-colonial politics. Similarly, as Smith (2006, 2010) notes, the complex and varied aspects of colonialism mean that our understandings of coloniality must be reconfigured to ask, What are the practices of coloniality today that can be determined within our institutions? How do we account for the continued sway of such practices of coloniality? What is the logic of coloniality?

Central to the preceding questions and possible responses is the inherent dominance of particular bodies, histories and practices. This is the logic of coloniality. Moving beyond the dynamic of the colonizer and the colonized, the colonial project is ongoing and unending. Settler sovereignty, often without naming its inherent whiteness, has proceeded by incorporating Aboriginal and non-Indigenous bodies into Western models of citizenship. Matrilineal societies, the use of ritual as an extension of the body and the transmission of cultural knowledge through Elders are often omitted from these citizenship models.[1] We account for the failure of the logic of settler colonialism in the unfinished business of trying to subvert all colonized bodies and their histories into a dominant narrative or even colonized bodies partaking of a politics of difference that weakens their solidarities against the Euro-dominant (see Dei 2016, in press). Rather than building communities and solidarities, many colonized bodies often spend tremendous efforts either occupying the space of innocence or claiming how our own colonial oppressions are more foundational to understanding global anti-colonial struggles. The colonized cannot negate or deny their histories, the nature and extent of power relations and the power of cultural memories as we seek collective anti-colonial resistance. We must know what we are doing and at whose bidding our cause serves. Energies are used more effectively when colonized peoples devote their energies to examining alternative counter claims and assertions of Indigenous sovereignty, learning from the lessons of coalition politics and cross-community alliances. Of course, there are different, alternative and counter articulations of sovereignty, Land and culture that are anti-colonial, but even inhabiting these intellectual spaces of difference offers up the possibility for new forms of praxis.

The urgency of the anti-colonial practice can be traced to some disturbing trends in the contemporary era, particularly with respect to the emergence of homogenizing capitalism. The mobility of labour and capital factors in the colonized, oppressed and Indigenous experiences across transnational spaces. Drawing from Bhabha (1994), claims of hybridity must be critically examined in relation to the 'third space,' as racialized bodies are both seen and come to see themselves in the contexts of their blackness/Indigeneity/brownness/racial Otherness and the global political economy. Any intellectual placement in the so-called third space must allow for aligning the practice of global capitalism with neo-colonialism.

The coloniality of education in the context of a global capitalist modernity raises critical concerns about the survival of Indigeneity. The hegemony of free markets, deregulation, competition, individualism, privatization and a restrictive definition of education serve corporate market interests and can reduce shared local, particularly Indigenous, knowledge. Drawing from Mundy (2008) and Quijano (2007), we see the emergence of a transnational knowledge economy that resists the localization and rootedness of Indigenous knowledge, unless such knowledge might be commodified through the appropriation of Indigenous Lands, resources and epistemologies.[2] The selling of knowledge for economic gain, often a process considered to be separate from the pricelessness and inherent value of cultural knowledge, is viewed as an economic benefit, a profitable venture; however, such commodification has the potential to erode further efforts of cultural resistance.

With class and gender-based privileges being intertwined with the market economy, we see their impact in the academy, especially in terms of how higher education rewards the proximity to the West and its influence. The characterization of alternatives to neo-liberalism and its educational agenda is often presented as anti-intellectual or economically irresponsible. Possibilities of decolonized education are not discussed or openly welcomed in many of our educational institutions. With the emergence of the transnational knowledge economy, the local, specific and Indigenous are often forfeited in the pursuit of economic advantage. Consequently, not much work has gone into the counter-visioning of education. This counter-visioning offers the intellectual space for Indigeneity to emerge as a site of authentic knowledge production and protection. We must be receptive to a space of critical, often uncomfortable, questioning of knowledge. Critical anti-colonial education for learners needs to be posited to help foster a strong sense of identity, self and collective agency and empowerment to communities. How have Indigenous forms of knowledge been taken up as alternatives or complements to Western/conventional approaches to schooling, learning and education? Rather than a challenge to the creation of new forms of learning, this question provokes introspection by both advocates and opponents, offering a source of robust dialogue.

Noting how hegemonic forms of education are taken up as examples of "development," this discourse reifies "democracy," "good governance," "human rights" and "development" in the contexts of the free market and capitalism (Dei, 2013). Rather than ask questions about what types of education should be pursued and the radical possibilities for change, education is simply seen as a core avenue for "global redistributive justice" (Mundy, 2008). Education plays a key role in these retributive efforts, especially in terms of the literacy of women and girls as a source of personal agency and social justice, but critical questions need to be asked about the content, nature and implications of this education. What type of education? What form should such education take and how? For example, we do not want to suggest that English-language instruction should be removed from all educational efforts, but how might Indigenous languages play key roles as part of this educational mandate? What voices are being unheard in a Westernized development curriculum, and what are the implications of this silence? Asking these questions moves us from a defensive position of silencing to a dialogue about the place of various languages and forms of local knowledge within educational and development projects.

Just as English is problematized, there is also the dismissal of the anti-development thesis: the idea that *development*, as we know it, is part of the problem. Conventional "development" is defined in terms of what people lack or what we are expected to become—a "catching up" to Western measures of development and economic sustainability. We need to reframe measures of development to include indices that are locally defined and determined by Indigenous peoples' aspirations, needs and concerns, all within an ecologically sustainable manner and within the prism of respect for social justice, equity and fundamental rights and freedoms. It is only by pursuing an anti-colonial reading of development that such counter-voices can gain legitimacy. Lordan (2013) observes that this pushing back against Western measures of development is evidenced by increasing activism, including the use of effective social media campaigns, to challenge the denial of Indigenous voices and approaches to development and sustainability. Silence is no longer an option, as Indigenous groups who feel excluded from official policy dialogues are using social testimony and protest to advance their causes. Effective and engaged anti-colonial theory and decolonial praxis require us, as researchers, allies, observers and social agents, to reconsider how the space of social change is being occupied.

Anti-colonial praxis is itself a type of pushing back against the politics of knowledge subversion and the politics of refusing to accept the current norms. There is no single model of anti-colonial praxis. If we accept that colonialism is varied and operates in different contexts, then our responses have to be multiple, and we are obliged to acknowledge the inherent tensions between competing visions of anti-colonialism. We must appreciate the diversity of Indigenous anti-colonial responses. We must understand the nature of colonial impositions and Indigenous struggles and resistances in order to know both the colonial and anti-colonial moments. The Indigenous can be questioned in our anti-colonial practices. What does it mean to disavow 'Indigenous' because it is contentious and tension filled? How do we read 'Indigenous' from the subaltern and not the dominant position? Sometimes a resistance to anti-colonial praxis comes with a de-legitimation of the knowledges of the colonized. It is a popular refrain to insist that anti-racism work must acknowledge and go beyond these categories of race, gender, class, sexuality and (dis)ability. What does going beyond the categories mean? What are we afraid of? Are the categories the problem, or are the meanings placed on these categories the real challenges? As we embrace questions of identity, we must be conscious of the ways individualism and competitiveness come up against discourses of relations and relationality. To see relationality as with/among peoples, the Land and the metaphysical world, there is the power of racial codes and colonial discourses that inform these codes. There is the need to separate or disentangle Indigenous articulations of 'Aboriginality' or 'Indigeneity' and the dominant articulations or conceptions of Aboriginalism/Indigenous, including calls for Indigenous resistance as opposed to tropes of primitivity and authenticity that can be accorded to the Indigenous.

We need to rethink the anti-colonial discourse by troubling our articulations of modernity and Eurocentric knowledge. Western discourses are relevant but woefully inadequate to understand the complexities of human experience and history. There is the need to decolonize Western epistemologies and the canons. As critical anti-colonial scholars, we cannot appeal to liberal articulations of justice and diversity. We must be asking new questions. This is the importance of grounding our scholarship in subaltern perspectives and the epistemic traditions of knowledge of the colonized/oppressed/Indigenous peoples. Anti-colonial projects need to be subjected to a critical interrogation, including nation-building and nationalist projects that are oppressive of women and other marginalized groups. A differentiated approach to theorizing the anti-colonial moment, one that accounts for the multiplicity of perspectives, presence and diversity even in neo-liberal contexts, considers and theorizes the multiple modes of colonization: colonial presence, influence, occupation *and* resistance.

The link between Indigeneity and anti-colonialism cannot be assumed but must be theorized. There was a world before European colonization. European colonization is not the end, nor the beginning, of history. Indigeneity allows us to think through options, possibilities and limitations. Something different is possible when thinking through Indigenous openings and counter possibilities. Indigeneity is about an identity and the process of becoming/being (Dei, in press). For colonized bodies there is the importance of asserting our Indigenous presence everywhere. We must raise questions about how Indigeneity is being theorized, and how the demarcations of race, gender, class, sexuality, disability, culture and history are accounted for in such theorization. In effect, we must bring complex meanings and readings to Indigeneity. We must also work with how Indigenous scholars are theorizing Indigeneity. Questioning culture, tradition and histories is a critical pursuit, enabling us to evoke culture in complicated ways. Situating Indigeneity in anti-colonial politics allows us to separate Indigenous understandings of the 'Indigenous/Indigeneity' from dominant/racist/colonial conceptions of the term while rejecting romanticized, mythologized versions. We must also re-conceptualize our understandings of Indigeneity as far more complex, going beyond 'Nativism' and the relations of Land. There is a co-implication of Land and race, as well as sexuality, gender, class, (dis)ability, religions and linguistic differences, in discussions of Indigeneity and Indigenous resistance and resurgences. The anti-colonial theorist must embrace all of these subjectivities as part of the political project of praxis.

Land and decolonization struggles are central to theorizing the anti-colonial. Land is a place of coming to know and experience connections with others in our worlds. Claiming Land, capitalized here as an epistemic assertion of its salience, is an assertion of selfhood and collective identity. Land also constitutes a basis of onto-epistemological existence and pursuing strategies of resistance and anti-colonial politics. The claims we make over Land must allow for alternative forms of sovereignty that are neither state- nor citizenship-based. Indigeneity and the question of Land are significant unifiers of the colonial encounter and experience for Indigenous and colonized peoples. As Dei (2016) concedes, it is always important when engaging in political struggles everywhere to recognize Lands on which we stand and work in solidarity with Indigenous peoples. However, claims to Land do not operate with hegemonic orthodoxies or from a hegemonic knowledge base.

We must bring multiple readings of the relations to Land so as to trouble and complicate hegemonic claims to the primacy of the settlement of stolen Lands as a starting point for all decolonial/anti-colonial engagements. While Land is sacred and revered by Indigenous peoples, it is also important to understand Land as a site of violence, pain and suffering. We must challenge ongoing racial and colonial displacements that implicate questions of Land and race. Land and racial dispossessions are intertwined. The dispossession of Indigenous Lands everywhere is intertwined with racial, gender, (dis)ability, class and sexual politics. Our categories are co-constitutive, so one cannot position race against Land. Quijano's (2000) "coloniality of power" conception cites race as a fundamental organizing principle structuring the multiple and varied hierarchies of the global system (see also Grosfuguel, 2007, p. 217). We see in colonial power the way race, including its unspoken whiteness, organizes our worlds.

Dei (2016) challenges us to pause and ask, Why do many black/African and other Indigenous bodies react differently to their designation as "settlers" on stolen Aboriginal Lands? Is it simply a question of denial of complicity or the erasing of innocence? In Canada, while recognizing the specificity of Indigenous realties of colonialism and external settlers, our anti-colonial struggles must be informed and guided by the prospects for decolonized solidarity. Questions about colonial/racial displacements, Euro-colonial and imperial pre-occupation of African soils and the impoverishment of black neighborhoods cannot be dismissed lightly. Negating such concerns is tantamount to racism. We should be able to grasp Land, and the complexity of human relations to the Land, so as to begin to push ourselves to a state of decolonized imaginations and relationships. Solidarity among colonized peoples is about building collective hopes and futures. There are dangers of collapsing the paradigm of hope and optimism, rendering it an exercise in futility or rhetorical escapism. For colonized and oppressed peoples, hope and the ability to envision new political, social and economic possibilities are critically important. We must nurture our hopes and dreams while embracing imaginings and possibilities.

Decolonization must be broader than simply being about relations to the Land. Questions of materiality and ontology go hand in hand. One of the major problems is the subjectification of Indigenous and colonized bodies and how these constitute significant aspects of educational practice. In questioning how the subjects are seen, along with how they see themselves, anti-colonial practice creates a critical dynamic between fixed colonial definitions and emergent anti-colonial ones. Tuck and Yang (2012) point to the importance of going beyond decolonization of the curriculum and schools. Decolonization is much more and implicates the Land in significant and fundamental ways. As a site of identity and culture, the Land is a salient educational space. Reconnecting to the Land and learning the stories therein are valuable tools for decolonization. Operating both formally and informally, officially and unofficially, these education sites provide spaces for the comparison of colonial and anti-colonial definitions to emerge. As part of these educational practices, there is the importance of reclaiming Indigenous traditions and histories as a continuity of past, present and future. For example, Fanon (2004) speaks of the colonizer's distortion of the Indigenous/colonized past. Should the colonized arrest this distortion and resist such amputation? Reclaiming Indigenous cultures as a way of life transcends the material and technological, encompassing metaphysical, spiritual, economic and social conditions. Transcendence creates spaces for exploration and possibility.

This collection explores decolonial struggle and anti-colonial praxis in a wide range of theoretical and geographic terrains with context-specific analyses, including Somalia, Nigeria, the African diaspora, Palestine, St. Vincent and Canada. These diverse perspectives offer multiple contexts for the exploration of anti-colonialism as both theory and praxis, inviting readers, whose own complicity is questioned, to consider how theory and praxis operate within the power dynamics of the diaspora. Colonial legacies endure, but they are challenged through these examples of praxis.

Challenging the hegemonic notions of the settler and the settled, mixed-raced theory creates a critical space for the re-engagement of the subject of colonization and the agent within anti-colonial politics. In Chapter 1, Emily A. Moorhouse begins by questioning the nature of mixed-race studies. Moorhouse uses anti-colonial and feminist theories, particularly within colonial-settler states, to raise questions about race and mixed-race identities. The discussion raises doubts about the usefulness of post-colonial and cultural studies and their inability to articulate the ways black and Indigenous bodies are related to, defined by and legally connected to Land. Challenging celebratory multicultural narratives of mixed race, along with the "settler move to innocence" (Tuck & Yang, 2012) and its inherent colour blindness, the discussion outlines ways to re-politicize mixed-race identities while working to undo anti-blackness and neo-colonial violence.

Continuing the theoretical analysis, Yessica D. Rostan invites readers to participate in a fundamental theoretical shift in Chapter 2, moving from the colonial distinction between the settler-as-self and the colonial-as-Land. Rostan outlines a study of *humxn* nature. Contesting the limiting Eurocentric notion of biology, the discussion sees the intersection of human-and-nature—*humxn* nature—as a framework for new formations of anti-colonial connections between self and Land. Acknowledging the growing global dialogue about sustainability, new forms of individual-collective and natural-human relations may emerge. Especially during an era concerned about global warming and the necessity of effective environmental stewardship, these new possibilities create theoretical and political spaces for inclusive anti-colonial relationships and negotiations.

In Chapter 3, Christopher L. Cully deepens the theoretical analysis with an exploration of the discussion between anti-colonial theory and anarchist theory. Because these are often misunderstood by the mainstream media and popular discourse, particularly anarchist theory, Cully traces these theories' central tenets. Cully notes the contested state as a point of convergence for both theories, offering a place for the negotiation of new models of political organization and pedagogy. Informed by Frantz Fanon, Taiaiake Alfred, Richard Day and Mikhail Bakunin, anarchist theory is considered a possible ally to anti-colonial theory in their shared social critiques.

With the preceding theoretical analyses offering frameworks for analysis, in Chapter 4 umar umangay asks readers to consider how subjects of colonization are seen by themselves and by the colonial legacies surrounding them. Engaging in a reflexive study of the understanding of identity, umangay grounds theory as part of Aboriginal cultural expression and self-identification. The chapter considers the quantitative data and qualitative lived experiences emerging from the 1991 Aboriginal Peoples Survey. This Canadian survey is significant for the importance of its social legacy, especially its construction of Aboriginal identity and related cultural processes. The chapter examines how the colonized and post-colonized bodies are seen and unseen, both in 1991 and beyond, offering implications for Aboriginal education training policies, the development of teacher candidates and how data are produced and consumed by Aboriginal communities.

Extending the pedagogical analysis of the interplay of culture, Land, indigeneity, power and identity, in Chapter 5 Cristina Jaimungal explores the construction and colonial legacy of whiteness within the context of English as a Second Language instruction. English is a dominant colonial language, and Jaimungal exposes the link between teaching English as a Second Language and its intrinsic connection to whiteness. Using African Indigenous perspectives on the question of language, especially the work of Achebe, Chow, Dei, Fanon and wa Thiong'o, Jaimungal considers whiteness and claims to linguistic legitimacy. Contextualizing the discussion within UNESCO's influential *Education for All Global Monitoring Report*, the author reveals the *race to whiteness* as part of a global educational agenda, denying opportunities to consider varying approaches to education for all. Challenging the racialized structure of English language education, the chapter offers strategies to resist this inherent racism and to reclaim a truly diverse, inclusive understanding of education for all as theory and praxis.

Moving from UNESCO's national and international influence, in Chapter 6 Muna-Udbi Abdulkadir Ali invites readers to enter the realm of the nation-state. Ali resists prevailing constructions of Somalia as a failed state, positing new ways to make meaning from nationhood. Contesting the notion of a failed state as an extension of privileged Western experiences, the author, informed by the work of Wai and Hill, uses an anti-racist methodological approach and an anti-colonial theoretical framework to challenge failed state discourses. Using the Republic of Somalia as its focus, the discussion questions the hegemonic Eurocentric state model. This rupturing of the failed state creates spaces in which to rethink statehood.

Exploring how statehood and identity are culturally negotiated, especially in the context of the post-independence period, Chizoba Imoka examines cultural identification and preservation in Nigeria through the voices of its youth in Chapter 7. Imoka creates a space wherein these voices reveal some of the tensions between different ethnic groups. Highlighting the colonizing experiences of students in private Nigerian secondary schools, education is shown to use colonizing logic, including the marginalization of some minority ethnic groups and dismissal of Indigenous knowledge in favor of Western epistemology. The performance of Nigerian identity is contested, read through the varying layers of ethnic and epistemic privilege. Noting a pedagogical possibility, the chapter offers suggestions to honor a wider range of voices and experiences.

Writing in Chapter 8, Annette Bazira-Okafor moves from the negotiation of nationhood and national identity to the African diaspora. Bazira-Okafor considers the place of hip hop as a site for identity negotiation and resistance for African diasporic youth. Many young people of African descent, including migrant youth and first generation youth in Canada, appropriate hip hop as a tool of resistance. Hip hop provides an accessible cultural space within which to articulate and explore identity. Referencing such artists as Arami The Corrector, Eddy Kenzo and K'naan, the discussion examines how these artists use local Indigenous histories and experiences to inform their work. The cultural act of hip hop expression creates the possibility for anti-colonial praxis. Advocating the educational merits of this expression, the chapter offers such suggestions for pedagogical growth as student and teacher exchange programs and the inclusion of rap as a form of black cultural resistance within the curriculum.

Extending the discussion of Indigenous communities in Africa, in Chapter 9 Suleyman M. Demi examines coalition building for decolonization struggles. Inspired by effective environmental protection coalitions, Demi considers how Indigenous and black communities might participate in coalitions for decolonization. Using anti-colonialism as the theoretical basis, this chapter considers "settler" and "settlerhood" in the North American context, outlining a shared ontology that makes these groups interconnected through similar, though not identical, histories and struggles. Practical examples of coalition building in Canada and the United States are cited.

Writing in Chapter 10, Mischa Berlin furthers the study of settlement as political practice and theoretical tool. Berlin uses an archeological model to provide meaning and to "unearth" colonial narratives and their potential implications for Aboriginals and Palestinians. Tracing the complicity of archaeology and anthropology as makers of colonial narratives and influencers of policy in Northwestern Ontario and Jerusalem, the discussion cites Annibal Quijano, Audra

Simpson, Nadia Abu El-Haj and Radhika Mohanram to situate these disciplines within a totalizing colonial epistemology. The discussion uses these geographically and archeologically distinct case studies to examine the notions of coloniality and the politics of repatriation. Informed by the work of Coulthard, Dei, Kempf and Simpson, the discussion examines reconciliatory politics, itself an extension of contemporary colonial discourse, and the archeological space of the museum as sites of knowledge production and cultural repatriation.

Moving from the colonial legacies of archeology and museum displays to the depiction of racialized bodies within modern capitalism, in Chapter 11 Stacey Papernick moves the focus from the personal to the collective, from anthropological unearthing to the contemporary movement and economic ties of a racialized form of capitalism. Papernick provides an anti-colonial media analysis of a troubling event involving the mayor of Leamington. In this small agricultural community southwest of Toronto, in July 2013 the mayor expressed contentious, divisive beliefs about Jamaican migrant farmworkers who are employed annually as temporary foreign workers in the agricultural sector of this community. Critics characterized the comments as racist, while the mayor and his political supporters viewed the remarks as expressions of concern. While not indicative of the movement of all goods and people within capitalism, this incident and its economic context are emblematic of the unequal social and economic relationships existing between migrant Jamaican farmworkers and local (largely white) citizens in Leamington. The movement of human capital within a global system and the willing participation of the Canadian and Jamaican governments demonstrate the domination of ideological and structural forms of colonial domination. This is a new form of colonization—the colony of the global marketplace. The chapter examines how racialized bodies come to be seen within media and local political discourses. Anti-colonial analysis is offered as a source of awareness and social change for farmworkers and unions, thus enabling them to use their agency to reposition themselves within global capitalism. Anti-colonial theory offers a space for mobilization around self-definition and labour rights for Jamaican agricultural workers.

Chapter 12, the concluding chapter, moves us from the racial and neo-colonial implications of transnational capitalism to local, situated sources of community resistance. Rebekah Tannis-Johnson examines the history of the Garifuna people of St. Vincent and the Grenadines. Tannis-Johnson examines the Garifuna cultural revival of the past forty years as a demonstration of cultural resistance within the larger power dynamics of decolonization. Influenced by the works of Anderson, Cabral, Corntassel and Coulthard, the discussion considers the claiming of Indigeneity as a process, one that sparks a Caribbean-focused conversation about the nature of decolonization and anti-colonial responses in that region.

As the diverse contexts and anti-colonial forms of resistance in these chapters reveal, there is no single authoritative reading of praxis, no one way to see or be seen within the anti-colonial prism. We, as scholars, teachers, learners and social change agents, must see and question the fragments of meaning, identities, experiences, power dynamics and new forms of being within this simultaneously and paradoxically post-colonial, neo-colonial and anti-colonial world. The prism offers glimpses of praxis. Each of the thirteen chapters offers new glimmers of critical engagement, each with varying contextual analyses to move us into deeper, fuller and richer contestations and new possibilities. Here is the challenge we share as we bring these glimpses together—making meaning from, questioning and resisting the legacies of colonization through our praxis.

NOTES

1. Matrilineal societies trace descent and family origin through a person's maternal line. This contrasts with the Western tendency to trace lineage and family names through the paternal line.
2. Commodification of Aboriginal knowledge takes many forms, including denial of full treaty rights, inequitable Land and resource agreements involving First Nations and the state and the misappropriation and selling of Aboriginal cultural experiences, including sweat lodge and potlatch experiences, without full cultural context or community endorsement.

REFERENCES

Bhabha, H. (1994). *The location of culture*. London: Routledge.

Brimpong, M. (2009, April). *Fanon, gender and sexuality*. Course paper SES 3914: Frantz Fanon and Education: Pedagogical Possibilities. Ontario Institute for Studies in Education of the University of Toronto, Toronto, Canada

Dei, G. J. S. (2000). Rethinking the role of Indigenous knowledges in the academy. *International Journal of Inclusive Education, 4*(2), 111–132.

Dei. G. J. S. (2013, April 30). *The global "economics of schooling" in the context of Africa and the Caribbean.* Keynote address, AERA Caribbean and African Studies in Education (CASE) Special Interest Group (SIG), San Francisco, CA.

Dei, G. J. S (2016). *Reframing blackness, anti-blackness and black solidarities through anti-colonial and decolonial prisms*. New York, NY: Springer.

Dei, G. J. S. (in press). Indigenous philosophies, counter epistemologies and anti-colonial education. In W. Lehman (Ed.), *Reader in sociology of education*. London, England: Oxford University Press.

Dei, G. J. S., & Asgharzadeh, A. (2001). The power of social theory: Towards an anti-colonial discursive framework. *Journal of Educational Thought, 35*(3), 297–323.

Fanon, F. (2004). *The wretched of the Earth*. New York: Grove Press.

Grosfuguel, R. (2007). The epistemic colonial turn: Beyond political economy paradigms. *Cultural Studies, 21*(2), 211–223.

Lordan, M. (2013). The race to self: Critical anti-racism theory in a global change era—lessons from Rio+20—the United Nations Conference on Sustainable Development. In G. Dei & M. Lordan (Eds.), *Contemporary issues in the sociology of race and ethnicity*. New York, NY: Peter Lang.

Mundy, K. (2008). Global politics and local realities in the realization of the universal right to education. In S. Moor & R. Mitchell (Eds.), *Power, pedagogy and praxis: Social justice in the globalized classroom*. London, England: Routledge.

Quijano, A. (2000). Coloniality of power, ethnocentrism, and Latin America. *Nepantla, 1*(3), 533–580.

Quijano, A. (2007). Coloniality and modernity/rationality. *Cultural Studies, 21*(2/3), 168–178.

Smith, A. (2006). Heteropatriarchy and the three pillars of white supremacy. In INCITE! Women of Color Against Violence (Ed.), *The color of violence: The INCITE! anthology* (pp. 66–73). Boston, MA: South End Press.

Smith, A. (2010). Indigeneity, settler colonialism & white supremacy. *Global Dialogue, 12*(2). Retrieved from http://www.worlddialogue.org/content.php?id=488

Tuck, E., & Yang, K. W. (2012). Decolonization is not a metaphor. *Decolonization: Indigeneity, Education & Society, 1*(1), 1–40. Retrieved from http://decolonization.org/index.php/des/article/view/18630

CHAPTER ONE

Who Needs Hybridity?

An Anti-Colonial, Feminist Theorization of Mixed Race

EMILY A. MOORHOUSE

INTRODUCTION

This chapter fuses anti-colonial, feminist and critical race theories to think differently about multiracialism or "mixed race." Mixed-race theory has been dominated by academics from post-colonial studies and cultural studies, often theorizing multiracial subjects as "hybrid identities." Though I see the post-colonial usage of "hybridity" as a counterpoint to the idea that race is a fixed, bounded category, I also see a number of limits to its utility.

Theories of hybridity have not allowed us to critically interrogate the politics of settler colonialism, anti-blackness, or the pervasive representation that continuously disappear Indigenous peoples. The frameworks from post-colonialism and cultural studies are insufficient methodological tools for theorizing how different groups relate to land, and the way that land plays a central role in Indigenous survival and resistance. Many studies using these frameworks also fail to contextualize the way that celebrating "hybridity" serves nationalist multicultural policies that operate as a tenet of "colour blindness," while bolstering the increasing number of media narratives that claim the presence of mixed-race people is an indicator that Canada is entering a "post-racial" era. These narratives thrive on a historical amnesia that forgets Canada's colonial past and neo-colonial structured violence and control that continuously target racialized bodies. Celebrating the presence of mixed-race individuals is also a "settler move to innocence" (Tuck & Yang, 2012) that attempts to undermine the saliency of race/racism while requiring people of colour and mixed-race bodies to subscribe to a Politics of Recognition (Coultard, 2014).

To remedy this in my own work, I turn to anti-colonial theorists to map the way that racialized and legal categories affect Indigenous and black bodies, allowing us to see the ways that identity can have material consequences. For example, many Indigenous people in Canada have difficulty identifying as mixed because doing so de-politicizes identity. There are also dangers associated with mixed blood and loss of status, both through the Indian Act and their community protocols. For multiracial black bodies, mixed-race identity can be invoked as a way to denounce racial parts, and blackness in particular. Taking critiques from Sexton (2008) and Mahtani (2014) into account, the chapter ends with ideas for mixed-race studies that go beyond the black/white binary, and work in solidarity with Indigenous and racialized people to dismantle anti-blackness and neo-colonial violence in its multiple forms.

ACKNOWLEDGING POSITIONALITY: MY PLACE IN THE STORY

In one of my undergraduate classes, a white female classmate continuously discounted the experiences of women of colour as they expressed their feelings of discomfort in certain academic spaces. My white classmate exclaimed, "School is not *actually* a dangerous space to be in. Maybe if you stopped *assuming* people are targeting you, we'd feel more like a community." I recounted the stories to another white classmate, who was surprised at the way I explicitly named my classmates' whiteness and white privilege. She stared at me blankly, saying, "But Emily ... you're a white person too! Kind of?" Despite my irritation, I disregarded her comments in the moment but continued to be puzzled by them as my day went on. This was not the first time a situation like this one had occurred, and I was tired of people assuming that I would be offended or unable to critique whiteness and/or white privilege because I have a white father, and am considered "half white."

I am also half Asian, with family roots in Singapore, Malaysia, Indonesia, and China. I spent the earlier years of my childhood in a predominantly white suburb, and I was constantly racialized as Asian, often in derogatory and/or fetishizing ways. I still get lots of questions—"What are you?" or "Where are you from?"—because I apparently "look mixed" or "exotic" (a term I will problematize later on in the chapter).

Conversations such as this, and an increasing interest in critical race theory spurred my interest in the field of critical mixed-race studies. While I remain interested in the complexities of identification that the field presented in a variety of studies, my interests in theorizing "mixed race" have always been grounded in an understanding that race and racism impact the way we self-identify. Analyzing the complexities of diasporic identification *must* include a detailed analysis of how settler colonialism and colonial structures have shaped the way we think about race, exclude people from racial identifications, and produce knowledge on race.

Though I have developed more critical views over time, I was not always able to do so. I too have gone through the Canadian colonial education system that purposefully excluded histories of colonial conquest and state-sanctioned violence. My schoolteachers, who were predominantly white, knew nothing of Indigenous forms of knowledge and often promoted multiculturalism and colour blindness. I did not learn how to question the ongoing settler colonial system until I was in the second year of my undergraduate degree, and I still have much to learn and unlearn.

METHODOLOGICAL JOURNEY: CRITIQUING THE "POST-COLONIAL" AND EXAMINING THE ANTI-COLONIAL

Most of the studies done on "mixed race" and multiracialism use frameworks from cultural studies and post-colonialism under the guise that both make space for "hybridity"—a term I problematize in a later section. A great number of multiracial or "hybrid identity" studies use guiding questions that focus on identity formation and what it means to be a mixed-race subject. Many frame mixed identity using Stuart Hall's idea that

> identity is not as transparent or unproblematic as we think. Perhaps instead of thinking of identity as an already accomplished fact, which the new cultural practices then represent, we should think, instead, of identity as a "production," which is never complete, always in process, and always constituted within, not outside, representation. (Hall, 1990, p. 222)

Post-colonial scholarship also looks at identity formation, focusing on new relations of power and how they emerge with new conjunctures (Hall, 1996, p. 249). Hall problematizes anti-colonial theories, claiming that they assume binary forms of representation that focus on nationalistic grand narratives (p. 246). He compares this with post-colonialism, which invites us to re-read the binaries as forms of trans-culturalism and cultural translation, while troubling binaries through decentered, diasporic rewritings (p. 247). Hall describes the post-colonial as a time of difference, asking what the implications of this difference mean for political formations and for the way in which subjects are defined.

Similar to Shohat (1992) and McClintock (1992), there is a valid critique of post-colonial scholarship for its theoretical and political ambiguity, and for the way that it blurs distinctions between the colonizer and the colonized. By not clearly articulating the systems of domination and making a clear call for opposition, political resistance can easily dissolve. The elusive nature of post-colonialism also leaves itself "open to the charge of ahistoricism" (Bahri, 1996, p. 138), particularly

postcolonialism as docoto

when scholars do not contextualize exactly *when* the post-colonial happened, or articulate the specific meanings for different post-colonial regions. Other critics also recognize that the "post" in post-colonial is a "temporal fiction that obscures neo-colonizing activities after the declaration of independence in many countries" (Bahri, p. 141).

Dirlik (1994) critiques post-colonialism for its ambiguity and for its "marketability" in academia (p. 347), claiming that it is a discourse that constitutes the world in the self-image of intellectuals who view themselves as post-colonial intellectuals with newfound power in the First-World academia. Sexton's (2010) piece "People-of-Color-Blindness: Notes on the Afterlife of Slavery" reminds us that if our focus on subversive relationships is making it "digestible," we reproduce colonial relations in place of resistance. Loomba (1998) takes a similar stance, asking why post-colonial scholarship has ignored the wealth of Indigenous texts and methodologies, and how this may be central to the psychological and spiritual healing of Indigenous peoples, black folks, and non-black people of colour.

Hall (1996) also describes post-colonialism as a general process of decolonization because the post-colonial subverts colonizing/colonized binaries in new ways (p. 246). I question the difference between subversion and an active dismantling, and wish Hall had elaborated on the issue more in order for us to evaluate whether subversion is a viable form of resistance. As Hall also fails to elaborate on why binaries are the problem, I am suspicious of the post-colonial claims that "the subject" and "identity" are "radically transformed" in their decentered positions that attempt to distance colonial narratives, and "go beyond it," structuring the "in-between." Part of this "in-between" that post-colonialism claims to be attuned to is *hybridity*, cultural un-decidability, and complexities of diasporic identification (p. 250).

Acknowledging the complexities of identification is one issue, but a more important part for me is the attendance to the saliency of race and racism, and the impact this has on how we choose to racially identify. Analyzing the complexities of diasporic identification *must* include a detailed analysis of how settler colonialism and colonial structures have shaped the way we think about race, exclude people from racial identifications, and produce knowledge on race. If the post-colonial is, as Hall (1996) claims, a "culturalism" (p. 256), then the post-colonial understanding of identity should be useful for diasporic subjects in understanding their identity. As Leila Angod (2006) expressed, I am somewhat dissatisfied with some of the essentialist movements which seem to have rigid definitions of community that do not allow spaces for my identity; but I am even more dissatisfied with depoliticized, ambiguous post-colonial theories that attempt to theorize more inclusivity by including different identities and their reconfigurations.

I am also uncomfortable with the way that mixed-race "hybrid" subjects in Canada are often seen as promoting unity. We are held up as examples—the literal production of people who have integrated by "overcoming" their anger and embracing multiculturalism. The presence of mixed-race bodies is not an effective form of anti-racist resistance in itself. As Andrea Smith reminds us in her article "Heteropatriarchy and the Three Pillars of White Supremacy," it is false to think that "if we just *include* more people, then our practices will be less racist. Not true." This model does not address the nuanced structure of white supremacy, such as through the distinctive logics of slavery, genocide, and Orientalism" (p. 70).

Multiculturalism and the celebration of multiracial people entail a very specific purpose—a historical amnesia (Razack, 2004)—one that forgets Canada's colonial past and the neo-colonial forms of violence that continue to target racialized bodies and exclude them from justice. Bonita Lawrence and Enakshi Dua (2006) remind us in "Decolonizing Antiracism" that post-colonial theory, for the most part, has not interrogated an understanding of Canada as a settler colonial state (p. 123). In failing to address this, post-colonialism performs historical amnesia and is no longer a sustainable form of resistance.

If theories are to be considered as progressive and ethical, they must be useful in tangible ways, not simply in theory. More important, they should be useful to the individuals or communities on which the research focuses. Zainab Amadahy and Bonita Lawrence (2009) give us an example of how this was not always the case in relation to post-colonial texts. Lawrence (1999) writes that the "exclusion of Native realities and Indigenous epistemologies in post-colonial and anti-racist theory was never so contradictory to me as it was that [Toronto] winter" when welfare rates were cut by 20 percent (p. 111). As Lawrence recalls this period in Toronto during the late 1990s, an era of amalgamation and funding reductions at the municipal and provincial levels, it is instructive to consider that these policy decisions resulted in increased numbers of homeless individuals, all while post-colonial discourse was praised in the academy as cutting edge and equity minded.

Post-colonialism has also failed Indigenous people by under-theorizing land, and how different bodies have different relationships to land. Post-colonial scholars have also failed to see how reclaiming a relationship to the land has been at the core of Indigenous survival and resistance in Canada. Indigenous peoples have fought to maintain their identity despite five centuries of colonization, and a great part of this "derives from the fact that they have retained knowledge of who they are due to their longstanding relationship to the land" (Lawrence & Dua, 2006, p. 127). Post-colonial writings on diasporic visions of a "home away from home" in North America are also premised on the ongoing colonization of Indigenous peoples and their land (p. 129).

Anti-colonial scholarship, in contrast, often places land at the center of the analysis. Eve Tuck and K. W. Yang (2012) explain that land is central in settler colonial societies, because land is

what is most valuable, contested, required. This is both because the settlers make Indigenous land their new home and source of capital, and also because the disruption of Indigenous relationships to land represents a profound epistemic, ontological, cosmological violence … and human relationships to land are restricted to the relationship of the owner to
his property. (p. 5)

Dakota scholar Elizabeth Cook-Lynn (1998) also problematizes post-colonial concerns with identity because of the way it frames Native identity in an individualistic
sense, instead of individuals seeing themselves as members of a collective community with shared responsibilities to one another and to the land (p. 125). Bonita
Lawrence's earlier work (1999) echoes Cook-Lynn's (1998), contextualizing how
"Bodies of law … distorted and disrupted older Indigenous ways of identifying the
self in relation not only to collective identity but to the land" (Lawrence, p. 4). In
re-thinking how mixed-race theory can create rather than divide communities, I
turn to anti-colonial theories and methodologies. I extend Audra Simpson's (2014)
call for knowledge production to recognize the colonial project (pp. 12, 13) and ask,
*How has colonization influenced our conceptualization of the label "mixed race" and how
do we attend to the way this category has affected groups differently?*

MULTIRACIALISM AND THE POLITICS OF DISTRACTION

Bahri (1995) notes that the growth of post-colonial studies "has been coeval with
the growing interest in multiculturalism … and cultural transnationalism" (p. 150).
She also references the increasing number of hires and promotions in "Post-
Colonial Studies" as substitutes for tangible social change while allowing universities
to gain points for "cultural diversity" (p. 153). I argue that this celebration of cultural
diversity is part of the "illusion of inclusion" (Corntassel, 2012, p. 92) in which the
presence of racialized people, and particularly *mixed-race* people, becomes a sign
that we are entering a "post-racial era." Celebrating mixed-race people and cultural
diversity also pushes the national narratives and policies of multiculturalism. Collectively, these become symbols of liberal progress, not only "in comparison to the
monocultural nationalism of other countries but also in comparison to earlier eras of
monocultural nationalism in Canada" (Coleman, 2006, p. 7).

Multiculturalism and celebrations of multiracialism are also examples of what
Tuck and Yang (2012) call "settler moved to innocence," defined as "strategies or
positionings that attempt to relieve the settler of feelings of guilt or responsibility
without giving up land or power or privilege, without having to change much at all"
(p. 10). The narratives and policies of multiculturalism also produce in the imagination the idea that immigrants of colour can now belong to a nation that has overcome its racism, while mixed-race bodies in Canada have permission to "belong" to
the white nation, as opposed to the age of anti-miscegenation and the one-drop rule.

This plays into the politics of recognition and accommodation that Glen Coultard (2014) explores in "From Wards of the State to Subjects of Recognition?" in Simpson and Smith's *Theorizing Native Studies*. Coultard explains that colonial relations in Canada are not usually imposed, but rather occur "through an asymmetrical exchange of mediated forms of state recognition and accommodation" (p. 62). Coultard reminds us that this "cultural recognition" never acknowledges Indigenous sovereignty; it is only recognition of cultural differences organized under one political formation—the colonial state. This embeds rather than contests the idea that white settlers are legitimate owners of Canada who grant others permission to live on the land. In addition to assuaging white settler guilt, multicultural immigration policies turn to immigrants "in order to capitalize on their labor, economic and educational strengths as Canada shores up its national prosperity and global competitiveness" (Coloma, 2013, p. 586).

The different, but inter-related, discourses of multiculturalism and multiracialism are invoked as a politics of distraction (Hingangaroa Smith, 2000), diverting "our energy and attention away from community resurgence" (Corntassel, 2012, p. 91) while "[framing] community relationships in state-centric terms" (Alfred & Corntassel, 2005, p. 600). Corntassel (2012) identifies three main themes in the politics of distraction: rights, reconciliation, and resources. These tend to divide communities, and in the case of Indigenous nations, push them towards a state of assimilation of co-adaptations (Corntassel, p. 91) Rather than focusing on state-centric discourses of rights, such as multicultural policy, Corntassel urges us to focus our energies on our responsibilities to our communities, to the land, and to Indigenous resurgence movements.

Eve Haque (2010) explores how multicultural policy used language as a softer, more "nuanced" approach to policy, even though it continued to operate using racial logic. Multiculturalism within a bilingual framework created "a racial order of difference and belonging through language in the ongoing project of white settler nation-building" (p. 5). Multicultural policy has always been conceived of in a bilingual framework that reinforces the legitimacy of the two colonizing powers and languages: English and French. This allowed language and culture to be the new terrain on which racial exclusion occurred, as opposed to the biologically based racial exclusions that were becoming less socially acceptable

Former Canadian Prime Minister Pierre Trudeau's "Canadian Policy Statement on Multiculturalism" stressed the importance of national unity but has no firm commitment to anti-racist politics and objectives. We can see clear examples of this in the *Official Language Act* (1969), wherein policy makers purposefully omitted "substantive contestation from both Indigenous communities and 'other ethnic groups'" (Haque, 2010, p. 6) in order to continue their assault on Indigenous languages. Multicultural policy also strengthened Canada's attempts to cease formal recognition of Indigenous peoples by reducing Indigenous people to a "cultural group" within the multicultural mosaic (Amadahy & Lawrence, 2009, p. 115) instead of a group of nations who suffered land theft and cultural genocide at the hands of colonial white settlers.

Following this analysis, it becomes clear that multicultural policy is not "progressive" but instead a new form of nationalism that contributes to the ongoing colonization and de-legitimization of Indigenous nationhood. National narratives of multiculturalism that promote colour blindness also relegate colonialism to an event of the past instead of a structure (Wolfe, 2007, p. 388). Using a right-based approach, multicultural policy often works to destroy the possibility of coalition building between Indigenous people in Canada and immigrants of colour by inviting them to participate in the ongoing colonization of indigenous people and their lands in what is now North America. Any multicultural, ethno-nationalist identities for new immigrants are "articulated through the colonization of Aboriginal peoples, or the ways in which the project of appropriating land shaped the emergence of black/Asian/Hispanic settler formation" (Lawrence & Dua, 2006, p. 128). This means, as perplexing and complex as it is, that

> colonial subjects who are displaced by external colonialism, as well as racialized and minoritized by internal colonialism, still occupy and settle stolen Indigenous land. Settlers are diverse, not just of white European descent, and include people of color, even from other colonial contexts. (Tuck & Yang, 2012, p. 7) *POC live on stolen land*

It is deeply troubling for many immigrants of colour to think of themselves as settlers, particularly for those who are refugees, those whose ancestors were forced into systems of slavery, or those who have been forced to migrate as a result of neo-colonial relations in their own country. Amadahy and Lawrence are cognizant of this in their article, "Indigenous Peoples and Black People in Canada: Settlers or Allies?" They explain that

> for groups of people to be forcibly transplanted from their own lands and enslaved on other peoples' lands—as Africans were in the Americas—does not make enslaved peoples true "settlers." (2009, p. 107)

Critical scholars cannot categorize "settlers" into one category. We must consider the geographical and temporal specificities of our arguments, including historical and present-day systems of anti-blackness that includes the dispossession and denial of access to land, opportunities, and resources. In her book *Exalted Subjects: Studies in the Making of Race and Nation in Canada* (2007), anti-racist feminist scholar Sunera Thobani argues that we cannot disregard the fact that immigrants and refugees also benefit from Canada's colonial project (p. 16).

What we need to be conscious of is the fact that *immigrants of colour and refugees do not benefit from the colonial project in the same way in which white settlers do*. People of colour, particularly black bodies, are consistently faced with and excluded from the national imaginary in relation to white migrants and white settlers. I also acknowledge the difficulty for immigrants and refugees who were forced to migrate because of the ongoing (neo) colonial relations in their country of origin. These issues of forced migration that displace people from across the globe cannot be read as a separate issue from the ongoing colonial processes that continue to disenfranchise Indigenous peoples in North America.

"Who is a settler?" This is no longer the important question. Instead it is this one: *"How can we work in solidarity with one another to dismantle white supremacist and (neo)colonial powers?"* Self-identifying as a settler instead of a Canadian citizen or an immigrant does little in itself to change colonial systems of domination. What is more important is the mobilization of knowledge that allows people of colour to become aware of the ways in which they can support movements against settler domination, colonial power, and white supremacy. Amadahy and Lawrence's "Indigenous Peoples and Black People in Canada: Settlers or Allies?" (2009) was useful because it was an attempt to break down positions of innocence (p. 105), in which both black *and* Indigenous people insist that their own suffering is so unique and encompassing that it erases the possibility of relationships of oppression between groups (Razack, 2004, pp. 10, 14).

One of my ongoing research interests is exploring the relations between black and Indigenous peoples in relation to "mixed race." In exploring this, it is important to see the ways in which "Indians and Black people in the US have been racialized in opposing ways that reflect their antithetical role in the formation of US society" (Wolfe, 2007, p. 387). Tuck and Yang (2012) expand on this, stating that

> through the one-drop rule, blackness in settler colonial contexts is *expansive*, ensuring that a slave/criminal status will be *inherited* by an expanding number of 'black' descendants. Native-American-ness is *subtractive* … constructed to become fewer in number and *less* Native, but never exactly white, over time. (p. 12)

This is done purposefully by settler governments with the goal of diminishing the possibility of land claims and Indigenous sovereignty over time while attempting to replenish the slave/criminal population that has been so central to the colonial project. What both forms of racialization have in common is that they ensure that white settlers are seen as the true and rightful owners of the land. Invoking multicultural "recognition" for Indigenous peoples and people of colour only furthers the colonial project. Multicultural "recognition" does not convey the sense of urgency to dismantle systems of anti-blackness and white supremacy, nor does it force us to actively protest the ongoing theft and extraction of Indigenous land. Celebrating the presence of mixed-race bodies as a solution to the problem of racism invokes similar dangers.

THE MULTIRACIAL SUBJECT AS A FETISH OBJECT—
PROBLEMATIZING *MESTIZA/MESTIZAJE*

In one of my graduate classes, I was assigned Gloria Anzaldúa's (1987) work *La Conciencia de la Mestiza: Towards a New Consciousness*. I found parts of the piece problematic but decided not to comment until the student presenting was finished. Much to my dismay, another student called upon me during the discussion period, asking, "Do you feel like a mestiza, able to cross boundaries? Do you feel like you can use *El camino de la Mestizo/The Mestiza Way* (p. 104) as a methodology for how you navigate your mixed-race identity?"

Disturbed by the question, I explained that I thought the question was both uncritical and eerily fetishizing, using terminology such as "hybridity" that infers the premise that race is something biological with "pure" categories that can be mixed to produce specific "breeds" and outcomes. Anzaldúa's reference to race as biology is clear when she writes that "the *mestiza* is a product of crossbreeding, designed for preservation under a variety of conditions" (1987, p. 103), alluding to the dangerous argument that mixed-race people and queer folks are the next step in "evolution" because of their supposed ability to mediate tensions by tolerating ambiguity (p. 107).

Anzaldúa's post-structuralist approach to "walking out of one culture, and into another, because I am in all cultures at the same time" (1987, p. 99) seems to de-politicize the meanings of Indigeneity and the colonial implications of crossing racial boundaries for Indigenous people, such as losing status and land. I also felt sick reading Anzaldúa describe the "inner strife" of the mestiza, whose "dual or multiple personality is plagued by psychic restlessness" (p. 100), and who "flounder[s] in uncharted seas … subject to a swamping of her psychological borders" (p. 101). This reminded me of the claim that mixed-race people have no racial "home" and are constantly confused about their identity, a claim that Olumide (2002) and Mahtani (2014) critique for the way it pathologizes multiracial identity.

I was happy to later read a critique of *mestiza* hybridity in Bonita Lawrence's earlier work. Lawrence argues that developing hybridized identities has never been an effective strategy for Indigenous survival in the Americas, particularly because of the way that "mestizo populations of all of the Latin American countries routinely deny their connections to their Indigenous roots, and are often complicit in the exploitation and destruction of Indigenous communities" (Lawrence, 1999, p. 28). She also suggests that it is important that we not read Native societies closing themselves off as "ethnic absolutism" that many post-structuralist and post-colonial scholars write against. Instead, we need to contextualize in relation to colonial policies that continuously "disappear" the Native, thus making it a form of survival.

MIXED RACE AND INDIGENEITY IN CANADA

Although I was provided a good introduction to critical race theory and anti-colonialism within my undergraduate studies, I struggled to connect the theories to my lived experience as a mixed-race person. My first real look at a re-politicized analysis of multiracialism came from Minelle Mahtani's work, specifically her book *Mixed Race Amnesia. Resisting the Romanticization of Multiraciality* (2014). Mahtani begins with the assertion that the Canadian mixed-race identity is "the product of colonial formations, created and reflected through cultural representations and facilitated through certain forms of cultural amnesia or strategic forgetting" (p. 3). She also reminds her readers that multiracial studies "continues to enact a form of epistemic violence against Indigenous peoples because of its refusal to carefully and thoroughly dissect the metaphor of mixing" (p. 56).

Andrea Smith (2011) writes in "Queer Theory and Native Studies" that "when Indigeneity is not foregrounded, it tends to disappear in order to enable the emergence of the hybrid subject" (p. 57). Mahtani (2014) reminds us of ways that racialized and legal categorizations have negatively affected Indigenous populations in Canada by outlining how the Indian Act of 1876 reinforced romanticized notions of "Indianness." It categorized people as Aboriginal, Metis, or Inuit in order to withhold legal recognition, access to land, and treaty rights. Craig Womack (1998) also writes about the difficulty for Indigenous peoples to identify with "mixed race" because he wonders whether "identifying as mixed blood, rather than as part of a tribal nation, diminishes sovereignty" (p. 32). By minimizing the number of registered "Indians" and maximizing land theft, the Indian Act drew divisions between status Indians and other Indigenous peoples and fostered fetishized notions of what an "authentic Indian" was. Individuals who were excluded from the Indian Act also struggled to compete for state funding, and their claims to Indigeneity were often viewed as fraudulent (Amadahy & Lawrence, 2009, p. 114).

It is also important to contextualize how colonial structures like the Indian Act interpreted Indigeneity on racialized *and* gendered lines. Audra Simpson (2014) provides an example of this in the Canadian context. Kahnawá:ke, a code established in 1984, required community members to have at least 50 percent Mohawk blood quantum. The code was established in response to the decade-long battle with the United Nations Commission on Human Rights that removed the bias of determining membership in Native bands along patrilineal lines (p. 57) that disenfranchised Native women and children. To an outsider, this appears to be a simple issue of gender equity, but to Kahnawá:ke community members it was an issue of accepting that white men could hold land in the community, the state setting the rules for who could be an "Indian."

Though taking away the rights of Mohawk women in this instance was about attempting to protect the community from elimination rather than active discrimination, Mohawk women have been the ones paying the legal price "through their disenfranchisement and legal exile from their natal homes, which must have been an enormous cost to the traditional structure of community given the clan-bearing, clan-transmitting, and property-owning status of women" (Simpson, 2014, p. 60).

In some cases, these women became stigmatized "as relatives who were 'polluted'—who had gone outside the conceptual and legal borders of the reserve, and in doing so, had acquired the stigma of betrayal" (Simpson, 2014, p. 61), and responsible for cultural loss (Alfred, 1996, p. 164). Women are positioned as being at fault for their own disenfranchisement from their community, rather than targets of a colonial system that created race and gender-based practices of exclusion. We can see here the importance of attending to the specificities within the category of mixed race, but also to the materiality of particular racialized identities in relation to the nation-state. As Bonita Lawrence states, "Everybody in Canada is intermarrying but nobody else is losing their citizenship as a result" (quoted in Rutherford, 2010, p. 11).

MIXED RACE AND BLACKNESS: VISIBILIZING BLACK-INDIGENOUS PEOPLES IN CANADA

Amadahy and Lawrence (2009) also highlight how gender-based Indian status has divided communities and excluded particular people. The children from off-reserve intermarriages between black people and Mi'kmaq in the Maritimes, and black people and Ojibway in Ontario are often not counted as "real Indians" (p. 114), particularly when the Native parent is non-status. This intense control often prevents black people with Native roots from participating in Native communities, and continues the silencing of "black Indians," which Amadahy and Lawrence say has yet to be significantly broken (p. 115). Blood-quantum policies and anti-blackness have also been internalized by many Native community members, making it difficult for them to see individuals who are black and Native as legitimate members of the community (p. 125).

While citing this example, Amadahy and Lawrence made an important connection between Indigeneity in Canada and Indigeneity in Africa (2009, p. 119), as both groups are under attack as Indigenous people. They are put into contradictory relations within North America, because one displaced group of Indigenous peoples risks becoming the displacers of another if mutually supportive relationships are not negotiated. Rather than seeing the situation as a conflict, this is a call for solidarity across groups to focus collectively on a global Indigenous resurgence and the dismantling of colonial structures.

While Indigenous communities in North America must unsettle internalized notions of anti-blackness, Amadahy and Lawrence are also critical of scholars who erase Indigeneity in their historical writings (2009, p. 120), including advocating for land grants to black Loyalists on land that the Mi'kmaq people never ceded, or the erasure of black Mi'kmaq people by only referencing them as "black" (see Walcott, 1997). They are also wary of scholars who invoke a settler move to innocence (Tuck & Yang, 2012, p. 10), by "position(ing) black settlers simply as noble in their fortitude in clearing the land (see Daniel Hill, 1992), not as those who are displacing Indigenous peoples in the process," or as people who had several interactions and learned survival skills from Native people in Canada (Amadahy & Lawrence, 2009, p. 121). They examine how these writings create a "double loss" for black people with Native heritage—the suppression of their North American Indigeneity and the broken African Indigeneity. I recognize the power in the "strong affinities between North American Indigenous knowledge and spirituality and African Indigenous knowledge and spirituality ... that may be a crucial source of empowerment for Black people" (p. 123). When they write of the "failure among Indigenous leaderships to provide an alternative vision for racialized peoples who may have little real allegiance to the Canadian settler state but have no option for their survival" (p. 126), it is not simply a cry of despair but an opportunity for coalition building.

MIXED RACE AND ANTI-BLACKNESS

Proclaiming mixed-race identity can also be seen as a way to claim higher status by denouncing racial parts in order to gain proximity to whiteness and white privilege. Mahtani's (2014) studies found that identifying as mixed allowed some individuals to be seen as racially unique or "exotic" (something that few of them even problematized, and none of them related to colonial fetishization) while they failed to adopt an anti-racist stand or progressive politics. This racial ambiguity of "I'm mixed" can become a way for some individuals to opt out of racial politics.

Jared Sexton's book *Amalgamation Schemes: Antiblackness and the Critique of Multiracialism* (2008) also makes this argument. Sexton's book provides a thorough critique and analysis of the post–civil rights multiracial movements in the United States. His usage of the term "multiracialism" includes the political initiatives of the multiracial movements, the academic field of multiracial studies, and the media discourse about "race mixture" in contemporary culture and society. Sexton critiques multiracialism for failing to challenge the living legacy of white supremacy and for promoting (implicitly and explicitly) tenets of colour blindness.

Sexton argues that by claiming "mixed race" individuals become associated with freedom from the constraints of being identified with racial blackness (2008,

p. 6). At times, multiracialism also renders the discourse of race as a matter of personal identity, despite the politicization and development of historical consciousness (p. 7). Sexton reminds us that this includes the historical relation between white supremacy's tolerance for multiracial formation and the strength of black liberation struggles. When black resistance was thought to be contained or neutralized practically and symbolically, the colour line became more fluid. When black activism moved against white supremacy (such as the end of the Jim Crow era and the rise of the Black Power movement), "mixed-race" status was again revoked as a viable source of identity, and racial blackness was understood again as a spectrum (p. 12).

Multiracialism can also be read as a patriarchal negation of racial blackness because of the way it promotes the phobic imagery of black as profound sexual threat. White supremacists (especially in the United States) have consistently been obsessed with policing inter-racial sexuality out of fear of the "pollution" or "genocide" of the white race (Sexton, 2008, p. 23). The sexual politics of multiracialism typically imply the production of heterosexuality, nominating reproductive sex as the principal mediation for racial difference, maintaining a system of racial "breeding" (p. 37). Concerns about interracial couples are usually concerns about their children, but little theorization is done on interracial couples who do not have children or on queer interracial couples. This creates what Sexton calls a "de-sexualization of race, and a de-racialization of sexuality" (p. 38). His clearest argument on this was illustrated through the idea of a "healthy" interracial relationship being an ideological lure (p. 154). This is because de-pathologizing the interracial couple is only accomplished by highlighting the healthiness of mixed-race people. This shifts the discourse to the terrain of reproduction, not sexuality, while reinforcing the dynamics of the two-parent nuclear family (p. 158).

Reading Sexton's and Mahtani's critical analyses left me disenchanted with mixed-race studies that focus on narratives of "passing" because I do not see "passing" as a viable form of anti-racist or anti-colonial resistance. I agree with Sexton (2008), who argues that the right to pass and to self-identify in different ways at different times is a "misleading comfort," allowing individuals to avoid "an engagement with struggles of racial inequality for those who are, in society's eyes, 'all black, all the time'" (pp. 76, 78). This also furthers the idea that black identity is always in "a state of lack or insufficiency, and barring some escape, a state of *confinement*" (p. 76), particularly because of the way that racial communication takes place in geographical spaces, constricting, refusing, allowing, or creating opportunities for different kinds of racial re/configurations (Mahtani, 2014, p. 19).

Taking Sexton's and Mahtani's critiques into consideration, the research question for scholars in critical mixed-race studies should shift. The research question for scholars in multiracial studies then shifts from "How do mixed-race individuals negotiate across racial boundaries?" to "How are mixed-race individuals actively resisting white supremacy, settler colonialism, anti-Indigeneity, and anti-blackness?"

The article "Geotheorizing Black/Land: Contestations and Contingent Collaborations" (Tuck, Smith, Guess, Benjamin, & Jones, 2014) was one useful starting point to think through this question. The study described in the article explored the way black people in the United States relate to land. The purpose of the study was to rewrite the narratives of black bodies as displaced, or "un-geographic/becoming geographic" (McKittrick, 2006, p. xiii; Tuck et al., 2014, p. 53) while attending to the "lack of descriptive work about how black people defined their own relationships to land beyond constructions of dispossession and environmental degradation" (Tuck et al., 2014, p. 55).

As land is a central part of Indigenous identity, sovereignty, and historical revitalization within the context of Canada and the United States, I think it could be an important entry point for mixed-race black subjects to connect with their familial histories. Research participants in Tuck et al.'s (2014) study explained the "profound relationship between people of African descent and the land because we come from a people that didn't really look on land and ownership being the way we approach material gains here. I think that the relationship of people to land is a part of who we are" (p. 66).

Black relationships to and with land existed pre-colonization, and can be reclaimed without damage and displacement-based narratives if the stories are given a space within which to unfold. With these considerations in mind, I have begun to understand how the knowledge I am producing on mixed-race theory must be grounded in the anti-colonial, anti-racist, feminist frameworks, and I look forward to mapping "mixed race" in a way that goes beyond previous limitations and into a transformative field of study. Audra Simpson's questions resonate with me the most: "Can I do this and still come home; what am I revealing here and why? Where will this get us? Who benefits from this and why?" (Simpson, 2014, p. 78). Answering them provides an epistemic map for the ongoing project of questioning hybridity.

REFERENCES

Alfred, T. (1996). *Heeding the voices of our ancestors: Kahnawake Mohawk politics and the rise of native nationalism*. Toronto, Canada: Oxford University Press.

Alfred, T., & Corntassel, J. (2005). Being Indigenous: Resurgences against contemporary colonialism. *Government & Opposition, 40*, 597–614.

Amadahy, Z., & Lawrence, B. (2009). Indigenous peoples and black people in Canada: Settlers or allies? In A. Kempf (Ed.), *Breaching the colonial contract: Anti-colonialism in the US and Canada* (pp. 105–136). New York, NY: Springer.

Angod, L. (2006). From post-colonial to anti-colonial politics: Difference, knowledge and R v R. D. S. G. J. S. Dei & A. Kempf (Eds.), *Anti-colonialism and education: The politics of resistance* (pp. 159–174). Rotterdam, the Netherlands: Sense.

Anzaldúa, G. (1987). "La Conciencia de la Mestiza: Towards a New Consciousness. Borderlands: La Frontera. The new Mestiza." In *Borderlands/La Frontera*, (99–120). San Franscisco, CA: Aunt Lute Books.

Bahri, D. (1996). Coming to Terms with the "Postcolonial". In D. Bahria and M. Vasudeva (Eds.) *Between the Lines: South Asians and Postcoloniality*. (137–164). Philadelphia, PA: Temple University Press

Coleman, D. (2006). *White civility: The Literary Project of English Canada* (pp. 3–45). Toronto, Canada: University of Toronto Press.

Coloma, R. (2013). 'Too Asian?' On racism, paradox and ethno-nationalism. *Discourse: Studies in the Cultural Politics of Education. 34* (4), 579–598.

Cook-Lynn, E. (1996). Intellectualism and the new Indian story. In D. A. Mihesuah (Ed.), *Natives and academics: Research and writing about American Indians* (pp. 111–138). Lincoln: University of Nebraska Press.

Corntassel, J. (2012). Re-envisioning resurgence: Indigenous pathways to decolonization and sustainable self-determination. *Decolonization: Indigenity, Education & Society, 1*(1), 86–101.

Coultard, G. (2014). From wards of the state to subjects of recognition? Marx, Indigenous peoples, and the politics of dispossession in Denendeh. In A. Simpson & A. Smith (Eds.), *Theorizing native studies* (pp. 65–107). Durham, NC: Duke University Press.

Dirlik, A. (1994). The postcolonial aura: Third World criticism in the age of global capitalism. *Critical Inquiry, 20*, 328–356.

Hall, S. (1990). Culture, identity and diaspora. In J. Rutherford (Ed.), *Identity: Community, culture, difference.* London, England: Lawrence & Wishart.

Hall, S. (1996). When was 'the post-colonial? Thinking at the limit. In I. Chambers & L. Curti (Eds.), *The post-colonial question* (pp. 242–260). London, England: Routledge.

Haque, E. (2010). *Multiculturalism within a bilingual framework. Language, race, and belonging in Canada.* Toronto, Canada: University of Toronto Press.

Hill, D. (1992). *The freedom seekers: Blacks in early Canada.* Toronto, Canada: Stoddard.

Hingangaroa Smith, G. (2000) "Protecting and respecting Indigenous knowledge." *Reclaiming indigenous voice and vision.* Ed. M. Battiste. Vancouver, BC: UBC Press, 209–224.

Lawrence, B. (1999). *"Real" Indians and others: Mixed-blood urban Native peoples, the Indian Act, and the rebuilding of Indigenous Nations* (Unpublished doctoral dissertation). University of Toronto, Canada.

Lawrence, B., & Dua, E. (2006). Decolonizing antiracism. *Social Justice, 32*(4), 120–143.

Loomba, A. (1998). Challenging colonialism. In *Colonialism/post-colonialism* (pp. 184–258). London, England: Routledge.

Mahtani, M. (2014). *Mixed race amnesia. Resisting the romanticization of multiraciality.* Vancouver, Canada: University of British Columbia Press.

McClintock, A. (1992). The angel of progress: Pitfalls of the term post-colonialism. *Social Text, 31*(32), 84–98.

McKittrick, K. (2006). *Demonic grounds: Black women and the cartographies of struggle.* Minneapolis: University of Minnesota Press.

Olumide, J. (2002). *Raiding the gene pool: The social construction of mixed race.* London, England: Pluto.

Razack, S. (2004). *Dark threats and white knights: The Somalia affair, peacekeeping, and the new imperialism.* Toronto, Canada: University of Toronto Press.

Rutherford, S. (2010, July). Colonialism and the Indigenous present: An interview with Bonita Lawrence. *Race and Class,* 9–18.

Sexton, J. (2008). *Amalgamation schemes: Antiblackness and the critique of multiracialism.* Minneapolis: University of Minnesota Press.

Sexton, J. (2010). People-of-colour-blindness: Notes on the afterlife of slavery. *Social Text, 28*(2), 31–56.

Shohat, E. (1992). Notes on the postcolonial. *Social Text, 31*(32), 99–113.

Simpson, A. (2014). *Mohawk interruptus—political life across the borders of settler states.* Durham, NC: Duke University Press.

Smith, A. (2006). Heteropatriarchy and the three pillars of white supremacy. Rethinking Women of color organizing. In INCITE! Women of Color Against Violence (Ed.), *The color of violence: The INCITE! anthology* (pp. 66–73). Boston, MA: South End Press.

Smith, A. (2011). Queer theory and native studies: The heteronormativity of settler colonialism. *GLQ: A Journal of Lesbian and Gay Studies, 16*(1–2), 41–68.

Smith, G. H. (2000). Protecting and respecting Indigenous knowledge. In M. Battiste (Ed.), *Reclaiming indigenous voice and vision* (pp. 209–224). Vancouver, Canada: University of British Columbia Press.

Thobani, S. (2007). *Exalted subjects: Studies in the making of race and nation in Canada.* Toronto, Canada: University of Toronto Press.

Tuck, E., Smith, M., Guess, A. M., Benjamin, T., & Jones, B. K. (2014, Spring). Geotheorizing black/land: Contestations and contingent collaborations. *Departures in Critical Qualitative Research, 3*(1), 52–74.

Tuck, E., & Yang, K. W. (2012). Decolonization is not a metaphor. *Decolonization: Indigeneity, Education & Society, 1*(1), 1–40.

Walcott, R. (1997). *Black like who? Writing/Black/Canada.* Toronto, Canada: Insomniac Press.

Wolfe, P. (2007). Settler colonialism and the elimination of the native. *Journal of Genocide Research, 8*(4), 387–409.

Womack, C. (1998). Howling at the moon: The queer but true story of my life as a Hank Williams song. In W. S. Penn (Ed.), *As we are now: Mixblood essays on race and identity* (pp. 28–49). Berkeley: University of California Press.

CHAPTER TWO

Erasing Colonial Lines
BETWEEN *Humxn* AND Nature

Mobilizing Settlers

YESSICA D. ROSTAN

The history of my people needs to be told. We need to present accurately what happened in the past, so that we can deal with it in the future ... I don't like what has happened over the last 500 years. We can't do much about that. But what are we going to do about the next 500 years? What are we going to do about the next ten years?
—GEORGE ERASMUS, DENE 1990 (QUOTED IN WRIGHT, 1992, P. 346)

INTERROGATING THE BIOECOLOGICAL-CULTURAL COMPLEX WITHIN ANTI-COLONIALISM

If you were to take a stroll along the Humber River trails in Toronto, you would be met with signs that warn you not to enter the water. As a kid growing up in the city, visiting these trails and parks was a summer ritual to me but I never wondered why the river waters were off limits. Running through sky-high trees and multi-coloured fields with my brothers and my cousins, I learned that tadpoles would morph into leaping frogs and that out of tiny eggs would spring forth baby birds that soon learned how to fly. These relationships to Nature provided an ontological and spiritual connection between my Self and all the wonders of the living world—a connection that faded in and out as I grew older and adopted social roles and norms. Even in my years as a biology student, studying Life from various macro- and microscopic lenses, I lived largely disconnected to my place within Nature except during brief moments of awe and imagination.

Since this discussion argues for a reimagining of what it means to be alive, I use the word *humxn* in my work to imply a new understanding of being human—a reclaiming of identity from all the things 'human' has come to mean. As I focused my lens on social justice and pedagogy, the humxn[1] relationship to Nature (both in ideological and material forms) grew vital in my questions about culture and has led me to ask myself: How is it possible that we have allowed Life itself to be redefined to the point that our streams, rivers and lakes are *un-enterable* and that humxn Life is not valued in its sacredness more than social power or material gain? What is it about this biological-cultural complex—our relationship to Life and Nature—that prevents us from individually and collectively abandoning destructive, dehumxnizing cultural norms and embracing possibilities for more creative Life- and people-sustaining organization (Albuquerque & Medeiros, 2013, p. 2)? In the current historical moment of humxn and planetary evolution, and among the multiple diverse identities and stories that coexist within today's rapidly changing world, we can no longer deny that the dominant story of humxn beings, Nature and progress put forth by Eurocentric and Western logic has profoundly shaped our collective imaginations and material organization through historical and ongoing colonial pursuits.

For this reason, among the assortment of questions that need to be asked, it is important that we question how colonial conceptions of the humxn within Nature have delineated the way we identify ourselves today in relation to Life, Land and each other. These questions are increasingly being asked around the world. As more and more voices are raised globally in defiance of our current systems' oppressive and unsustainable nature, it is in these spaces with our capabilities for adaptability and inventiveness that we can help bring anti-colonial possibilities to the forefront (Guevara, 1961).

Anti-colonialism means different things to different people (see Kempf, 2010, p. 14), and I have found that its misunderstanding can result in its quick dismissal in discursive conversations, particularly in colonial spaces within the academy, in our communities and in our schools. Necessarily, anti-colonialism immediately states resistance to white supremacy and Eurocentric cultural organization, but the transformational possibilities of this discourse and practice risk going unnoticed by those simply skimming the surface of anti-colonial thought. Anti-colonialism looks for possibilities of resisting and transforming cultural systems of oppression and domination, or imposed ways of knowing, being and living (Dei, 2010)—because of this, it speaks to us all.

In Canada, environmental justice concerns are rising amongst diverse groups—many led by or linked to Indigenous voices, whose evolving cultural knowledges and "authority reside in origin, place, history and ancestry" (Dei, 2002, p. 121). Political and corporate leaders are increasingly being asked to answer questions that have been silenced for far too long. Complementing public, youth, labour, and immigration movements and reorganization around the globe, the Canadian environmental stage is quickly becoming a space for cultural exchange between communities with anti-colonial and sustainable visions for the future. Lovelace (2009) writes, "Environmental and Aboriginal justice converge on many levels and often share ground during direct-action events," asserting that in their unified hopes, they are fighting to eliminate the colonial norm that "supports the Canadian dominion as a system that claims the privilege of pillaging the earth and displacing the original human beings for its own wealth and security" (p. xvii). In other words, this shared responsibility to preserve the sacred humxn relationship to Life and Land, despite diverse histories and identities, is allowing us to work together.

This revolutionary front is not devoid of humxn error, intersections or power dynamics, but it includes all Indigenous and non-Indigenous diasporic or immigrant settler individuals and communities living here, and at the very least it hopes to achieve common ground on the most fundamental level—the interconnectedness and sovereignty of all Life. A young couple from Toronto, from families who had immigrated to Canada, shared with me their experiences of joining an anti-pipeline encampment on First Nations land in western Ontario. When I asked them how they had felt resisting alongside Indigenous communities as non-Indigenous immigrant settlers to Canada, their answers echoed Cannon (2012), who writes that since "the history of colonization is a problem facing all Canadians, then it is each and every Canadian who needs to acknowledge and understand how this is so" (p. 22). On a profound individual and collective level, all of us around the world are being called to action. As immigrant settlers in Canada, we are implicated in the colonial destruction of peoples, cultures and Land, and responsible for defending our humxn connection to Nature—to Life, to Land, to our Self and to One another.

Social justice issues are directly caused by this disconnection of the humxn to Life, of the humxn to the Land. This separation is evident today in the stubborn and irrational decisions among the majority of lawmakers and citizens to continue humxn and environmental destruction, and what this means for the fate of us all, collectively. It is evident in the growing number of refugees that are forced to flee and settle on stolen continents, the ongoing wars creating terror and taking lives in the name of material and cultural power, the institutionalizing and normalizing of white supremacist patriarchy in our increasingly interconnected cultural, political and economic organization, and the larger global capitalist empire's utter indifference for the humxnity of others or the health of our communities in its cold, business-like proceedings. All of these immediate concerns of social justice are linked irrevocably to the unnatural conceptions of the humxn within Nature fueled by European modernity and hierarchical ideas of progress.

Frantz Fanon (1963), a crucial leader in African anti-colonial thought, exposes the "falsity" in the colonial concept of individualism (p. 11) and interrogates the compartmentalization of the world into "species" or race (p. 5). He describes decolonization as a profound social reorganization, one that creates a new dominant species and that requires brotherhood, sisterhood and comradeship—the collapse of individualism (p. 11). How are we going to get there in a world so divided? Where will this new humxn species come from? Arturo Escobar (2004) warns that colonial conditions "have by no means disappeared" (p. 207). He affirms that "the need for international solidarity is greater than ever before, albeit in new ways," and that these alliances have the task of resisting "a new global market-determined economy that commands, in more irrefutable tone than in the past, the world be organized for exploitation and that nothing else will do" (p. 208). In order to "imagine beyond modernity" (Escobar, 2004, p. 210) and create possibilities for the kind of decolonization that involves "the creation of new men" (Fanon, 1963, p. 2), we need to interrogate the conditions that have led us here, and reflect on how we organize our world—both mentally and physically. If the humxn species harbours the potential within it to create such monumentally destructive changes in the material and cultural dimensions of our world, then does not within that same potential lie the power to transform the world for the better? It is time we take up our roles in creating these possibilities together, especially if we hope to support anti-colonial agendas.

Many of us within our communities, even some social justice scholars and activists who argue most passionately against the myriad of colonial and capitalist oppressions, are caught in the snares of consumption, financially supporting and ideologically normalizing many unsustainable colonial 'values' hidden behind cunning advertisements and empty promises. Although it is understandable that addressing our consumption habits requires time, energy and mental space, especially for marginalized and already struggling communities and individuals, this reluctance amongst so many of us to take responsibility for our consumption and reification of capitalist colonial norms serves to highlight a global cultural phenomenon. The colonized consciousness and identity have been detached from the humxn's interconnectedness to Nature, Land, Self and One another. Somewhere deep down we must have been persuaded that the only way forward is capitalistic, based on individualism, linear growth and excess material wealth. Somewhere along the line we have disconnected or conveniently forgotten the dangerous colonial tensions in our consumption. Even as we decry capitalism and call for humxnism in our politics we live a Life of material excess and disconnection that is directly responsible for ongoing destruction of humxn cultures, their Lands and the Life-sustaining systems of the Earth. Why?

If we understand that capitalism is a vehicle for old and new forms of colonization and oppression, then we need to question our investment in it and find real alternatives in our everyday lives. Do we not see that many of the tyrannies of capitalism would be impossible without our participation as consumers? As social justice learners, advocates and pedagogues we foil our own work by falling

amen!

for these cultural commodities and financing further destruction. The strength of capitalism and neocolonialism lies largely in their ability to seduce us, to create vagueness and doubt, and to hide and disconnect the oppressive systems behind the material things we produce and purchase.

By leaving these unsustainable relationships to people, Land, material resources and power unchallenged, we cannot pretend to talk about decolonization. In doing this, we are ignoring that those most affected by the destruction of colonial capitalism are the very people we are fighting with, including Indigenous, racialized and marginalized communities, and we are ignoring the possibility that a growing global ecological and social consciousness could help foreground Indigenous voices and anti-colonial perspectives. Indeed, it is already doing so on many fronts. The College of Menominee Nation, for example, is known for its sustainability focus, research and activism. Through its partnerships with various sustainability agencies and networks, it is working to foreground Menominee wisdom and knowledge and to bring the crucial element of spirituality into sustainability discourse. Melissa Cook, Menominee director of the tribally controlled Sustainable Development Institute, says that spirituality, or "the connection you have with yourself, with the world" is a "core concept of sustainability" (Cook, quoted in Ambler, 2010, p. 73). This is only one example of a growing number of projects across the planet in which the challenges and possibilities of sustainability are bringing Indigenous voices and anti-colonial perspectives to the forefront of social change.

Thinking about social justice requires thinking about how we identify with being alive. It requires us to identify with the changing biological and cultural ecosystems we rely on and co-create. Finally, it requires thinking about how various peoples from around the planet are implicated colonially in these Life systems. Choosing not to engage these pressing questions of our time in anti-colonial thought and learning is short-sighted and could be counter-productive considering the momentum of environmental justice movements that are raising questions about our cultural relationships to Land, Water, Air, each other and an oppressive political economy. Sustainability and anti-colonial struggles are interconnected far more profoundly than we realize if only because they coexist and struggle simultaneously for change in the relations among Land and living peoples. There is a unique and hopeful opportunity for collaboration here, one that holds within it many dreams of possibility.

DISRUPTING SETTLER NORMALCY AND BRINGING COLONIALISM 'HOME'

The African struggle for independence from Europe was a key site for producing much of the beginnings of anti-colonial literature, developed with the revolutionary ideas of authors and social reformers such as Aimé Césaire, Frantz Fanon, Albert Memmi, Mohandas Gandhi and Che Guevara (Dei, 2010). Over time, anti-colonial thought has come to encompass and speak to the struggles of cultures in a much broader context and simultaneously for our particular individual struggles within colonial relations (Kempf, 2010, p. 14). Dei (2010) describes anti-colonial thought as an old idea with resurfacing or new political, cultural and intellectual possibilities that "reflect the values and aspirations of colonized and resisting peoples/subjects" (p. 11). As activists and educators, we can encourage engagement with anti-colonial ideas by highlighting possibilities for solidarity and transformation.

It is with this purpose in mind that I explore the possibilities of a bioecological framework as a means to effectively introduce and engage non-Indigenous peoples with their own implications in colonialism, and for encouraging participation in anti-colonial objectives. As a Uruguayan-born immigrant settler to Canada navigating within a globally destructive colonial and consumerist system, I am concerned with how all anti-colonial thinkers—each coming from our own locations with our own talents and knowledges—can work together, looking and pushing in the same direction rather than against each other. It is ultimately from this perspective that I question how a bioecological approach to anti-colonialism can "encourage people to engage with their privilege" (Cannon, 2012, p. 24) as settlers complicit in colonialism. I believe it can do so by interrogating where we draw the lines between humxns and Nature, and where these ideas came from. This approach helps to create spaces for asking anti-colonial questions and centering identification with settler colonialism in our learning. What are the diverse ways of exploring our colonial and anti-colonial relationships as humxns to Nature, to Land, to each other and to ourselves? As teachers, how can we bring different perspectives to these questions?

Settler colonialism is unique in that the colonizer has moved in and come to stay (Tuck & Yang, 2012). In Canada, settler colonialism means Indigenous communities are being forced to coexist in an oppressive dehumxnizing relationship with colonists, diaspora and immigrant settlers. In order to address how bioecological lenses can help centre anti-colonialism in settler education, we can begin by looking at how the humxn-Nature relationship is theorized in anti-colonial thought. For me, it is helpful to understand colonialism as acting on minds, bodies and materials. It imposes ways of knowing and being with ourselves, with each other and with(in) Nature. Tuck and Yang (2012) offer that settler colonialism remakes *Land* into *property*, and that consequently "human relationships to land are restricted to the relationship of the owner to his property" (p. 5). This physical, psychological and spiritual disconnection to Land, which forms a key part of settler colonial oppression, helps to explain the consumerist trajectory of our globalizing culture. In order to validate the colonial order, "epistemological, ontological, and cosmological relationships to land are interred, indeed made pre-modern and backward" (Tuck & Yang, 2012, p. 5). How else could oil and mining companies bulldoze through communities without legal and political ramifications?

Reading Jean-Paul Sartre's preface to Fanon's *The Wretched of the Earth* (1963), I can see parallels between the way settler colonialism maintains the settlers disconnected from their colonial implications and the way external colonialism— where lands and peoples are exploited and shipped back to the colonizers (see Tuck & Yang, 2012)—physically disconnects the everyday Life and consciousness of the distant metropolis from the ongoing violence in the colonies. Sartre writes, "It's true, you are not colonists, but you are not much better ... they made you rich ... you pretend to forget that ... massacres are committed in your name" (Fanon, 1963, p. xlix). If humxn and environmental destruction is committed in our names as settlers and participants in a global consumerist empire, then we are in solidarity with colonial agents until we do something about it. Is there a link between this physical/mental disconnection from violence and our ability to feel responsibility? If so, what does it mean when settlers feel this violence in their immediate surroundings in the form of increasingly urgent humxn and environmental justice issues? What can happen when colonial violence comes to affect their own lives? It appears to me that rising local and global bioecological concerns—concerns about humxn Life and Nature—may have a role to play in settler awareness and mobilization, precisely by bringing the colonial violence 'home,' so to speak.

How can we nurture settler responsibility by drawing attention to changing colonizer-colonized spatial relations? In a moment when globalization has become a new form of conviviality and interdependence, colonizers, colonized, diaspora and settlers are suddenly finding themselves on the same deteriorating planet. Mbembe (1992) sees in conviviality the possibility of imagining new ways to resist or compromise within colonial state-social relations. He also interrogates how we understand our own acts of resistance and whether we consider these acts to be transformative. Although ideological resistance is important to help heal colonial damage and reclaim agency, the material base of the state also needs to be reclaimed. For this to happen, I believe it is our humxn relationship to Land and Nature that needs to be interrogated and changed. The growing question of sustainability forces us to think about these relationships on individual and collective, local and global levels. It forces us to be accountable for our pasts and futures. In the words of Fanon (1963), we are facing a "colossal task, which consists of reintroducing man into the world, man in his totality" (p. 62). The only way to do this, he writes, is to "confess" our different modes of participation in colonialism, to "decide to wake up, put on [our] thinking caps and stop playing the irresponsible game of Sleeping Beauty" (p. 62). Bioecological entry points to anti-colonialism are one way to offer a space and sense of urgency in which settlers may call to judgment their colonial implications and their responsibilities in decolonization.

A CASE FOR THE BIOECOLOGICAL ENTRY POINT

I anticipate that some may argue that framing anti-colonial transformation through the lens of biological concepts does an injustice to the diverse ways of knowing and relating to what being humxn means. After all, they would be justified in pointing out that biology, as a Western-validated scientific form of knowing, was a potent force for notions of race, progress, Eurocentric modernity and colonialism. Thésée (2006) argues that science was "developed to drive the European man to dominate nature" and "anchored into the colonial enterprise in multiple ways" (p. 28). She rightly points out that science and technology were instrumental in expanding colonization efforts with "tools of exploration, penetration, domination and economic development, but also the scaffolding of militaristic and cultural superiority" (p. 28). The oppression of peoples has been justified by the Eurocentric scientific and philosophical images of humxns within Nature since perhaps even before Plato's and Aristotle's notoriously damaging hierarchical great chain of being. It is evident in the feeble religious excuses of colonization and in the 'scientific' theories that made racism acceptable for so long (see Maldonado-Torres, 2004).

These colonial conceptions work to create concrete colonial realities out of abstract philosophies because of the undue power that science confers. Thésée (2006) insists that the mind is colonized through science and that it "is more efficient than even physical violence in perpetuating domination over peoples and nations" (p. 39). She then goes on to offer that "the school is the main site of propagation for these discourses," and that it is precisely there it can be tackled (p. 39). As an immigrant settler who studied biology in Canada for years, I can think of hundreds of places in which important questions about colonialism and non-Western perspectives could have arisen ... but of course, they didn't. If these questions are silenced in most history classes, why wouldn't they be silenced in the sciences—the colonial tools for domination?

We learned countless details and processes of humxn and natural biology, but even as we learned about ecosystems and sustainability, the humxn relationship to Nature, Life, Self and Others was never specifically addressed in biology class. There was no room for these ontological and spiritual questions in science. I thought about these relationships on my own until I had the chance to discuss them—*finally*—in a postgraduate philosophy class. This is only my personal example, but as Dei (2002) points out, there are many dimensions to the individual learner—psychological, spiritual and cultural dimensions—that are not addressed in conventional education. As I learned about the creation of Life, watching cells grow, divide and diversify before my eyes into what would become a multicellular, living, breathing Existence, how could I *not* see myself reflected? How could the biological study of living things—of Life—*not* discuss this deep connectedness? Why would our very relationship to Nature, which is such a profound aspect of humxn culture and experience, be silenced and remain unquestioned in education? Perhaps it is because interrogating the humxn relationship to Nature could have serious consequences for Western modernity and contemporary colonial systems.

For this reason, I believe that to refuse to question, speak to and decolonize the impacts of biological underpinnings in colonial relations is to refuse the connection between how we have collectively, and yet differently, been conceived as living humxn beings by this dominant discourse, and how Eurocentric conceptions of Life have been internalized by cultures and peoples around the world. Intersections of racism, gender, sexism and ableism in our histories are all informed in diverse ways by these hegemonic biological concepts, making them urgent ideas to interrogate in order to reclaim our individual humxn stories and identities. Kempf (2010) writes, "While anticolonialism works with the knowledge of the oppressed, it also works with a holistic understanding of oppression and of resistance" (p. 20). It is with this holistic understanding in mind that I suggest that science's record as having been practiced and wielded destructively in oppressive colonial politics does not make it an irrelevant space for the politics of resistance. Its deconstruction can help us interrogate profound internalizations of what it means to be humxn and help us connect with each other in a way that redefines how we engage with our world.

BIOPOWER, SOVEREIGNTY AND RESPONSIBILITY

Hierarchical conceptions of humxns and Nature are utilized to confer power and punishment in what Mbembe (2003) describes as necropolitics—the politics of Life and death. Analyzing Foucault's notion of biopower, Mbembe argues that "to exercise sovereignty is to exercise control over mortality and to define life as the deployment and manifestation of power" (p. 27). Put another way, biopower and sovereignty are "the capacity to define who matters and who does not, who is disposable and who is not" (p. 27). He describes racism as "a technology" of biopower that divides the humxn species through "the establishment of a biological caesura between the ones and the others" (p. 17). This holds heavy implications for thinking about both past and ongoing forms of oppression of humxn Life and all other Life on Earth. What kinds of biological lines have we drawn? Are they Life-sustaining or destructive? Can erasing these colonial lines help foreground interconnectedness? I believe we must deconstruct and rebuild how we understand our own sovereignty as living beings (and as settlers) if we have any hope of manifesting responsibility, power and cultural change. Morgensen (2011) writes, "As scholars increasingly theorise biopower as definitive of our times, we must confront our inheritance of settler colonialism as a primary condition of biopower in the contemporary world" (p. 52). It is important to discover how, exactly, settler colonialism is a "primary condition of biopower" in today's world.

Settler colonialism silences and normalizes the oppression of peoples and Life in various ways. It works to legitimize the settler as "holding dominion over the earth and its flora and fauna, as the anthropocentric normal, and as more developed, more human, more deserving than other groups or species" (Tuck & Yang, 2012, p. 6). Violently taking Indigenous Land and then making it produce unsustainably to maintain the settler identity of "civilization" through excess is a form of biopower since it declares the settlers' Life more valuable than both Indigenous Life and the Life of the Land (p. 6). Corntassel (2012) confirms that the "commodifying and marketizing" of Indigenous Land is destructive to Indigenous ways of knowing and relating to Land, which understands "homelands and communities as a complex web of relationships" (p. 92). What is remarkable about Corntassel's perspective, however, is that even given these destructive colonial forces that have "disrupted individual and community relationships with the natural world," he calls on Indigenous communities to "confront the ongoing legacies of colonialism" and to take up their responsibility as leaders in sustainability as a way to work towards decolonization (p. 87).

But Indigenous communities are not the sole humxns responsible. As Cannon (2012) points out, it is imperative that we come to understand "environmental sustainability as a problem we all share" (p. 26). This means engaging *everyone* involved, all humxn Life in its full sovereignty, co-creating a decolonizing cultural rebirth that moves "beyond political awareness and/or symbolic gestures to everyday practices of resurgence" (de Silva, 2011, as cited in Corntassel, 2012, pp. 8, 9). As promoters of social justice, it is not enough to talk about the intricacies of colonialism and capitalism or to lead loud marches against neoliberalist austerity measures in our communities. This is very important work, yet it accomplishes very little if we continue to feed the great industrial-colonial machine. We first need to take responsibility for our individual roles as *workers* and *consumers* implicated in colonial systems, and then begin to relearn sustainable humxn relationships to Nature—to Land, to Life, to ourselves and to each other—informed by the local Indigenous ways of knowing and being with the Earth.

PEDAGOGICAL POSSIBILITIES

Cannon (2012) critiques that much of pedagogical literature fails to address ways in which non-Indigenous peoples can be engaged with their participation in settler colonialism. He argues that the reality of our Canadian educational spaces is that the majority of learners are privileged and that we need to find ways for these individuals to reflect and take ownership of their identity as settlers. In Toronto and large urban centres especially, diasporic peoples and immigrants make up a large portion of learners. In 2011, Statistics Canada reported that one out of five people in Canada's population were "foreign-born" and identified themselves as a visible minority (p. 14). (Here, I must digress to point out that the government's description of any humxn on Earth as "foreign-born" only serves as further indication of the colonial attempts in Canada to draw lines amongst people and Land and to assign privilege.) It is also important to note that in 2011, 13.7 percent of newcomers were born in Europe, 3.9 percent were born in the United States, whereas the remaining 82.4 percent of immigrants to Canada came from Asia, the Middle East, the Caribbean, Central and South America, Africa, Oceania and other regions (p. 15). This means that in larger urban cities, where most newcomers choose to settle (p. 11), most diasporic and immigrant settlers are coming to Canada from countries affected by past and contemporary forms of colonialism.

As Morgensen (2011) points out, "We are all caught distinctly in the hierarchies that structure its [Western law's] persistently colonial formation" (p. 72). In some cases, families have arrived forcefully as part of a diaspora or have sought refuge in Canada and learners come from situations that can be linked back to an oppressive globality "from which subaltern groups attempt to reconstitute place-based imaginaries and local worlds" (Escobar, 2004, p. 210). We face increasingly complex groups of learners that identify in increasingly complex ways to settler colonialism in Canada and to colonialism back home. Haig-Brown (2009) writes that "the simple binary distinctions of colonizer/colonized or Indigenous/immigrant fail to address the range of ways that people are a part of this country" (p. 14). She also points out that the "everyday lack of consciousness" in settler Canadians' education "create[s] the conditions that allow them the same possibility of forgetting their pasts and their relation to Indigenous peoples" (p. 12). Métis scholar Kathy Hodgson-Smith (1997) writes that to be in "good relation" "requires us to know one another, to acknowledge our relation now and historically to each other, to all things living and nonliving, especially to the earth that sustains us physically, intellectually, emotionally and spiritually" (as cited in Haig-Brown, 2009, p. 13). Each of us, individually, must come to understand our own location within this bioecological-cultural and colonial experience of the world.

In Canadian educational spaces that serve a large and growing population of diverse immigrant settlers, anti-colonial perspectives could benefit from a bioecological entry point and the interrogation of biocultural humxn relationships to Nature. In my own community work with settlers, immigrants and refugee newcomers to Canada, beginning with a bioecological conversation has helped bring the transformative purpose of anti-colonialism to the forefront. It creates spaces of exchange for imagining new ways to resist, and allows non-Indigenous settlers to become engaged by encompassing the pluriversal worlds (see Mignolo, 2007) that come together to make up our collective reality as living, breathing humxn beings on a living, breathing planet.

During an arts-based peacebuilding summer program for youth (ages eleven to eighteen), I struggled with bringing anti-colonial social justice concerns to light in a way that successfully engaged and encouraged old and new settlers and immigrants to Canada. For numerous reasons, their families had come to Canada from all over the world, having carried with them diverse individual experiences and perspectives. Together, we told stories and explored identity, drew out anti-oppressive community commitments, learned to share space by playing music and games, and deconstructed social norms through theatre, but I could not inspire in them more than a brief acknowledgment and discussion about some vague role they had to play in some seemingly nonexistent social revolution. How could I inspire more in these youth? How could I encourage real responsibility and ownership for their implications in colonialism? How could I stoke the fire of indignation and a need to question profoundly their identities and contributions within humxnity? It was here that I learned the value of the humxn relationship to Nature. Above all else, no matter what differences we had, here was one story to which we could all relate on a profound individual level.

We began to go outside together. We began to play and notice things we had not noticed before. Walking around our community, I asked them to look for and write down or photograph examples of conflict, oppression, divisions and power, followed by examples of community, diversity, creativity, interconnectedness and peace. Suddenly the words we had been throwing around in discussions began to come alive. But it was not until Nene, a Ghanaian elder and chief, came to teach us one day that colonialism was really brought 'home' and we could see our responsibilities as settlers more clearly.

As we sat in a circle outside, Nene asked us all what we knew about the Earth. In a way that captured our imaginations, he placed each one of us in the heart of Nature. First, he told us that the Earth was on an axis as it rotated around the sun. He told us the Earth was vibrating and spinning at one thousand miles an hour and then asked us how it was possible for us to be sitting so still and unmoved. He interrogated our explanations of gravity and then linked us irrevocably to the electromagnetic field of the Earth's core. As he spoke, he asked us to question our relationship to the Earth through a bioecological and cultural story that engaged us and connected us to trees, to animals, to the sun and moon, to plants, to water, to each other, to Life and finally, to colonialism—humxn and ecological destruction—and to our responsibility as humxns of the Earth. As I watched the conversation unfold, I could see Nene had awakened in the youth not only a sense of wonder and awe but more importantly a sense of collective power.

He had managed to connect them to Nature and to engage them in anti-colonial thought, and by pointing out that youth have for generations been the leaders of social transformations he inspired them to dream and imagine possibilities. From that day forward, our discussions were charged with a different kind of energy and from the young people's artwork, plays, poems, stories, interactions and peace-building initiatives radiated a new understanding of themselves within history and Nature—an old idea, a new dream.

There are possibilities within formal and community educational spaces of introducing anti-colonial questions through questions about Nature—Land, Air, Water—and our relationship to it (Tuck, McKenzie, & McCoy, 2014). A bioeco-logical understanding of our nature as living humxn beings and of our relationship to each other, other species and the Earth, observed critically with a mind that recognizes histories, contradictions, differences and power relations, can be useful for highlighting the very interconnectedness that anti-colonialism and Indigenous voices and movements aim to bring to the forefront. In thinking about solidarity, it can be transformative to learn about humxnity as a species among species—and consider ourselves literally dependent on all other living and non-living things. This bioecological lens, beginning with the sustainability of Life, peoples and Land, can help us to collectively imagine new ways of organizing our structural, social, eco-nomic and cultural ways of being, sharing and knowing in a way that centres inter-dependence rather than destruction—power *with* rather than power *over*.

Biologically, we can show how our learning relies on exchange and communi-cation between people and between Nature and people. Cesaire (1972) asks, "Of all the ways of establishing contact [between civilizations] was it [colonization] the best?" to which he answers simply "no" (p. 2). How can a bioecological anti-colonial approach help us begin to establish contact with each other and the Land in ways that honour our interconnectedness? How can it help us understand sites of difference and to view them as embodiments of a diverse and healthy cultural ecosystem rather than fear them as threats to our own existence? Most importantly, by helping to relocate both colonized and colonizer within Nature and our everyday local and global communities, what potential does it have for healing and mobili-zation, particularly within settler colonial contexts? A bioecological entry point to anti-colonial thought can provide a holistic, multicentric approach to understanding the interconnected relationships between peoples in our natural biocultural context and prevent the propagation of colonial relations (of inclusion and exclusion) in our struggle for the one thing we undoubtedly have in common: Life.

Centuries of colonization have eradicated forms of Life and of knowing, categorized and divided us with Eurocentric constructions of mxn, womxn and Nature that are destructive of Life itself. Colonialism interpreted in this way is NOT progress but the explicit, antagonistic and violent inhibition of the sover-eignty of Life. This is essentially what Cesaire is arguing when he talks about the colonizer proceeding towards savagery, this "thing-ification" of people and Nature and Life, where mxn is turned into an instrument of production (1972, p. 6). But humxns are not instruments or things or machines; we are the embodiments of Life's Power; Life's diversity, subjectivity and communion; Life's resilience, adaptability and creativity. In all our Life-inspired forms, ways of knowing and stories of being, we have unique individual roles to play in the participation of humxnity in the larger ecology and evolution of Earth.

We are Powerful. We are Sovereign. We are Free.
Together, we can inspire the rebirth of humxnity, a new species
"united in diversity"[2] and in justice.
Together, we can be responsible for the co-creation of a culture of possibilities.

NOTES

1. The 'x' is used rather than the 'y' seen in some feminist literature (humyn) because in biology the male sex chromosomes are represented as XY, while the female sex chromosomes are represented as XX. Both male and female sex genes contain the X chromosome passed down from the mother and then either an X or Y chromosome passed down from the father. Feminists using the progressive 'humyn' are still (through a biologist's perspective) retaining the maleness of the word because the 'y' is exclusive to the male sex genes. I choose to use 'humxn' throughout my work to highlight the importance of this common 'x' among people regardless of gender or sexual identity, but also to foreground ethnobiological approaches (and our current lack of these approaches) in imagining and bringing forth the new humxn. Additionally, it is a way of honouring our mothers.
2. Freire, 2007.

REFERENCES

Albuquerque, U. P., & Medeiros, P. (2013). What is evolutionary ethnobiology? *Ethnobiology and Conservation, 2*(6), 1 4.

Ambler, M. (2010). Teaching sustainability: The role of math and science at College of Menominee Nation. In P. Boyer (Ed.), *Ancient wisdom, modern science* (pp. 63–74). Pablo, MT: Salish Kootenai College Press.

Cannon, M. J. (2012). Changing the subject in teacher education: Centering Indigenous, diasporic, and settler colonial relations. *Cultural and Pedagogical Inquiry, 4*(2), 21–37.

Cesaire, A. (1972). *Discourse on colonialism.* New York, NY: Monthly Review Press.

Corntassel, J. (2012). Re-envisioning resurgence: Indigenous pathways to decolonization and sustainable self-determination. *Decolonization: Indigeneity, Education and Society, 1*(1), 86–101.

Dei, G. J. S. (2002). Spiritual knowing and transformative learning. In E. O'Sullivan, A. Morrell, & M. O'Connor (Eds.), *Expanding the boundaries of transformative learning* (pp. 121–133). New York, NY: Palgrave Macmillan.

Dei, G. J. S. (2010). Fanon and anti-colonial theorizing. In G. J. S. Dei (Ed.), *Fanon and the counter-insurgency of education* (pp. 11–28). Rotterdam, the Netherlands: Sense.

Escobar, A. (2004). Beyond the Third World: Imperial globality, global coloniality and anti-globalisation social movements. *Third World Quarterly, 25*(1), 201–230.

Fanon, F. (1963). *The wretched of the earth.* New York, NY: Grove Press.

Freire, P. (2007). *Daring to dream: Toward a pedagogy of the unfinished.* A. M. A. Freire (Ed.). Boulder, CO: Paradigm.

Guevara, E. C. (1961). *Guerrilla warfare.* New York, NY: Monthly Review Press.

Haig-Brown, C. (2009). Decolonizing diaspora: Whose traditional land are we on? *Cultural and Pedagogical Inquiry, 1*(1), 73–90.

Kempf, A. (2010). Contemporary anticolonialism: A transhistorical perspective. In A. Kempf (Ed.), *Breaching the colonial contract: Anti-colonialism in the US and Canada* (pp. 13–34). New York, NY: Springer.

Lovelace, R. (2009). Prologue. Notes from prison: Protecting Algonquin lands from uranium mining. In J. Agyeman, P. Cole, R. Haluza-DeLay, & P. O'Riley (Eds.), *Speaking for ourselves: Environmental justice in Canada* (pp. ix–xix). Vancouver, Canada: University of British Columbia Press.

Maldonado-Torres, N. (2004). The topology of being and the geopolitics of knowledge: Modernity, empire, coloniality. *City, 8*(1), 29–34.

Mbembe, J. A. (1992). Provisional notes on the postcolony. *Africa, 62*(1), 3–37.

Mbembe, J. A. (2003). Necropolitics. *Public Culture, 15*(1), 11–40.

Mignolo, W. D. (2007). The rhetoric of modernity, the logic of coloniality and the grammar of de-coloniality. *Cultural Studies, 21*(2–3), 449–514.

Morgensen, S. (2011). The biopolitics of settler colonialism: Right here, right now. *Settler Colonial Studies, 1,* 52–76.

Statistics Canada. (2011). *Immigration and ethnocultural diversity in Canada, 2011* (No. 99-010-X2011001). Ottawa, Canada: Author.

Thésée, G. (2006). A tool of massive erosion: Scientific knowledge in the neo-colonial enterprise. In G. J. S. Dei & A. Kempf (Eds.), *Anti-colonialism and education: Politics of resistance* (pp. 23–42). Rotterdam, the Netherlands: Sense.

Tuck, E., McKenzie, M., & McCoy, K. (2014). Land education: Indigenous, post-colonial, and decolonizing perspectives on place and environmental education research. *Environmental Education Research, 20*(1), 1–23.

Tuck, E., & Yang, K. W. (2012). Decolonization is not a metaphor. *Decolonization: Indigeneity, Education and Society, 1*(1), 1–40.

Wright, R. (1992). *Stolen continents: The "new world" through Indian eyes.* Toronto, Canada: Penguin Books Canada.

CHAPTER THREE

Against All Authority

Critical Convergences in Anarchist and Anti-Colonial Theory

CHRISTOPHER L. CULLY

INTRODUCTION

The impetus for this chapter stems from the idea that Anarchism and Anti-Colonial theory share certain points of convergence, thus engaging with one another in ways that may not yet be fully realized but are developing. This discussion intends to add to the number of voices that are emerging to put these two bodies of knowledge into conversation and consider what the convergences and divergences are and where the points of learning and transmission are. Through a sustained discussion, comparison, and analysis it becomes evident that Anti-Colonialism and Anarchism share much in the way of convergences and stand to gain from an engagement with one another.

This discussion begins by providing a brief overview of what exactly is meant by Anarchism and Anti-Colonialism in this context, and where these two bodies of knowledge can trace themselves. This will be particularly important in the case of Anarchism, as it is a theory and a practice that has been susceptible to distortion through media representation, academic writing, and public discourse. The discussion then interrogates Anarchism as a body of knowledge that is still at a risk of reproducing colonial relations given its genealogy in Western schools of thought. This risk can be mitigated by engaging with Anti-Colonial theory, and understanding Anarchist history and theory that extends beyond the West. The discussion then investigates the points of convergence that Anarchism and Anti-Colonialism share based on some key aspects of theory, with attention paid to writers/theorists such as Fanon, Alfred, Day, and Bakunin. The discussion concludes by considering some questions about what the conversation between Anarchism and Anti-Colonialism reveals in terms of political and pedagogical implications. The intention is not to answer these questions here but rather to have this be a launching point for a wider discussion and, ultimately, larger pieces of writing and scholarship.

It is important that I situate myself in this discussion as a white-settler residing on stolen/occupied land and have benefited from more than five hundred years of colonization on the North American continent. I realize that I can claim no totality in understanding some of the struggles I shall discuss, but I hope that this chapter can operate as an act of solidarity as a genuine interrogation of how Anti-Colonialism and Anarchism both work to contest inequitable relations across settler society and around the globe.

ANARCHISM

Anarchism in theory and praxis has suffered much misrepresentation and criticism as a viable state of social relations, as well as being irrelevant given that it is difficult to define. Anarchism has been accused of being unrealistically utopian, ill defined, and an extreme violence bent on an extreme form of individualism. These misconceptions can partly be attributed to Anarchism itself, as it is anti-canonical in nature, meaning there isn't a "single body of written work [unlike in the case of Marxism], that clearly and cohesively maps out a common position" (Suissa, 2010, p. 7). Despite the anti-canonical nature and difficulty in finding a precise definition, there are four points of agreement consistent across all strands of Anarchism:

1. All anarchists share a principled rejection of the state and its institutions, and in doing so they:
2. Do not reject the notion of social organization or order per se;
3. Do not necessarily regard freedom—specifically, individual freedom—as the primary value and the major goal of social change, and;
4. Do not propose any "blueprint" for the future society. (Suissa, 2010, p. 14)

For the purposes of this discussion, the Anarchist position being described is based on these four general principles, but is also guided more specifically by the Social Anarchist school of thought, broadly made up by thinkers such as Peter Kropotkin and Mikhail Bakunin. Social Anarchism emphasizes a collectivist vision and has made up the majority of theoretical work produced by Anarchists. There are two major strands that make up Social Anarchist thought: Anarcho-Communism and

Anarcho-Syndicalism. Anarcho-Communism "is the view that the products of labour should be collectively owned and distributed according to the principle of from each according to his ability, to each according to his needs" (Suissa, 2010, p. 14). Anarcho-Syndicalism makes central the issues surrounding labour, and contends that trade unions, as an expression of the working class, should form the basis for a new social reality (Suissa, 2010). While it is clear that one can make immediate connections between Social Anarchism and Marxism, the defining distinction is the Anarchist's rejection of the state. Ultimately, Anarchism works to resist all interlocking forms of oppression and domination.

ANTI-COLONIALISM

We should understand that Anti-Colonialism "challenges any form of economic, cultural, political, and spiritual dominance" (Dei & Kempf, 2006, p. 5). Cannella and Manuelito (2008) summarize Anti-Colonialism in the following way:

> a) Reveals and actively challenges social systems, discourses and institutions that are oppressive and that perpetuate injustice … and explore ways of making these systems obviously visible in society; b) support knowledges that have been discredited by dominant power orientations in ways that are transformative … and c) construct activist conceptualizations of research that are critical and multiple in ways that are transparent, reflexive and collaborative. (Cannella & Manuelito, 2008, p. 56)

Anti-Colonialism "challenges the colonizer's sense of reason, authority and control" (Dei & Kempf, 2006, p. 5). With this orientation in mind it is also crucial to understand that Anti-Colonialism challenges the intersecting and interlocking axis of oppression and domination. Anti-Colonialism is an epistemic disruption to colonial knowledge production; ultimately, Anti-Colonialism seeks to theorize colonialism and dominating social relations through the lenses of Indigenous knowledges and worldviews. As Dei (2006) notes, "Such a perspective seeks to subvert the dominant relations of knowledge production that sustain hierarchies and systems of power" (Dei & Kempf, 2006, p. 5). Anti-Colonialism, then, is a deeply political project and cannot be wrestled from that impetus.

While these descriptions in no way capture the totality of either body of knowledge, it is illustrative to identify some of the ways in which Anti-Colonialism and Anarchism have points of important convergence. Fundamentally, both are highly skeptical of dominating social relations and seek alternative practices to resist and reconfigure these relations in more equitable/just embodiments. Both Anarchist and Anti-Colonial projects are deeply political and it is often impossible to dissect the theory from the praxis.

RACE, INDIGENEITY, AND ANARCHISM

Historically, Anarchism has had a tenuous relationship when it comes to supporting radicalized social movements. Most often, Anarchism has been identified as a white middle-class movement that cares little for everyday oppression and instead focuses unrealistically on grand utopian visions. These visions mostly subsume questions of race and indigeneity under the broader umbrella of total class liberation.

> Clearly, a movement which is all White, middle-class, self-absorbed, and naive about our struggle is not one we can unite with. In addition, it is a movement which can do very little for itself, let alone for our struggle. So it is time for some frank talk with Anarchists if we are to move forward from here toward the realistic possibility of a social revolution. (Ervin, 2015, para. 2)

This commentary emanating from the first issue of a journal on black autonomist politics, the *Journal of Anarchy and the Black Revolution*, clearly lays out the critique and the challenge to Anarchism in the form of "frank talk"—for Anarchism is to take seriously the questions of difference it has historically ignored, in particular race and indigeneity. Part of Anarchism's problem in this instance is that for some time it has been primarily concerned with liberation and emancipation under the umbrella of "class," deeming this to be the overarching and most encompassing area of struggle. Questions of difference then are often left aside to attend to a totalizing vision of working-class liberation and self-determination.

Scholarship on questions of Anarchism and race is seemingly lacking; however, Maia Ramnath (2011) does take up the question of race and caste as it relates to the Indian Anarchist context, although this is a small part of her larger project. The case must be made for how Anarchist scholars and activists dedicated to Anti-Colonialism move to take on the questions of race and indigeneity. The domination of class politics in Anarchist circles needs to end. Anarchists and Anarchist theory need to begin to take seriously questions of difference through intersectional and interlocking frameworks. One area of Anarchist Studies that offers some hope in light of this challenge is "Post-Anarchism."

There is risk here in positing Post-Anarchism as a potential starting point for Anarchist theory to begin to take seriously questions of race and indigeneity. The unease arises in Post-Anarchism, in its most simple form, and is the meeting and dialogue created by Classical Anarchist theory and Poststructuralism and knowing that both of these traditions find their origins in Western ontologies. Similarly, Poststructuralism is often criticized as being devoid of political praxis; however, when seen in conjunction with both Anti-Colonial thought and Anarchist theory, there is space created for the political project to emerge. The linkage with Poststructuralism provides a reorientation for Anarchism to question universality and modernity, troubling Anarchism into dealing more astutely with intersectionality and social relations. Despite this seeming paradox with the rest of this chapter there is something of importance here, and it begins with the questions of power and the state.

Anarchist sociologist Richard Day (2005) has worked to explain the relationship between Foucault's conception of power and how it can relate to Anarchist practices of resistance. Day (2005) brings together Foucault's conception of power with his views on governmentality, describing how Foucault illustrated that the scope of government over time moved from being a focus on the regulation of the individual to a focus on the regulation of the population in total. This practice of governmentality focused on regulating behavioural norms whether they be sexual, familial, or broader in scope. This normalization of social behaviour then becomes the coercive force, one that is decentralized and no longer located in one place. What this implies then is that the "state" as a focus of singular domination and power no longer exists as such. Rather, when we speak about the state, we are talking about a "state" of relations (Day, 2005, p. 16). If we understand that the main contention of Anarchism historically is the state, then what does a shift away from the state as the single focal point of domination mean for Anarchist practices of resistance? This is where Post-Anarchism arrives as the new formulation of Anarchist practice which seeks to question the Western canonical tenets of Anarchism, embracing Foucault's conception of power and governmentality to make the claim that if we think of the state as a "state" of relations, then a totalizing revolution becomes ineffectual. The change must be brought in the realm of discourse, of everyday practice, taking advantage of the silences and ambiguities that discourse creates. Important for understanding Post-Anarchist resistance, Foucault writes,

> I'm not saying that all forms of power are unacceptable but that now power is necessarily acceptable or unacceptable. This is anarchism. But since anarchism is not acceptable these days, I will call it anarcheology, the method that takes no power as necessarily acceptable. (Day, 2005, p. 137)

Here, for Anarchists, Foucault illustrates that "life without the state form is an ongoing actuality rather than an impossibility or as a utopian point to be reached in a far off future" (Day, 2005, p. 137). In other words, life without or beyond this state is a living reality/potential, and Anarchist practices of resistance need to change to respond to this; the time for liberation is now and in continuum. Anarchist theory thus must refocus to the "state" of social relations, necessitating a change in tactics from totalizing revolution to diversified, localized, and multiple practices of resistance that are responsive to specific locales and struggles. This may also go a long way in liberating Anarchism from a rigid class-based position and moving it towards an understanding of other subject positions.

A move to a focus on the "state of relations" is particularly important to an Anarchist discussion of race. For if we understand race as a social construct that is deeply embedded in our social state of relations, then Anarchists who are on a mission to resist all oppression and domination must take up this question with serious intention. Anarchist theory needs to challenge the "state of relations," part of which is informed by racialized narratives and discursive and social practices.

The state of relations is also fundamentally important to taking up a discussion of Anarchism and Indigeneity. Central to this discussion of Indigeneity and the state of relations is the centrality of place and land for Indigenous peoples. Following from Barker and Pickerill (2012), who draw on Kanien'kehá:ka scholar Taiaiake Alfred in thinking through the terms Indigenous and Indigeneity, it remains clear that, in fact, "Indigenous remains a contested term, in no small part because it is the imposition of colonial domination and dispossession that renders an Indigenous collectivity or commonality across diverse places visible" (Barker & Pickerill, 2012, p. 1709). Drawing on Alfred's (2005) articulation of Indigenous identity as founded on an "oppositional, place-based existence, along with the consciousness of being in struggle against the dispossessing and demeaning fact of colonization by foreign peoples" (Barker & Pickerill, 2012, p. 1709), place-based existence is a type of being for Indigenous peoples—the anchor for identity, relationships, and spirituality. The colonial projects globally worked hard to displace Indigenous peoples from their lands and reduce their spiritual, material, and life-sustaining connections to place and land. Barker and Pickerill (2012, p. 1706; see also Ferguson, 2011, pp. 103–106) go on to note:

> Anarchist and Indigenous peoples' movements do have a great deal in common. They share the goal of creating decolonized societies, defined by the mutual sharing of place, maintenance of social-spatial organizations commensurate with their respective cultures, and mediated through respectful protocols designed to maintain alliances across, rather than in spite of, difference. However, these lofty and commonly held goals are frequently sabotaged by taken-for-granted spatial perceptions with major impacts on the practices and processes of pursuing decolonization. For as much as it is commonly understood that decolonization is a place-based process, an attempt to counter centuries of settler colonial usurpation of Indigenous lands, there remains a lack of engagement with colonization as a highly spatial process.

Barker and Pickerill (2012) propose that Anarchists and Anarchist theory must take into account that a spatial and place-based ethic is essential to understanding the specific histories of colonization in a given locale. Traditionally, Anarchism has been primarily concerned with questions of universalism and internationalism— with social class positioned as the cohesive factor. However, this ignores or silences the ways in which struggles are not only positioned by class, but also how specifically struggles for decolonization and freedom from oppression are based in very specific historical contexts of place. When it comes to Anarchists and Anarchist theory looking to be involved with Anti-Colonial politics/theory, it is not only an understanding of the immediate and contemporary context that is urgent and necessary. A long view of history and context that encompasses pre-colonial understandings must also be included. Anarchists and Anarchist theory must seriously reckon with colonial histories and how spatial and place-based relationships have been altered and disrupted to ensure that their work around spatial relations does not further this disruption or reinscribe colonial relations. Self-determination being a key factor in Anarchist ethics must be extended to take seriously the self-determination of Indigenous peoples even if it does not align squarely with Anarchist goals.

Barker and Pickerill (2012) also caution that the Anarchist activist cannot simply appropriate Indigenous knowledge, ways, and place-based relationality, for that would be disingenuous and further damaging; however, Anarchists must critically interrogate their place in relation to Indigenous Anti-Colonial struggles. This critique extends to Anarchist theory as it challenges its Western academic orientation and universal analysis to be mindful of how Anarchist theory and practice will inevitably have to look different through place and space.

SHIFTING ORIENTATIONS

Despite being one of the most radical and anti-authoritarian theoretical standpoints, Anarchism has not always been able to adequately evaluate and centre Anti-Colonial struggles in its theory and praxis. Emanating mostly from European Socialism, Anarchists have historically been preoccupied primarily with Capitalism and its manifestations in the West and have only lightly touched on Anarchist Anti-Colonial struggle in its historiography. As mentioned, Anti-Colonialism theorizes colonialism and domination through the lenses of Indigenous knowledges and worldviews. That draws our attention to the fact that Anti-Colonialism as theory travels between time and space and across borders, drawing on a multiplicity of "centres." This is a point in which Anarchist theory has the potential to glean much from Anti-Colonialism to actually rediscover the historical linkages between Anarchist struggle and Anti-Colonial struggle and theory. Anarchism in this sense needs to begin to read itself through an Anti-Colonial lens to rediscover its own lost historiography that places struggles against colonial and imperial rule at the forefront and de-centres itself from Europe and the West in general. Much like Mignolo (2007) calls for an epistemic de-linking from modernity for decolonization (Mignolo, 2007, p. 3), Anarchists need to de-link from the idea that Anarchism is simply a phenomenon of Europe and the West.

Anarchist scholar Süreyyya Evren (2012) calls attention to the idea of Anarchism being a simply European phenomenon "as an example of what J. M. Blair calls 'geographical diffusionism,' where progress is seen to flow endlessly out of the centre (Europe) towards the otherwise sterile periphery"—perpetuating Anarchism giving into the "colonizers model of the world" (Evren, 2012, p. 314). To move away from this colonizing mind-set, Anarchism needs to engage itself from an Anti-Colonial perspective to rediscover how Anarchism has rather been a flow of ideas transnationally and is not a unique outcome of European social relations. Evren (2012) calls on us to discuss "third world anarchisms" and treat them in their own agency and not just as simple applications of European ideas. Contemporary Anarchist theorists have already begun the work of shifting the orientation of Anarchism from Europe and the West, but much work is still to be done. Benedict Anderson (2005) in his work *Under Three Flags* discusses how Anarchists from Spain worked in solidarity with Anti-Colonial struggles and that Anti-Colonialism was at one time a priority for Anarchists despite the staunchly nationalist goals of the Anti-Colonial struggle at the time. In a similar vein, Maia Ramnath (2011) in her book *Decolonizing Anarchism* takes on Anti-Colonial struggles in the South Asian context from an Anarchist perspective, highlighting how South Asian Anarchists played a defining role in these struggles (Ramnath, 2011). This reveals to us that Anarchism and Anti-Colonialism have in fact sustained a long-standing conversation and points of solidarity that have somehow been lost in the historiography. In this sense, the call to understand the convergences between Anti-Colonialism and Anarchism is not "new" but rather more of a reawakening to or a rediscovering of those connections. The priority that both Anti-Colonialism and Anarchism place upon resisting all that is dominating and oppressive lays the framework no doubt for why these two bodies of knowledges share an affinity, which a rereading of history reveals.

REVOLUTION AND COLONIAL OVERTHROW

Limited work has been done to bring together some of the key theorists of Anti-Colonialism and Anarchism, but some interest has emerged in looking at the convergences between a theory of Anarchist social revolution as developed by Mikhail Bakunin and the theory of Colonial overthrow put forward by Frantz Fanon. Ryan Allen Knight (2013) argues, "When we examine Mikhail Bakunin and Frantz Fanon's revolutionary theories, we see very stark overlapping thoughts regardless of the different time and place in which they were writing" (p. 275). Knight further argues that unlike traditional Marxist interpretations of social revolution predicated on the emancipation of the working class as the only revolutionary force, it is Bakunin's understanding that the peasantry, were and are a revolutionary force in history. "Bakunin understood domination and resistance outside of the bourgeoisie and proletariat antagonism that is inherent in Capitalism" (Knight, 2013,

p. 275). Oppression and domination are manifested in multiple sets of conditions; thus Bakunin indicates to us that Anarchism is willing to envision a larger picture of multiple interlocking forces. Much like Bakunin, Fanon went beyond classical Marxist theories to understand colonialism and domination from the psychophysical realm, paying close attention to the overall mental state of colonized peoples under colonial rule (Knight, 2013, p. 276). The willingness of both Bakunin and Fanon to look beyond simple dichotomies in the processes of domination points us to the notion that both Anti-Colonialism and Anarchism can be understood to be engaged in projects of multiplicity whereby multiple understandings, viewpoints, and conditions need to be engaged to be able to form a complete picture of domination and an ability to resist it.

The drive to go beyond typical understandings is not the only line of convergence that Bakunin and Fanon open up to us between Anarchism and Anti-Colonialism. It is also their thoughts on transfers of power at the end of revolution or overthrow. Both Bakunin and Fanon were highly skeptical "of bourgeois elements emerging during and/or after the revolution" (Knight, 2013, p. 282). Bakunin, an Anarchist, was highly uncomfortable with the idea of any return to state power during or after the revolution with the fear that this would stamp out any of the truly radical reorientations put forth by the people (Knight, 2013, p. 282). Fanon was less concerned with a return to state power and more concerned that any play by the nationalist bourgeoisie, who were too close with the colonizer, to gain position for themselves should be treated with great skepticism and disregard. In *The Wretched of the Earth*, Fanon (1965, p. 110) observes:

> The national bourgeoisies, however, ... in region after region, are in a hurry to stash away a tidy sum for themselves and establish a national system of exploitation. ... [T]his is why we must understand that African Unity can only be achieved under pressure and through leadership by the people, i.e., with total disregard for the interests of the bourgeoisie.

Fanon's warning here demonstrates the intolerance that Anti-Colonialism has for reproducing domination of social relations and that Anti-Colonial struggle must go beyond simple reform. It needs, of course, to accept leadership from the people and to reject the colonizers' vision, even if that vision is coming from the mouths of fellow countrymen. What one sees in this quote as well is distrust in illegitimate authority, another point in which Anarchism and Anti-Colonialism coalesce. Mikhail Bakunin, writing on the goals of revolution, stated:

> The immediate, if not the ultimate, goal of the revolution is the extirpation of the principle of authority in all its possible manifestations; this aim requires the abolition and, if necessary, the violent destruction of the state. (quoted in Knight, 2013, p. 282)

While Fanon (1965) might not necessarily be calling for an end to statehood per se, the anti-authoritarian streak and disregard for illegitimate authority present in these two passages demonstrate how both Anti-Colonialism and Anarchism are not interested in replacing one oppressor for another, but rather seek to go beyond and work to redefine social relations genuinely for the people in the collective interest. The echoes of Fanon and Bakunin here have found resonance with many Anti-Colonial and Anarchist theorists now working to redefine the links of solidarity between these two traditions.

ANARCHO-INDIGENISM AND BUILDING ALTERNATIVES

Though links of solidarity are beginning to be made between Anti-Colonialism and Anarchism there is still debate regarding what the actual possibilities are given Anarchism's long-standing relation to Western modes of thought. Much of this theorizing has come from Indigenous North American scholars working on issues of Indigenous Resurgence. While this theorizing cannot speak for all colonized peoples across the globe, it is posited as an example of where Anarchist and Anti-Colonial ideas are coming together to prefigure and create alternatives. Nishnaabeg scholar Leanne Simpson (2011, p. 31) reminds us that

> western theory, whether based in post-colonial, critical, or even liberator strains of thought, has been exceptional at diagnosing, revealing, and even interrogating colonialism. ... Yet western theories of liberation have for the most part failed to resonate with the vast majority of Indigenous peoples, scholars, or artists.

Leanne Simpson's skepticism here is an important lesson when talking about the convergences between Anarchism and Anti-Colonialism, for if these two bodies of knowledge are truly to be able to be in conversation, it is essential that Anarchism recognize Colonialism as a starting point in analyzing systems of oppression, particularly in settler-colonial contexts. Despite this skepticism, though, there is still great opportunity for developing a framework that brings together Anti-Colonial and Anarchist conceptions. Kanien'kehá:ka scholar Taiaiake Alfred (2005) in his work *Wasáse: Indigenous Pathways of Action and Freedom* put forth the concept of "anarcho-indigenism" and describes it in the following way:

> Two elements that come to my mind are *indigenous*, evoking cultural and spiritual rootedness in this land and the Onkwehonwe struggle for justice and freedom, and the political philosophy and movement that is fundamentally anti-institutional, radically democratic, and committed to taking action to force change: *anarchism*. (p. 45)

What is so striking about Alfred's conception is not only that he brings together a concept of Indigeneity with Anarchism, but also that he recognizes this as a positive political project, a point to which we will return. We should understand that Indigenous resurgence and Anti-Colonialism are not shaped by Anarchism, but in reality Anarchism has been very much shaped by Anti-Colonial and

Indigenous thought. Anarchists are heavily indebted to Indigenous peoples of the Americas and beyond—although Indigenous peoples faced struggles against colonial regimes, it was their contributions to discourses around democracy, autonomy, and self-determination that were being appropriated by the "enlightened" thinkers of the time (Lasky, 2011, p. 9). Any practice of struggle or liberation in a settler-colonial context, such as Canada, demands an alliance and prominence given to those to whom these lands belong. The alliances are being built between Anarchists and Indigenous peoples as they are both engaged in struggle against the state, specifically in Anti-Colonial and counter-globalization movements (Lasky, 2011). The struggle against the state is a key component to the contemporary convergences between Anti-Colonialism and Anarchism, and has characterized much of the recent scholarship surrounding discourses of reconciliation and Indigenous resurgence. In his work *Peace, Power, Righteousness: An Indigenous Manifesto*, Alfred (2008) calls for Indigenous peoples to reconnect with traditional value systems and ways of knowing as the very means by which to resist against colonialism and state power. Similarly, Dene scholar Glen Coulthard (2007) has warned against Indigenous peoples participating and seeking resistance only through state-sanctioned channels, because they run the risk of what he calls becoming "subjects of empire" (Coulthard, 2007). Ultimately, what scholars like Alfred and Coulthard want to recognize is that we must "deconstruct the notion of state power to allow people to see that the settler state has no right to determine indigenous futures" (Alfred, 2008, p. 71). Alfred calls for Indigenous peoples to seek a return to their own specific form of governance, and as such disengage from the state.

This idea of disengaging from the state is a notion that has preoccupied some contemporary Anarchist scholars. Anarchist theorist Richard J. F. Day (2005) has begun to develop a concept of social change that resists the old dichotomies and hegemony, instead focusing on a politics of affinity. Day (2005) calls for radical social change to begin to be based on a model of *affinity* as opposed to *hegemony*. Day (2005) describes these movements for radical social change as displaying an "*affinity for affinity* [emphasis added], that is, for non-universalizing, non-hierarchical, non-coercive relationships based on mutual aid and shared ethical commitments" (p. 9). Day's conceptions of a non-universalizing conception of social movement and change align with Anti-Colonialism's impetus towards understanding a multiplicity of knowledge forms and ultimately tactics for resistance. Day (2005) challenges old models of social change that consistently look towards the state as a site of recognition or a vessel to be taken over and appropriated; rather, this model of affinity calls for supporting one another in collective construction and experimentation free from totalizing ideas, not the destruction of the state per se but rather a disengagement. It is within the politics of affinity and disengagement then that one can begin to see some important linkages between contemporary Anti-Colonialism and Anarchism.

Indigenous activists, scholars, and others are at the forefront of constructing alternatives to colonial state power and beginning to disengage from the colonial institutions in order to return to traditional forms of governance; in a sense, this is a radical reorientation that threatens to undermine relations of power specifically in settler-colonial contexts. Although Anarchists do not have a rich tradition of spirituality and epistemology to draw upon, there is an opportunity here in the convergence of Anti-Colonialism and Anarchism, for Anarchists to forge and begin to develop more genuine relations of solidarity that put colonization at the forefront. Richard Day (2001) puts forward the Two-Row Wampum as a model for egalitarian social relations and describes it from the Haudenosaunee perspective in this way:

> These two rows will symbolise two paths or two vessels, travelling down the same rivers together. One, a birch bark canoe, will be for the Indian people, their laws, their customs and their ways. The other, a ship, will be for the white people and their laws, their customs and their ways. We shall each travel the river together, side by side, but in our own boat. Neither of us will try to steer the other's vessel. (p. 191)

The Two-Row Wampum is a manifestation of a philosophy regarding egalitarian social relations and sovereignty between groups of peoples. One need not look long into the history of settler states such as Canada to see that agreements such as the Two-Row Wampum have not been kept up in good faith. However, Richard Day brings Anarchist theorist Pierre-Joseph Proudhon into the discussion to demonstrate how this conception of relationship squares with Anarchist ideas surrounding federalism. Day (2001, p. 192) notes, "In federal systems based on a plentitude of autonomies, there is no hovering sovereign that would be capable of devolving or granting rights or privileges to subordinate entities." What Day (2001) brings attention to here is a conception in both Anarchist and Anti-Colonial theory that groups and entities can live alongside each other under the promise of mutual non-interference, enabling a multiplicity of sovereignties to exist as opposed to subsuming all into a single nation-state sovereignty, a system that has characterized the colonial encounter. In this sense, we must also consider that Anarchism and Anti-Colonialism are deeply political projects that place a focus on praxis as well as theory. One of the reasons these two philosophies square so well is that they harbour a hopeful politics that goes beyond critiquing power and ultimately looks for ways to subvert and transform power through social relations, multiple knowledge systems, and radical experimentation.

FUTURE QUESTIONS AND NEW LINES OF INQUIRY

While this discussion has not exhausted the conversation surrounding Anarchism and Anti-Colonialism, it is clear how these bodies of knowledge converge in some important ways, diverge in others, but ultimately have a lot to offer one another. Some key questions do emerge that offer some lines for future inquiries into the implications for the transmissions between these two. First, what are the political implications of building solidarity/action based on disengagement from the state? The radical politics of both Anti-Colonialism and Anarchism at least point us in the direction of beginning to consider quite seriously how the rally for state protection and inclusion so quickly runs the risk of further entrenching domination and oppression. In this sense, then, we must consider what radically Anarchist and Anti-Colonial/Decolonial politics can come to embody. Second, how would a shift towards centring Anti-Colonial and Anarchist historiography play out pedagogically? It would be important to consider how these politics may well be able to infiltrate spaces of education, challenging not only the very foundations in which these institutions rest but also how they could be engaged in radical transformation. How can Anarchist theory benefit from the spiritual aspects of Anti-Colonialism and Decolonization, or is this an inherent incompatibility? In the short run, at the very least an initial answer to this question may be found in Anarchists respecting their notions of self-determination for everyone. These questions, and many more, will, I hope, guide a larger project surrounding the possibilities that are made available by Anti-Colonial and Anarchist interventions.

Both Anarchism and Anti-Colonialism offer views into the importance of maintaining a politics and a positive political project. Neither Anarchism nor Anti-Colonialism can be separated out nicely between theory and practice and rather involve both intimately. Both seek to move beyond relations of domination by creating alternatives that are based on self-determination and collective autonomy. This is a politics of possibility—as Anarchism and Anti-Colonialism bring notions of social transformation and a new multiplicity of being with each other to these conversations.

REFERENCES

Alfred, G. R. (2008). *Peace, power, righteousness: An Indigenous manifesto*. Don Mills, Canada: Oxford University Press.

Alfred, T. (2005). *Wasáse: Indigenous pathways of action and freedom*. Toronto, Canada: University of Toronto Press.

Anderson, B. R. O. G. (2005). *Under three flags: Anarchism and the anti-colonial imagination*. London: Verso.

Barker, A. J., & Pickerill, J. (2012). Radicalizing relationships to and through shared geographies: Why anarchists need to understand Indigenous connections to land. *Antipode, 44*(5), 1705–1725.

Cannella, G. S., & Manuelito, K. D. (2008). Feminisms from unthought locations: Indigenous worldviews, marginalized feminisms, and revisioning an anticolonial social science. In N. K. Denzin,

Y. S. Lincoln, & L. T. Smith (Eds.), *Handbook of critical and Indigenous methodologies* (pp. 45–60). Thousand Oaks, CA: Sage.

Coulthard, G. (2007). Subjects of empire: Indigenous peoples and the "politics of recognition" in Canada. *Contemporary Political Theory, 6*, 437–460.

Day, R. (2001). Who is this "we" that gives the gift? Native American political theory and the Western tradition. *Critical Horizons, 2*(2), 173–201.

Day, R. (2005). *Gramsci is dead: Anarchist currents in the newest social movements.* London, England: Pluto Press.

Dei, G. J. S., & Kempf, A. (Eds.). (2006). *Anti-colonialism and education: The politics of resistance.* Rotterdam, the Netherlands: Sense.

Ervin, L. K. (2015). Speaking of anarchism, racism and black liberation. *Journal of Anarchy and the Black Revolution.* Retrieved from https://libcom.org/library/speaking-anarchism-racism-black-liberation

Evren, S. (2012). There ain't no black in the anarchist flag! Race, ethnicity and anarchism. In R. Kinna (Ed.), *The Continuum companion to anarchism.* London, England: Bloomsbury Academic.

Fanon, F. (1965). *The wretched of the earth.* New York, NY: Grove Press.

Ferguson, K. E. (2011) Becoming anarchism, feminism, indigeneity. *Affinities: A Journal of Radical Theory, Culture, and Action. 5*(1) 103–106.

Knight, R. A. (2013). Anti-colonial anarchism, or anarchistic anti-colonialism: The similarities in the revolutionary theories of Frantz Fanon and Mikhail Bakunin. In J. A. Meléndez Badillo & N. J. Jun (Eds.), *Without borders or limits: An interdisciplinary approach to anarchist studies* (pp. 275–284). Newcastle upon Tyne, England: Cambridge Scholars.

Lasky, J. (2011). Indigenism, anarchism, feminism: An emerging framework for exploring postimperial futures. *Affinities: A Journal of Radical Theory, Culture and Action, 5*(1), 3–36.

Mignolo, W. (2007). Delinking. *Cultural Studies, 21*(2–3), 449–514.

Ramnath, M. (2011). *Decolonizing anarchism: An anti-authoritarian history of India's liberation struggle.* Oakland, CA: AK Press.

Simpson, L. (2011). *Dancing on our turtle's back: Stories of Nishnaabeg re-creation, resurgence and a new emergence.* Winnipeg, Canada: Arbeiter Ring.

Suissa, J. (2010). *Anarchism and education: A philosophical perspective.* Oakland, CA: PM Press.

CHAPTER FOUR

Anti-Colonial AND Decolonizing Meaning Making OF Colonialism Through THE 1991 Aboriginal Peoples Survey

UMAR UMANGAY

A cannibologist is, at least in the first instance, any anthro exhibiting an obsessive desire to prove that cannibalism was—in some cases still is—an inherent feature of "primitive" societies.
—WARD CHURCHILL & PIERRE ORELUS, "CONFRONTING WESTERN COLONIALISM, AMERICAN RACISM AND WHITE SUPREMACY" (2012, P. 67)

INTRODUCTION

Like the obsession of the "cannibologist," this chapter challenges the ontology and mono-cultural perspective of large-scale quantitative research as an obsession/desire to impose particular identities on Indigenous communities, and as an expression of ongoing colonialism in the settler nation-state of Canada. It explores decolonization, anti-colonial, and post-colonial thought through a paradigm shift of the quantitative analysis and its interpretations of the 1991 Aboriginal Peoples Survey (APS) conducted by Statistics Canada, the federal Canadian agency mandated to collect qualitative and quantitative data about Canadians (Statistics Canada, 2012a, 2012b, 2012c, 2012d). The 1991 APS was selected because of the data liberation initiative at the University of Toronto, allowing for open access to the data set without pre-analysis from researchers at Statistics Canada. It was ethically useful because the data through the lens of an Indigenous researcher would provide trends and themes, rather than identifying or reifying Aboriginal communities in Ontario. This unobtrusive, open-access approach would provide a map to the dynamics of power from the colonizer and its historical significance as the initial national survey on Aboriginal People in Canada. This data legacy informed reconciliation projects such as the qualitative and witness-based approach of the Royal Commission on Aboriginal Peoples and the Truth and Reconciliation Commission.

The meaning making comes from the adaptation of Enriquez's (1992) "indigenizing from within," and the lived-experience of this author developing a decolonization and anti-colonial critique and transformation of quantitative analysis based on the nuances of Indigenous knowledge (IK). The discussion also expands on previous articles by Angod (2006) that explored the transitory and unstable nature of post-colonial and anti-colonial thought and relations as they related to Canada's legal system, and by Hales's (2006) examination of the cognitive imposition of colonial and modernist investigative techniques connected to white privilege that remain embedded in education research methodology.

This discussion follows the framework of the matrix in Figure 1.

Indigenous Creation Story *Holo Mai Pele* (Emerson, 1909; Kanahele, 2016)	Colonization	Decolonization	Anti-colonial Curriculum Development
Pele sends *Hi'iaka* to get *Lohi'au*	Rejection	Recovery	Epistemology
Encounter with reptiles	Invisibility	Mourning	Conceptual frameworks
Reanimation of *Lohi'au*	Replacement	Dreaming	Reflective practice
Hawaiian gods intercede	Façade of adaptation	Commitment	Knowledge production
Hi'iaka equal deity to *Pele*	Exploitation	Action	(Re)configuration

(left vertical axis label: Transformative Interface)

Application Matrix

Fig. 1. Transformative interface and application matrix.[1]

It was applied to the 1991 APS, so that the data and analysis were used in part as the colonizing process of Canadian First Nations, but they may also be used in part as the decolonizing process for Indigenous people. Referring to the "Colonization" column in Figure 1, the APS and contemporary quantitative research followed the process of rejection, invisibility, replacement, façade of adaptation, and exploitation. The subversion of the analysis (Dei, 2006, p. 3) comes with opening up the analysis using the decolonization column in which the APS becomes a tool for recovery, for mourning of the past and what could have been, dreaming, commitment, and action. The structure of this discussion uses the two columns as an adaptation to the contrapuntal relationship used in post-colonial discourse (Said, 1978, 1993), that is, rejection and recovery, invisibility and mourning, replacement and dreaming, façade of adaptation and commitment, and exploitation and action.

Using the awareness that colonization is anything dominating or imposing (Dei, 1996; Kempf, 2009), the quantitative summary of results from the APS and its developing implications became the moment of unpacking for an anti-colonial trajectory. By that I mean that the process of decolonization becomes subversive to the ideals and rigorousness of Western-based quantitative analysis. In summary, this discussion challenges the analysis of APS as being inside the object of study, and of producing knowledge about the cultural processes and policy of Aboriginal education training and development of teacher candidates and of First Nations students. By questioning the very nature of data production and consumption, the research flows from quantitative secondary analysis towards a decolonized framework as data come to be narrated through Indigenous bodies and their complexities, fluxes, and transitions.

REJECTION AND RECOVERY

The data set used for critical inquiry came through the use of the data liberation of the 1991 Aboriginal Peoples Survey (APS) at the University of Toronto. Historically and from a quantitative perspective, one of the factors in quantifying success in schooling comes from social reproduction theories. The class of worker, total income, gender, and age were noted as important predictors for education as defined as highest level of schooling (Anyon, 1997; Kozol, 1991; Willis, 1977). One of the historical purposes for the creation, development, and implementation of a large-scale survey such as the 1991 APS was to evaluate the adequacy of a theoretical correlation model in (re)explaining Aboriginal "problems" in education and other socioeconomic "deficits"—it was a census of Canadian First Nations.

However, one hypothesis on an anti-colonial approach to the data set comes from the epistemic stance that First Nations cosmology integrates Elders and the community (as a collective) into the family unit as sources of Indigenous knowledge and for social support. Thus, the intermediary variables dealt with associations defined by teachers, Elders, and exposure to Aboriginal language-based media regardless of the other independent variables. To restate the inquiry with regard to the microdata analysis of the 1991 APS, the anti-colonial analysis warranted an examination of the mediating factors of Indigenous knowledge transmission that contributed to the correlation of linking formal schooling and educational level for self-identified Aboriginal people in Ontario. If the analysis indicated a weak relationship between the *exogenous* (external) variables and the dependent variable, it would support the hypothesis that for Indigenous knowledge transmission, family, Elders, and language were more significant than variables such as total income, class, or gender. However, if the analysis indicates a stronger relationship between the exogenous variables such as income and class and the independent variable, then the economic reproduction model described the relationship.

Preceding the writing of this discussion, quantitative calculations on the following variables were completed:

- The Elder variable was "computed" as the sum of value labels of being taught to read, write, and speak by Elders. A high value corresponded to a high level of use of Elders in learning of Aboriginal language;
- Family and Teacher variables were the sum of value labels of being taught by family members and by teachers; and
- the Aboriginal Media variable was the sum of the values of listening to, reading, and watching media materials in Aboriginal languages.

These variables should have a mediating effect, whether positive or negative, on education level (highest level of schooling variable). These mediating variables were also connected with the qualitative analysis through a case study by Antone (1997, pp. 199–200):

> Language and culture are important to the Onyota'a:ka people. … [C]ultural values and goals that come from within the Onyota'a:ka community need to be incorporated into the educational programs that are administered to these students. A strong relationship between the home and school is essential to develop and maintain the learning process of the children. For this to happen it is necessary that traditional knowledge, values, skills, interests, and the wisdom of the Elders be validated.

However, from the author's analysis, the mediator variables for school success involved social interaction with Elders, teachers, and family. These were also mediating variables for individuals reaching the highest level of schooling even if they had a positive attitude about the formal aspects of education. The choice of variables was based on prior case studies and institutional ethnographies on Aboriginal people that were previously explored by the author. For this quantitative study, with the entry point of anti-colonialism, relationships were the strategic factor to schooling success. Specifically, it was the factor of Aboriginal Elders who were the physical and spiritual keepers of Indigenous tradition, worldview, and education, and they were the ones necessary to impart knowledge and skills through their interaction with the young in informal and formal settings. This supported Wilson's (1996, p. 49) observation: "Elders are not only passing on knowledge about specific skills and events but are conveying a way of life and a specific world view. ... [T]raditions of the people cannot be taught using European teaching styles." Therefore, in terms of recovery in the decolonization process, the results indicated that the highest level of schooling has a strong linkage between the individual (student) and Elders, in spite of the rejection of this factor as significant in the original APS research.

When the pathway of analysis reflected a decolonization perspective, the correlation of over-representation and under-representation of Aboriginal students in Ontario was linked to their connection to Elders and their knowledges. It would not be a hierarchical or a linear distribution. Previous research on Indigenous peoples was empirically sound; however, the results and recommendations of these reports have supported the Western academy's dependence on and conviction towards problem-based and correlation analysis. In other words, "[t]he power of nationalism ... lies precisely in its ability to successfully speak on behalf of all the people" (Loomba, 1998, p. 198). By using the colonization and decolonization pathways in a contrapuntal manner, the methodological problem emerged in that Western researchers could plot out correlation and not power dynamics (Blumer, 1969; Cohen, 1985; Creswell, 2003). Furthermore, a modernist interpretation could not offer any solutions towards concepts such as surveillance, emancipation, and transformation. That is, Western quantitative research had relied on structural changes without acknowledging the individual transformation and relational consciousness that must occur at the same time. The next section explores the contrapuntal relationship between invisibility and mourning as it relates to Indigenous bodies and Indigenous knowledge (IK) in the 1991 APS data and analysis.

INVISIBILITY AND MOURNING

The substance of this particular anti-colonial trajectory relies on the intersection of invisibility and genocide of Indigenous peoples. Although the Indigenous were/ are subjects for research, I would contend that the subject of study in relation to the Indigenous is not really there, and that the complicity and acceptance comes through the mourning of what was not really there in the first place. Suzuki (1992, p. xxviii) forewarned:

> But like the current spasm of species extinction, the destruction of indigenous people is now occurring with frightening speed. … [L]ike a species that has lost its habitat and survives only in zoos, indigenous people who lost their land and eke out a living in tiny reserves or urban slums lose their uniqueness and identity.

Within the Western cultural hegemony, the lived histories embodied in First Nations and IK were invisible in the questioning and design of the 1991 APS. There is a connection with the notion of the abyss between nothingness and the tragedy of being at a loss in a settler state (Angod, 2006, p. 163; Fanon, 1967). At that time, IK was being (in)corporated in the sustainable development initiatives from non-governmental organizations (NGOs) or in pseudo-documentaries/historical recreations performed for tourists visiting developing countries. These perceptions of development, although using IK, had rendered black and Indigenous bodies as absent (Dei, 2008a). Also, using the idea of mourning, the initial analysis of archival statistical data and research discussions confirmed the fact that Indigenous people in Canada had not realized the upward mobility of educational opportunities when compared with other minority groups having access to higher education opportunities. The government of Canada acknowledged that many Indigenous students do not stay in school (INAC, 1998a), and that "Aboriginal people continue to fare worse than non-Aboriginal people in terms of virtually all social and economic indicators" (INAC, 1998a, p. 15). Referring to Statistics Canada (1980), a close examination of Table 10.7 revealed that almost 80 percent of First Nations people had less than a secondary education and 5 percent entered college or university.

With the 1995 Royal Commission on Aboriginal Peoples (RCAP) (1996a, 1996b, 2003) and political changes to education policy for Aboriginal peoples, and the current Truth and Reconciliation Commission, there were significant changes in education attainment. In 2006, 50 percent of the First Nations people aged twenty-five to sixty-four living on reserve had not completed high school compared with 30 percent of off-reserve First Nations people. An estimated 9 percent of off-reserve First Nations people had a university degree, up from 7 percent in 2001. In comparison, 4 percent of First Nations people living on reserve had a university degree, up from 3 percent in 2001 (Statistics Canada, 2012d). There was improvement in educational attainment of First Nations people through statistical data, and First Nations control for their education has led to Aboriginal language programs. Siggner (1986, p. 8) noted that the ratio of Indigenous people with a higher education is only half that of the total Canadian population. Hull (1990, p. 3) determined that there was a gap between high socioeconomic scale (SES) Indians and low SES Indians in terms of their children completing high school. That is, 70 percent of children of high SES Indian parents completed high school compared with 30 percent of children of low SES Indian parents. MacIvor (1995, p. 73) summarized and reaffirmed the statistics that illustrate the marginalization of Indigenous students as compared with mainstream Canadians:

[T]he rate of functional illiteracy among on-reserve peoples is twice as high as that for other Canadians. Only 25 per cent of the on-reserve population earn high school diplomas, while among other Canadians, over 50 per cent of the population attain similar levels of education. In terms of university participation, only 6.2 per cent of registered peoples attend university, compared to 18.5 per cent of other Canadians. Only 1.3 per cent of registered Indians receive university degrees as compared to 9.6 per cent of the non-Aboriginal population. ... [A]t the secondary level, science education is characterized by low enrollment and achievement levels among our students.

Results were also used from the 1991 APS and were summarized in RCAP's Volume 5; this started the unpacking of invisibility and consequences of Aboriginal learners:

These efforts represent important changes in the environment for Aboriginal children. But data as recent as the Aboriginal peoples survey (1991) showed that a large percentage of Aboriginal youth was not completing high school. As discussed later in this chapter, of Aboriginal youth aged 15 to 24 years who left school, 68.5 per cent did not have a diploma. There are local variations and success stories of keeping students in school until graduation. Researchers who study retention issues maintain that leaving school is not a sudden event. Rather, it is a process that begins much earlier. In the education of Aboriginal children, the seeds of the future are being planted in early school experience. (RCAP, 2016, p. 424)

Invisibility was also seen in terms of the amount of the data set being accessed by the author, despite the data liberation license. Specifically, the problem with the APS data as presented in the E-Stat interactive tool for education and archived database (Statistics Canada, 2016) was that only basic and limited frequency analysis could be performed. Because the data had already been aggregated, the ability to create a model and use a multivariate analysis that incorporated the variables of age, sex, reserve/urban schooling, SES, ethnicity of teachers, and attitudes to Elders and to schooling became unattainable. Another problem is that the confidentiality policy at Statistics Canada prevented the release of individual-level data. The initial univariate analysis of the 1991 APS microdata of Section B Language and Tradition done by the author noted that the percentages used were not valid percentages. This meant that the percentages that were summarized reflected the percentage of the people in the sample, regardless of whether they were asked the question or volunteered an answer or gave a specific response. Those who did not respond, provide any answer, or were deemed not applicable were included in the calculation.

The frequency analysis of the Ontario data regarding solutions to community "problems" illustrated that 76.9 percent (N = 7073) did provide answers. However, those who did answer saw solutions in terms of more policing, family service counseling, improved community service, more employment, and improved education. This aligned with the idea that colonized bodies would adopt the dominant deficit-based problem-solving trajectory of the settler state (Cesaire, 1972; Dei, 2006; Dei & Asgharzadeh, 2000; Fanon, 1967). The chosen solutions were consistent in terms of census area with insignificant variation, and it seemed to reflect the conditioned response for bureaucratic improvement. The author noted that the more important underlying knowledge of the APS was the high frequency of non-answers to questions regarding Aboriginal "problems." This connects to the invisibility of the Aboriginal body in its participation, and a form of reflective mourning on the growing disillusionment, resistance, education, and activism against Western methodologies that focus on pathologies. It is also a reflection of how culture-specific wording of a survey may lead to a process of "invisibility" of the Indigenous: "in denying its need, marginalizing its adherents, and downgrading its research agenda" (Stone, 1995, p. 148). In a pragmatic sense, a non-answer may simply mean that there was no appropriate answer available for the respondent to select—it was invisible for data collection, and it was a loss to Indigenous agency voice.

The author's assessment of the univariate results may indicate that the loss of Aboriginal language(s) and culture(s) continued to this day despite Aboriginal activism, proactive native-focus schooling, and support/research documents on self-determination and Aboriginal social dynamics. The quantitative analysis of looking for invisible variables and causes had reinforced the conclusion that there exist definite social, economic, and cultural gaps between the Aboriginal population and non-Aboriginal peoples. This difference and inequality of opportunity for education and jobs were skewed against Aboriginal peoples. This mourning comes from the dream/imagination of "what could have been" for Aboriginal people and learners in Canada (Dei & McDermott, 2014). Even with this evidence, the Indigenous body as a learner and as contributor to settler society and in our mainstream education programming and schooling remains obscure. The next section suggests that invisibility of the Indigenous is connected to the replacement of IK and the Aboriginal body as part of the settler state and its knowledge production.

FAÇADE OF ADAPTATION AND COMMITMENT

The colonized do not have epistemic privileges

—MIGNOLO, 2007 (P. 459)

The moment of commitment may not be as real when viewed from the epistemic lens of the Indigenous. Dei and Asgharzadeh (2000, p. 299) noted that "a colonial process can actually reward the knowledge that inserts learners within existing hegemonic structures and practices … a false status to the colonial subject." It is this façade that the author would contend that the settler state has provided programming in Aboriginal language retention and resiliency.[2] The factor is that the Elders and caregivers who have the ability to speak and to teach the Indigenous language are diminishing in number, and are not part of schooling bureaucracy. For the province of Ontario, 17.3 percent (N = 7073) of self-identified Aboriginal people could communicate in an Aboriginal language. The highest percentage of Aboriginal speakers comes from Indian reserves/settlements, at 62.9 (N = 1371). The census metropolitan area (CMA)[3] of Toronto yielded 2.6 percent Aboriginal speakers. Interestingly, for the variable of not being able to speak but still understand Aboriginal language(s), the CMA of Toronto showed the highest percentage at 19.4 (N = 948). This suggested to the author that in large urban areas, self-identified Aboriginal people know the language but do not choose to use it in public discourse. It may link to the affordance of invisibility or may also correlate to the façade of adaptation for Indigenous people to be part of large-scale settler communities. Cities such as Toronto, Montreal, and Vancouver operate in the colonial languages of English and French. Day-to-day conversations and even college and university discourses are often conducted in English and/or French. The frequency analysis suggested that Aboriginal people realize that Aboriginal languages were not part of the mainstream discourse; yet resistance to the mainstream was manifested in their ability and commitment to understand an Aboriginal language.

Commitment to Aboriginal ways of being was noted through the data set on listening and watching media based in an Aboriginal language(s) and participating in Aboriginal activities. There was a high frequency for people in Indian[4] reserve/ settlements. Also, in terms of actual participation in traditional activities, there was a high frequency found in less urban areas. Interestingly, there was no significant difference in terms of liking to participate in traditional Aboriginal activities. The highest frequency of being taught to speak an Aboriginal language came from Indian reserves/settlements. This would support the idea that the commitment towards any form of projects and politics related to decolonization may have traction in rural communities/reserves. In fact, the lowest frequency occurred in the CMA of Toronto.

It is mainly immediate family—parents and grandparents—who foster commitment to Aboriginal languages and teach a family member to speak an Aboriginal language. Elders take a secondary role (in terms of frequency) in teaching Aboriginal language(s). Schoolteachers had a limited role in teaching people to speak Aboriginal language(s); in the best case it was 8 percent (N = 1371) in reserves/settlements. Areas that were not reserves/settlements have yielded frequency percentages of less than 7 percent of those being taught an Aboriginal language. These data support the current direction of self-determined language development occurring in reserves/settlements. This triangulates with Antone's (1997, p. 123) revelation that

> the parents and grandparents of the fluent participants spoke the Onyota'a:ka language and therefore promoted the use of this language to their children ... because she [First Nations Elder] was aware of the prophecy pertaining to language loss, she would be able

to make sure her children retained the language and could continue to pass it on to the next generation.

Other census areas indicated that schoolteachers were not significant in teaching students to read Aboriginal languages. The ability to read newspapers, newsletters, and magazines in Aboriginal languages(s) was more prevalent in reserves/settlements. In general, being taught to read and finding reading material in an Aboriginal language was less than 25 percent in a best-case scenario. The ability to write in an Aboriginal language(s) is highly concentrated in Indian reserve/settlements. Again, parents were the primary teachers of writing in an Aboriginal language; grandparents and Elders were the secondary support. Schoolteachers had a limited profile in teaching students to write in an Aboriginal language.

The analysis of the schooling environment for self-identified Aboriginal people in the province of Ontario indicated that a high percentage of respondents did not answer every question, so the percentages reflect the opinions of those who chose to actually put a response down. A total of 33.3 percent (N = 1371) of self-identified Aboriginal people living in reserves/settlements indicated that there was an elementary school in the same community and 39.8 percent (N = 1371) indicated that they lived with their own family. The previous calculation suggested that Aboriginal knowledge transmission occurred through immediate family. Combining that statement with the factor of "living with one's own family during the elementary school years," the best case scenario of learning and retaining Aboriginal culture, language, and worldview would occur in the reserve/settlement.

The Indian reserve/settlement area also yielded the highest percentage of Aboriginal teachers and Aboriginal languages being used by schoolteachers. In terms of personal support, Ontario data indicated that 26.1 percent (N = 7073) came from parents, 27.2 percent (N = 7073) came from a spouse, 15.4 percent (N = 7073) came from an Elder, and 15.2 percent (N = 7073) came from a native worker/agency. When the census areas were factored in, the highest frequency occurred for Indian reserves/settlements. A total of 51.1 percent (N = 1370) of support came from parents, 51.0 percent (N = 1371) came from a spouse, 44.3 percent (N = 1371) came from an Elder, and 44.9 percent (N = 1371) came from a native worker/agency. Lowest frequency occurred in the CMA of Toronto with 14.3 percent (N = 948) support from parents, 13.1 percent (N = 948) from a spouse, 4.2 percent (N = 948) from an Elder, and 2.0 percent (N = 948) from a native worker/agency. Again, narratives from the RCAP (1996a, 2003) triangulate the importance of critically interrogating the strength and reach of local Aboriginal support and resources. It may be a complex analysis, but there were shifts between the façade of adaptation/accommodations and the commitment of Aboriginal groups to remain sovereign and sustainable.

I would also interpret the results as the presence of and the potential for decolonization projects to gain traction. It would require local control of the social resources for Aboriginal support in reserves/settlements with an established infrastructure developed by the local Aboriginal community. Like learning and education, interactions for support with the Aboriginal world decreased as one moved to a more urban setting. The façade of adaptation was that education was important for Aboriginal learners through schooling. Corntassel (2012, p. 91) made a similar analysis, noting a "politics of distraction" that affected Aboriginal rights, reconciliation, and resources. The revisiting of the APS data set would suggest that relationships with parents and grandparents were important for education success. Colonization becomes a strategic enterprise by using a common point—education and then developing a Western ontology/rationale for insertion into an Indigenous context; but the analysis of the data set such as the APS was exclusionary of an authentic Indigenous inquiry framework. The next section reflects upon the replacement of knowledge forms and possibilities that could have been and that may yet be.

REPLACEMENT AND DREAMING

For the province of Ontario, the main dislikes of the "elementary school years" were being away from home, prejudice and racism, teachers/principals, and subject material. This supported the colonial project with the replacement of Aboriginal learning and schooling, and the Aboriginal people were aware of this. However, the responses from Indigenous participants in the APS were replaced by the coding and data summarization of Western research. For example, policies that were derived from the APS had influenced the development of Ontario's Aboriginal education strategy[5] in including First Nations history throughout the curriculum. This form of colonial rhetoric aligns with the burden of salvation that Mignolo (2007, p. 463) described. The self-determined voice and embodied IK remained elusive in the public curriculum, and by extension in the consideration of teacher training (St. Denis, 2011). The logical empiricism derived from the APS analysis illustrated the failure of Aboriginal learning, and the design to not take into consideration the colonizing project.

The idea of replacement is tied to the appropriation of knowledge and the redefinition of truth. Foucault (1995, pp. 27–28) hypothesized that

> power produces knowledge … that power and knowledge directly imply one another. …
> [I]t is not the activity of the subject of knowledge that produces a corpus of knowledge,
> useful or resistant to power, but power-knowledge, the processes and struggles that traverse
> it and of which it is made up, that determines the forms and possible domains of knowledge.

Foucault's assertion is important to the Indigenous researcher and educator because it is the processes and agency of self-determination, anti-racism, and anti-colonialism that signify the resiliency and emergence of local Indigenous knowledges/

worldviews. The contrapuntal arrangement to the replacement of the Indigenous is to engage the imagination and dreaming of the Indigenous. Within Du Bois's (1986, p. 1139) eloquent parable "A Mild Suggestion" there resided a profound statement: "Education means ambition, dissatisfaction and revolt. You cannot both educate people and hold them down." The 1991 APS may be unpacked/dreamed for critical understandings of social dynamics affected by the intersecting factors of race, colonialism, gender, and class. Indeed, it may be used to liberate the Indigenous student/researcher. Again, the dreaming concept is a rephrasing of King (1993, p. 43) who described a combination of "the forces of tradition and the forces of change to prepare their children to face the future securely grounded in their past, proud of their people's accomplishments of today, and capable in the future, with knowledge and skills of the mainstream culture."

According to Harvey (1986, p. 77), applied sociological research must build upon answerable questions and data. The APS data set had illustrated that despite the disadvantages that some Indigenous students are forced to endure such as poverty and racism, the support from their parents, counselors, teachers, and community can provide the motivation for them to achieve. Family, community, language, and identity are influential factors, providing the ethic of social mobility through education. They can provide lived experiences, motivation, and, most important, the context and reasoning toward First Nations autonomy. If these factors were significant, the result would be for Indigenous students to have a sense of self-worth and autonomy. This also raises a further question: To what extent do support structures for Aboriginal education come from the Indigenous community itself, and not just a façade of a colonizing body in those bureaucratic structures? That is, could the dreaming be authentic to the Aboriginal? The next section examines the contrapuntal discourse between exploitation of the settler state and possible actions.

EXPLOITATION AND ACTION

To control the conceptual scheme is thus to command one's world.
—GOLDBERG, 1998 (P. 9)

Despite the passage of two centuries since first contact, total cultural and societal assimilation into the colonizer's world did not occur. Perhaps this was due to the colonizers being more interested in the superiority and "rigorous" teaching of their Western worldview, their instilling of the Christian religion, and their ways of maximizing profits with an efficient yet inexpensive Indigenous labour force (Cesaire, 1972). The contrapuntal framing comes from informal and formal Indigenous education (re)emerging from Elders and the community. Acknowledging the legacy of the residential school system in Canada, action in the decolonization process comes through the understanding, learning, and adapting of Indigenous values brought about by the agency of Aboriginal parents to educate their own children because colonial/Western schooling provided the barest amount of learning (Hull, 1990; MacIvor, 1995; Simpson & Smith, 2014; St. Denis, 2011). Angod (2006, p. 165) noted this as "[a]nti-colonialism [taking] an ideological turn here in terms of agency." Thus agency became the responsibility of Elders to be the vital link in communicating the Indigenous worldview to succeeding generations (Wilson, 1996).

Aboriginal students who learn from their parents, grandparents, and Elders have a better chance of learning, reading, and speaking an Aboriginal language. The author would caution that learning the nuances of Aboriginal culture does not correlate well to the Western-defined educational level. The APS provided a superficial analysis of the social dynamics of Aboriginal life and education—colonial processes of replacement and exploitation. Nevertheless, the responses from Aboriginal people regardless of their geographical location indicated that a close connection to family and Elders would help in retaining Aboriginal languages and culture. A call to further actions comes with the development of First Nations curriculum materials and the transition of pedagogy toward understanding multiple-oppression in the classroom through inquiry and twenty-first-century multi-literacies. Workshops and lessons on stereotypes, and the presentation of valid and alternative worldviews are starting to be developed in Ontario's public curriculum. However, the change has not occurred in the praxis of mainstream educators and pre-service teachers who seem to have difficulty de-linking from modernist and liberal ideals (Mignolo, 2007, pp. 449–514).

My turn to state an equation: colonization = "thingification."

—CESAIRE, 1972, (P. 21)

I would argue that the colonial project of the 1991 APS had elements to make the Indigenous body/voice reduced to process/project of "thingification"—deficits of the colonized reduced to numbers and averages, and to be solved by the dominant non-Aboriginal settlers. Contrapuntally, the APS was also used to expose evolving forms of settler-state internalized colonization, and to promote and develop decolonization pedagogy and transformative research culture. Through a contrapuntal understanding, the Indigenous educator/researcher must accept the notion that Western epistemology, Aboriginal worldviews, colonizing knowledge, and Indigenous knowledges may be so fundamentally different that they share no related assumptions. To put it another way, I would agree with Ross's chapter title: "Being Indian Is a State of Mind" (1992, p. 70), but that state of mind does not have to be the same or meaningful to those of a Western mind-set. In fact, a cultural and knowledge synthesis and/or hybridity between Western and Indigenous spaces may not be necessary.

Within this discourse between exploitation and action, the promotion of Aboriginal languages and identities was not the only solution, nor was that the only variable. One would be committing the error of reductionism and using an essentialized Aboriginal body ready to be continually exploited. That is, the lived experiences of Indigenous students who have filled out the "highest level of schooling" question on the 1991 APS do not fit into some abstract, logical structure or unitary and romanticized category. Aboriginal learners in Western schooling encounter racism and exploitation merely by attending public schools. Why some Indigenous students do well in school is a complicated phenomenon, framed within the lived experiences of the students themselves, their peers, teachers, counselors, and parents. The implementation and research strategies as self-determined by local Aboriginal communities should occur in stages from ease of implementation towards complex social and organizational changes. In the process of evaluating quantitative data on Indigenous students, the author suggests that initial change occurs at the design level and progresses towards a change in the actual questioning and data-capturing strategies in reaching out to Indigenous students, to ultimately striving for Indigenous control of data analysis and reporting towards inclusive schooling of Indigenous students.

RETURNING TO THE COLONIZATION AND DECOLONIZATION MATRIX

Its story is a story of creation, of the process of interaction in science, art and culture and the integration of those aspects into the expression.

—CAJETE, 1999 (P. 13)

Bearing in mind the limitations of the 1991 APS data set, the following conclusions were calculated by the author:

- Indian reserves/settlements have a degree of cultural insularity and were invisible to mainstream policy and analysis.
- The teaching and learning of Aboriginal culture through reading, writing, speaking, and listening occurred for the most part in Indian reserves/settlements.
- It was primarily parents who transmitted Aboriginal knowledge with secondary support from grandparents and Elders.
- Schoolteachers played a limited role in Aboriginal knowledge transmission.
- The CMA of Toronto had a high percentage of self-identified Aboriginals who understand Aboriginal language(s) but do not speak it.

The colonization and decolonization matrix in Figure 1 relates the author's Indigenous Hawaiian creation chant with knowledge creation, specifically with the Ontario curriculum. As one revisits the political project of healing and subversion, the matrix becomes a story of creation, self-determination, and evolution. The results and analysis, like Hales's (2006) critique of her research methodology, were "concerned with processes of knowledge production, procurement, interrogation, validation and dissemination" (Hales, p. 243). The data analysis was transformed when the author/analyst also used a contrapuntal approach to illustrate the transformation of the distinctiveness of Aboriginal ways of learning. Dei (2006, p. 2) noted that "power of the anti-colonial prism lies in its offering of new philosophical insights to challenge Eurocentric discourses." The quantitative analysis and results were used to develop the conceptual framework and a priori understandings to develop the goals of Aboriginal education, to (re)vision an awareness to advance data capturing, and to conceptualize a pragmatic and authentic nexus of Aboriginal and non-Aboriginal conceptual frameworks. The dynamics of power in Hawaii and Canada were paralleled through the Indigenous, with the *mele* (chant) shown as a data set with open access to those willing to feel, listen, and learn. Traditional chants carried historical and social codes, and for this researcher the *Holo Mai Pele* specifically encoded the epistemic and moral relationships between people and spirituality. It was also a form of historical legacy that informed projects on Hawaiian language retention, culturally based curriculum, and sustainability practices on the Hawaiian Islands.

The future action phase of the decolonization project involves understanding the importance of voice and self to the self-study of teaching practice and to the curriculum training and development of the faculty of education. There is a need for an Indigenous form of quantitative research, and challenges to survey data would employ the factor of race/racialized identity as an independent and co-determinant variable (Dei & Asgharzadeh, 2000, p. 309). It would make explicit the following: that the use of storytelling and narratives at the community level filtered through the self was also an indicator of success. Further revelations of the quantitative secondary analysis would be used to develop a series of factors and themes of decolonizing the analyst and to develop future sustainable and 3sovereign iterations of the policy of education in a First Nations context. It is hoped that the complex convergences and divergences between decolonization theory, post-colonial theory, and anti-colonial theory become articulated through the challenge and contestations of using quantitative analysis with data taken from Indigenous groups.

NOTES

1. The matrix was derived from the author's analysis to summarize, connect, and visualize a contrapuntal relationship. The colonization and decolonization columns come from the author's

reading, re-interpretation, and synthesis of Enriquez's (1992) treatise on "cultural revitalization" and cross-cultural psychology.
2. http://www.edu.gov.on.ca/eng/curriculum/elementary/nativelang.html
3. "Area consisting of one or more neighbouring municipalities situated around a major urban core. A census metropolitan area must have a total population of at least 100,000 of which 50,000 or more live in the urban core." http://www.statcan.gc.ca/pub/93-600-x/2010000/definitions-eng.htm
4. Term used in Statistics Canada and federal government literature.
5. http://www2.edu.gov.on.ca/eng/aboriginal/

REFERENCES

Angod, L. (2006). From post-colonial thought to anti-colonial politics: Difference, knowledge and R. v. R. D. S. In G. J. S. Dei & A. Kempf (Eds.), *Anti-colonialism and education* (pp. 159–192). Rotterdam, the Netherlands: Sense.

Antone, E. M. (1997). *In search of voice: A collaborative investigation on learning experiences of the Onyota'a:ka* (Unpublished doctoral dissertation). University of Toronto, Canada.

Anyon, J. (1997). *Ghetto schooling: A political economy of urban education reform*. New York, NY: Teachers College Press.

Blumer, H. (1969). *Symbolic interactionism: Perspective and method*. Englewood Cliffs, NJ: Prentice-Hall.

Cajete, G. (1994). *Look to the mountain: An ecology of Indigenous education*. Skyland, NC: Kivaki Press.

Cajete, G. (1999). *Igniting the sparkle: An Indigenous science education model*. Skyland, NC: Kivaki Press.

Cajete, G. (2000). *Native science: Natural laws of interdependence*. San Diego, CA: Clear Light.

Cesaire, A. (1972). *Discourse on colonialism*. New York, NY: Monthly Review Press.

Churchill, W., & Orelus, P. (2012). Confronting Western colonialism, American racism and white supremacy. In P. W. Orelus (Ed.), *A decolonizing encounter* (pp. 56–112). New York, NY: Peter Lang.

Cohen, A. P. (1985). *The symbolic construction of community*. New York, NY: Tavistock.

Corntassel, J. (2012). Re-visioning resurgence: Indigenous pathways to decolonization and sustainable self-determination. *Decolonization: Indigeneity, Education and Society, 1*(1), 86–101.

Creswell, J. W. (2003). *Research design: Qualitative, quantitative, and mixed methods approaches* (2nd ed.). Thousand Oaks, CA: Sage.

Dei, G. J. S. (1994). Reflections of an anti-racist pedagogue. In L. Erwin & D. MacLennan (Eds.), *Sociology of education in Canada: Critical perspectives on theory, research and practice*. Toronto, Canada: Copp Clark Longman.

Dei, G. J. S. (1996). *Anti-racism education: Theory and practice*. Halifax, Canada: Fernwood.

Dei, G. J. S. (1998). The politics of educational change: Taking anti-racism education seriously. In V. Satzewich (Ed.), *Racism and social inequality in Canada*. Toronto, Canada: Thompson Education.

Dei, G. J. S. (2005). Critical issues in anti-racist research methodology: An introduction. In G. J. S. Dei & G. Johal (Eds.), *Critical issues in anti-racist research methodology* (pp. 1–28). New York, NY: Peter Lang.

Dei, G. J. S. (2006). Introduction: Mapping the terrain—towards a new politics of resistance. In G. J. S. Dei & A. Kempf (Eds.), *Anti-colonialism and education: The politics of resistance* (pp. 1–23). Rotterdam, the Netherlands: Sense.

Dei, G. J. S. (2008a). *Teaching Africa: Towards a transgressive pedagogy* [Adobe PDF ebook version]. New York, NY: Springer.

Dei, G. J. S. (2008b). *Racists beware: Uncovering racial politics in contemporary society*. Rotterdam, the Netherlands: Springer.

Dei, G. J. S., & Asgharzadeh, A. (2000). The power of social theory: Towards an anti-colonial discursive framework. *Journal of Educational Thought, 35*(3), 297–323.

Dei, G. J. S., & McDermott, M. (Eds.). (2014). *Politics of anti-racism education: In search of strategies for transformative learning* [Apple iBook version]. Dordrecht, the Netherlands: Springer. doi:10.1007/978-94-007-7627-2

Du Bois, W. E. B. (1986). *Writings: "The suppression of the African slave-trade." "The souls of black folk." "Dusk of dawn." "Essays and articles."* New York, NY: Literary Classics of the United States.

Emerson, N. B. (1909). *Unwritten literature of Hawaii: The sacred songs of the Hula*. Retrieved from http://www.ulukau.org/elib/collect/unwritten/index/assoc/D0.dir/doc222.pdf

Enriquez, V. G. (1992). *From colonial to liberation psychology*. Quezon City: University of the Philippines Press.

Fanon, F. (1967). *Black skin, white masks*. L. Markmann (Trans.). New York, NY: Grove Press.

Foucault, M. (1995). *Discipline and punish: The birth of the prison*. New York, NY: Vintage Books.

Goldberg, D. T. (1998). *Racist culture: Philosophy and the politics of meaning*. Malden, MA: Blackwell.

Hales, J. (2006). An anti-colonial critique of research methodology. In G. J. S. Dei & A. Kempf (Eds.), *Anti-colonialism and education: The politics of resistance* (pp. 243–256). Rotterdam, the Netherlands: Sense.

Harvey, E. B. (1986). The practice of applied sociology. In L. Tepperman & R. J. Richardson (Eds.), *The social world*. Toronto, Canada: McGraw-Hill Ryerson.

Hull, J. (1990). Socioeconomic status and Native education in Canada. *Canadian Journal of Native Education. 17*(1), 1–14.

INAC. (1998a). *Notes for an address by the Hon. Jane Stewart, Minister of Indian Affairs and Northern Development on the occasion of the unveiling of Gathering Strength—Canada's Aboriginal Action Plan. January 7, 1998*. Ottawa. Retrieved from http://www.inac.gc.ca/info/speeches/jan98/action.html

INAC. (1998b). *Gathering strength—Canada's Aboriginal action plan*. Retrieved from http://www.inac.gc.ca/strength/policy.html

INAC. (2011). *Indian status*. Retrieved from http://www.ainc-inac.gc.ca/br/is/index-eng.asp

Kanahele, P. (2016) *Holo Mai Pele Synopsis*. Retrieved from http://www.paulwaters.com/hulapele.htm

Kempf, A. (Ed.). (2009). *Breaching the colonial contract: Anti-colonialism in the US and Canada* [Adobe PDF eBook version]. New York, NY: Springer.

King, C. (1993). Omachewa-Ispimewin: Education and community in a northern Saskatchewan Cree village. In E. Newton & D. Knight (Eds.), *Understanding change in education: Rural and remote regions of Canada*. Calgary, Canada: Detselig Enterprises.

Kozol, J. (1991). *Savage inequalities: Children in America's schools*. New York, NY: Crown.

Loomba, A. (1998). Challenging colonialism. In *Colonialism/postcolonialism* (pp. 184–258). London, England: Routledge.

MacIvor, M. (1995). Redefining science education for Aboriginal students. In M. Battiste & J. Barman (Eds.), *The circle unfolds*. Vancouver, Canada: University of British Columbia Press.

Mignolo, W. (2007). Delinking: The rhetoric of modernity, the logic of coloniality and the grammar of de-coloniality. *Cultural Studies, 21*(2–3), 449–514.

Ross, R. (1992). *Dancing with a ghost: Exploring Indian reality*. Markham, Canada: Reed Books Canada.

Royal Commission on Aboriginal Peoples. (1996a). *Final report of the Royal Commission on Aboriginal Peoples: Vol. 3. Gathering strength* (pp. 433–584). Ottawa, Canada: Canada Communication Group.

Royal Commission on Aboriginal Peoples. (1996b). *People to people, nation to nation. Highlights from the Report of the Royal Commission on Aboriginal Peoples*. Ottawa, Canada: Minister of Supply and Services Canada.

Royal Commission on Aboriginal Peoples. (2003). *Final Report of the Royal Commission on Aboriginal Peoples: On-line edition*. Retrieved from http://www.ainc-inac.gc.ca/ch/rcap/sg/sgmm_e.html

Royal Commission on Aboriginal Peoples. (2016). *Final Report of the Royal Commission on Aboriginal Peoples: Web Archive. Volume 3, Chapter 5, Section 3.2 The Child in the Formal Education System*. Retrieved from http://www.collectionscanada.gc.ca/webarchives/20071211053020/http://www.ainc-inac.gc.ca/ch/rcap/sg/si43_e.html#3.2%20The%20Child%20in%20the%20Formal%20Education%20System

Said, E. W. (1978). *Orientalism*. New York, NY: Vintage Books.

Said, E. W. (1993). *Culture and imperialism*. New York, NY: Vintage Books.

Siggner, A. J. (1986, Winter). The socio-demographic conditions of registered Indians. *Canadian Social Trends*, 2–9.

Simpson, A., & Smith, A. (Eds.). (2014). *Theorizing native studies* [Kindle eBook version]. Durham, NC: Duke University Press.

St. Denis, V. (2011). Silencing Aboriginal curricular content and perspectives through multiculturalism: There are other children here. *Review of Education, Pedagogy and Cultural Studies, 33*(4), 306–317.

Statistics Canada. (1980). *Perspectives Canada III* (Catalogue No. 11-511E). Ottawa, Canada: Supply & Services.

Statistics Canada. (2003). *2001 census: Analysis series Aboriginal peoples of Canada: A demographic profile* (Catalogue No. 96F0030XIE2001007). Ottawa, Canada: Minister of Industry.

Statistics Canada. (2012a). *2006 census: Immigration in Canada: A portrait of the foreign-born population, 2006 census: Highlights*. Retrieved from http://www12.statcan.ca/census-recensement/2006/as-sa/97-557/p1-eng.cfm

Statistics Canada. (2012b). *2006 Aboriginal population profile—Ontario*. Retrieved from http://www12.statcan.ca/census-recensement/2006/dp-pd/prof/92-594/details/page.cfm?Lang=E&Geo1=PR&Code1=35&Geo2=PR&Code2=01&Data=Count&SearchText=Ontario&SearchType=Begins&SearchPR=01&B1=All&GeoLevel=PR&GeoCode=35

Statistics Canada. (2012c). *Aboriginal peoples survey. Detailed information for 1991*. Retrieved from http://www23.statcan.gc.ca/imdb/p2SV.pl?Function=getSurvey&SurvId=3250&SurvVer=1&InstaId=16692&InstaVer=1&SDDS=3250&lang=en&db=imdb&adm=8&dis=2

Statistics Canada. (2012d). *2006 census: Educational portrait of Canada, 2006 census: Aboriginal population*. Retrieved from http://www12.statcan.ca/census-recensement/2006/as-sa/97-560/p20-eng.cfm

Statistics Canada. (2016). *E-STAT (10F0174X)*. Retrieved from http://www5.statcan.gc.ca/olc-cel/olc.action?objId=10F0174X&objType=2&lang=en&limit=0

Stone, L. (1995). Feminist educational research and the issue of critical sufficiency. In P. L. McLaren & J. M. Giarelli (Eds.), *Critical theory and educational research*. Albany, NY: SUNY Press.

Suzuki, D. (1992). A personal foreword: The value of native ecologies. In P. Knudtson & D. Suzuki, *Wisdom of the elders* (pp. xxi–xxxv). Toronto, Canada: Stoddart.

Willis, P. (1977). *Learning to labour*. Lexington, MA: D. C. Heath.

Wilson, S. (1996). *Gwitch'in native elders: Not just knowledge, but a way of looking at the world*. Fairbanks: University of Alaska Press.

CHAPTER FIVE

A Race TO Whiteness

Revealing the Colonial Structure of English Language Education—What Kind of Education for All?

CRISTINA JAIMUNGAL

INTRODUCTION

When we speak the language of the colonizer, as Fanon (2008) calls it, the question is not just whose language is being spoken, but what values, ideas, and cultures are being reproduced and re-presented as universal or global ideals? Which languages have currency, and which are gobbled up, disciplined, and marginalized as a direct result of privileging particular languages (Phillipson, 1992, 2001, 2008, 2009)?

English is more than a lingua franca; it is more than simply a language of globalization. The discourse of national languages is built upon the idea that the nation requires English as a communicative form of social cohesion that negates questions of race and difference (Dei, 1999). We need to rethink language in the way Indigenous scholars and critical language scholars have been articulating to both name and challenge dominant (language) systems of oppression. We need to think of language as identity, language as a way of knowing, language as assimilation, language as resistance, and language as a lived experience with highly material consequences for non-dominant language speakers. As Dei and Kempf (2006) articulate, "Language is very important not only in the process of identity formation, but also in processes of learning and for the psychological, spiritual, mental and cognitive development of the self" (p. 16). We need to recognize that language is inherently political and has historically been used as a colonizing weapon to inculcate values and denigrate racialized bodies. Language is about who we are and how we come to know, understand, and act within our world. By expanding our understanding that the concept of language embodies more than merely instrumental communicative, we can begin to challenge the deeply rooted and often unquestioned belief that global (English language) education projects ought to be considered part of laudable, apolitical education objectives. Despite counterclaims from global English "scholarly cheerleaders," as Phillipson (2008) remarks, this chapter takes the strong position that English is still a dominant colonial language, arguing that there is absolutely nothing innocent or accidental about the global proliferation of English language education. With this view, we, as in interdisciplinary critical race and language scholars, cannot ignore that English continues to be a dominant colonial language, saturated with power and underpinned by whiteness.

Grounded in anti-colonial research methods, this chapter is organized in four sections: (1) Language, Legitimacy, and Race, (2) Anti-colonialism, Postcolonialism, and Limits, (3) "Global" English, Colonialism, and Whiteness, (4) English, Modernity, and Development. Since there continues to be purely descriptive scholarship by macro-sociolinguistics that clearly negates Indigenous perspectives by depoliticizing language shift, it is crucial that the first section of this chapter engages the foundational intellectual scholarship of African Indigenous scholars such as Frantz Fanon (2008), Chinua Achebe (1997), and Ngũgĩ wa Thiong'o (1994) by pointing to their contemporary relevance in critical discussions on language. In the second section, I discuss the conceptual utility of Dei and Kempf's (2006) anti-colonial lens and theoretical implications by addressing the limits of postcolonialism. In the third section, I draw on the work of foundational critical language scholars such as Phillipson and Pennycook in order to highlight the ways in which their work links "global" english to colonialism and, by extension, the systemic structure of whiteness. In section four, the objective is to flesh out the intrinsic connection between English language education and whiteness, illuminating how the racialized hierarchy of language as a colonial structure works to sideline other languages and uphold epistemic systems such as modernity and development. To illustrate this point, I call specific attention to the politically neutral discourse on language in three UNESCO Reports: (1) *Education for All Global Monitoring Report* (UNESCO, 2014), (2) *Beyond 2015: The Education We Want* (UNESCO-UNICEP, 2014), and (3) *Education for All 2000–2015: Achievements and Challenges* (UNESCO, 2015). Through attention to the discourse around language medium of instruction and testing, the reports reveal an agenda that boasts a *race to whiteness*, one that sidelines the political significance embedded in problematic conceptions of literacy and negates the consideration of *what kind of education for all*. In sum, the ideas, discussion, and analysis presented in this chapter are unapologetically direct in naming race, identifying contemporary forms of colonialism in education, and challenging privileged systems of knowledge that are annexed to the structure of whiteness. To echo Cesaire's (1972, p. 39) compelling words:

> What am I driving at? At this idea: that no one colonizes innocently, that no one colonizes with impunity either; that a nation which colonizes, that a civilization which justifies

colonization—and therefore force—is already a sick civilization, a civilization which is morally diseased.

The foregoing striking words reflect the need to take a critical stance in addressing contemporary colonial practices, reminding us that colonization, in any of its routine, everyday forms, has very real material consequences for people of colour *and* society. However, regardless of what the "petty bourgeois doesn't want to hear any more," English (language education) is one site where the exertion of colonial power can be traced and epistemologically examined and challenged (Cesaire, 1972, p. 53). For all intents and purposes, these are the key ideas that drive this work.

LANGUAGE, LEGITIMACY, AND RACE

The language of my education was no longer the language of my culture.
—WA THIONG'O, 1994 (P. 13)

Claims of language legitimacy work in tandem with education to delegitimize knowledge and perpetuate racial hierarchies of language. As wa Thiong'o (1994) writes, colonial alienation "starts with a deliberate disassociation of the language of conceptualisation, of thinking, of formal education, of mental development, from the language of daily interaction in the home and in the community" (p. 28). Colonial alienation, therefore, is a process that upholds the racial hierarchy of language and reproduces ideological perceptions in favour of English:

> The attitude to English was the exact opposite: any achievement in spoken or written English was highly rewarded; prizes, prestige, applause; the ticket to higher realms. English became the measure of intelligence and ability in the arts, the sciences, and all the other branches of learning. English became *the* main determinant of a child's progress up the ladder of formal education. (Wa Thiong'o, 1994, p. 12)

The above articulation of wa Thiong'o (1994) highlights the privileged position afforded to English. It highlights the fact that English was not merely communicative; it was a marker of status, a barometer of intelligence, and an indicator of progress. Interestingly, what wa Thiong'o (1994) originally pointed out during the formative post-colonial language debate is what would later be referred to as *symbolic power* by a critical language scholar: "[f]or in the routine flow of day-to-day life, power is seldom exercised as overt physical force: instead it is transmuted into a symbolic form, and thereby endowed with a kind of legitimacy" (Bourdieu, 1991, p. 23). The symbolic power afforded to English has also been echoed by other Indigenous scholars who engaged in the language debate. Achebe (1997) writes, "There is certainly a great advantage in writing in a world language" (p. 28). However, as much as Achebe demonstrates optimism about the communicative advantages of using a "world language," he remains cognizant and critical of the colonial violence "of the world language which history has forced down our throats" (p. 28). Achebe's critical undertones tend to be downplayed but certainly deserve highlighting. Shedding further light on the language debate, Fanon's (2008) analysis of colonial domination in *Black Skin, White Masks* also makes an invaluable contribution to the politics of language and race. Fanon (2008) articulates the experience of Blackness in Francophone Martinique, but he also explains the way in which "mastery of language affords remarkable power" (p. 18). However, one of Fanon's (2008) most thought-provoking articulations intellectualizes the link between language, humanity, and race. In his words,

> The Negro of the Antilles will be proportionately whiter—that is, he will come closer to being a real human being—in direct relation to his mastery of the French language (Fanon, 2008, p. 18).

Fanon's psychoanalytical approach to identity formation and its connection to language reveal that proximity to whiteness is determined by linguistic competency. For Fanon (2008), it is French that is imbued with symbolic power to grant such proximity. It is French that marks intelligence and ability, and it is also the French language that determines proximity to being human: "Nothing is more astonishing than to hear a black man express himself properly, for then in truth he is putting on the white world" (Fanon, 2008, p. 36). Fanon's (2008) articulation underscores the ways in which language has been utilized as a tool to mask (read: *whiten*) the bodies of racialized speakers, a point which Lippi-Green also makes: *You may have dark skin, we tell them, but you must not sound Black* (1997, p. 63, emphasis in the original). Clearly, Lippi-Green, like Fanon (2008), recognizes the colonial logic, and by extension racial logic, that governs language use.

In a different context, offering a contemporary view of the connection between language legitimacy and race, Amin (1997a, 1997b, 1999, 2006) focuses on the disempowerment of minority women of colour ESL teachers and connects it to the broader systemic structures that uphold whiteness. Her work corroborates a substantive amount of research on microaggressions among racialized ESL teachers. Amin (1999) compellingly argues that "ESL students in Canada are cognizant of the message that Canadian society is giving them about who is important and who is not important" (Amin, 1999, p. 102). Amin (1997) points out that the TESOL landscape is not an equitable playing field for those categorized as "non-native" English speakers. Furthermore, she points out that "growing up in a middle-class urban family in postcolonial Pakistan, English ruled our lives. It was equated with intelligence, knowledge, culture, and was also a way of getting ahead" (Amin, 1997b, p. 139). Moreover, Amin (1997b) expresses that "the 'you-have-an-accent' accusation has been a motif of my life in Canada (p. 139)." The totality of Amin's experience with teaching English reifies the racial-linguistic divide and points to a colonial logic that espouses a hierarchy among accents. Lippi-Green (1997) refers to this hierarchy as the language subordination process: "[A]ll accents associated with white countries or the North have a higher status than accents associated with non-white countries or the South" (Amin, 1997b). Providing a solid argument and revealing the socially constructed preference for White teachers, Amin (1997a) reveals that most of the teacher participants in her study admitted that they even perceived her to be a non-native speaker. Amin's (1997a) findings show that "the teachers believed that some ESL students make the following assumptions: (a) Only White people can be native speakers of English; (b) only native speakers know 'real,' 'proper,' 'Canadian' English; and (c) only White people are 'real' Canadians" (p. 580).

And there you have it—that annoying fly on the wall that Cesaire spoke of: the saliency of *race*.

The symbolic power ascribed to French in Fanon's (2008) context and English in wa Thiong'o's analysis (1994) brings the question of language legitimacy to the forefront and underscores the politicized, racialized nature of language that Amin (1997a, 1997b, 1999, 2006) seeks to expose. With this in mind, an anti-colonial lens is particularly resourceful in demonstrating how dominant colonial logic operates as a tool that grants legitimacy to particular speakers. *Because, as yuh does already know, all of dem English language is not treated da same.*

ANTI-COLONIALISM, POST-COLONIALISM, AND LIMITS

We take the oppressor's language and turn it against itself. We make our words a counter-hegemonic speech, liberating ourselves in language.

—HOOKS, 1994 (P. 175)

Now let us consider the concept of anti-colonialism in relation to reclaiming language by interrogating the limits of postcolonial theory with respect to issues of agency and voice.

While it is important to consider how efforts to reclaim heritage languages (Hindi and Yoruba in Trinidad, for example), revitalize language (Maori in New Zealand, for example), or reinvent language (Rastafarian English in Jamaica, for example) are indeed important and valuable sites of resistance, it is equally important to consider the implications of postcolonial discourse on language. In relation to postcolonial English language literature, for example, the issue of voice and individual agency can be overly emphasized as a site of resistance particularly when structures of domination are not challenged. For this reason, I draw on Dei and Kempf's (2006) anti-colonial thought to articulate the theoretical utility of an anti-colonial lens and explore the value and limits of postcolonial conceptions. For Dei and Kempf (2006, p. 2),

> Colonialism, read as imposition and domination, did not end with the return of political sovereignty to colonized peoples or nation states. Colonialism is not dead. Indeed, colonialism and re-colonizing projects today manifest themselves in variegated ways (e.g., the different ways knowledges get produced and receive validation within schools, the particular experiences of students that get counted as [in]valid and the identities that receive recognition and response from school authorities).

By expanding the notion of colonialism to include practices of domination and imposition, the anti-colonial perspective exposes the way contemporary (not just pre-emancipation) colonizing projects operate as social control. Anti-colonial thought shifts the focus from "agency and nationalist/liberatory practice towards a discursive analysis and approach that directs our attention to the intersection between 'western knowledge production' and the 'Other' and Western colonial power" (Shajahan, 2003, p. 5 as cited in Dei & Kempf, 2006, p. 13). By focusing on how knowledge is produced through systems of domination and how individuals themselves are complicit in the reproduction of colonial norms, anti-colonial thought makes critical political insights that are invaluable to examining social structures of education.

With this view in mind, anti-colonialism turns to the project of exposing how broader institutional and ideological systems work to enact racialization. For Dei and Kempf (2006), "the process of racializing is external and strategic, and is not the responsibility of the person who is targeted. This distinction is crucial because of the tendency for some to argue that those who do anti-racist work by working with race actually create the problem" (p. 10). For example, in the context of English language education, some might argue that there is nothing racialized about the conception of "native" and "non-native" speakers. It might be argued that race is peripheral to a discussion of language simply because anyone can learn any language they choose. However, upon closer examination, we see that racialization occurs when terms such as "native" and "non-native" English speaker are embedded in a capitalist education system that favours the White (or White passing) "native" speakers and treats them, as Chow (2014) calls, an "uncorrupted origination point" (p. 58). Therefore, from an anti-colonial perspective, why do particular bodies from particular places want to learn English (or another dominant language)? Why are certain bodies perceived to be "non-native" despite language fluency? To probe these questions, it is useful to consider Dei and Kempf's (2006) argument: "It is crucial in anti-colonial politics to maintain an important distinction between individual white identity and whiteness as a system of domination and structure of privilege" (p. 12). By addressing the macro-political factors, anti-colonialism emphasizes the structure, "the world outside of the subject" (Dirlik, 1997, 2000, as cited in Dei & Kempf, 2006, p. 15). Anti-colonial thought, therefore, highlights the material consequences of systems of domination without overly relying on celebratory concepts of colonized cultural practices of hybridity and liberation in a way that post-colonial discourse tends to do. Anti-colonial thought persuasively argues that we are not in a post-colonial era. Cesaire (1972) states that the "official apparatus [of colonialism] might have been removed, but the political, economic, and cultural links established by colonial domination still remain with some alterations" (insertion by author, p. 27). Therefore, even though many so-called post-colonial nations might appear to have been granted political independence, colonialism and colonial logic still animate the structural operation of whiteness. Using this line of thought, it is important to recognize that the task at hand is to recognize exactly how colonialism operates and to examine the implications of such operation. As hooks (1994) explains, "It is not the English language that hurts me, but what the oppressors do with it, how they shape it to become a territory that limits and defines, how they make it a weapon that can shame, humiliate, [and] colonize" (p. 168). Anti-colonial thought, therefore, names the oppressor—whiteness—and makes it visible. Teasing out the connection between English and whiteness is crucial to anti-colonial thought and a central aim of the next section.

"GLOBAL" ENGLISH, COLONIALISM, AND WHITENESS

At this point, it is helpful to engage the work of Phillipson (1992, 2001, 2008, 2009) and Pennycook (2007, 2014) to illustrate the way macro-sociolinguistics have interrogated English language dominance and argued in favour of more critical approaches to the "globalized" or "international" English language education landscape. Although Phillipson's and Pennycook's works are not positioned as anti-colonial, their scholarship, especially Phillipson's (1992) influential work *Linguistic Imperialism*, is incredibly proficient at examining and exposing imperialistic systems of domination around language planning and policy. This section draws on existing literature to illustrate how conceptions of whiteness and imperial domination operate simultaneously to maintain and uphold an inequitable distribution power.

To begin, Phillipson (2008) recognizes that descriptive sociolinguistic approaches to language change are inadequate for addressing the politicized nature of English language education and globalization. For Phillipson (2008, p. 1), "global" English and American expansionism "can be traced back over two centuries." With such irrefutable evidence, Phillipson (2008) notes that he is baffled by some linguists' lack of recognition and outright denial of English language politics. Such defensive approaches attempt to neutralize language politics and can be viewed as "settler moves to innocence" (Tuck & Yang, 2012) or "politics of distraction" (Coulthard, 2007). Both tactics neutralize and depoliticize language because they are attempts to make language issues innocent, they are attempts that distract from politicization, and they are attempts that negate the very material consequences of dominant language imposition. Phillipson (2008) similarly explains that by using politically neutral terms such as "language spread" or "language death," social conditions of control that contribute to language loss are portrayed as agentless and remain invisible (Skutnabb-Kangas, 2000, pp. 365–374, as cited in Phillipson, 2008, p. 29). For Phillipson (2008), linguistic neoimperialism is characterized by the maintenance and perpetration of language inequality, exploitive dominance, and supremacist ideologies that underpin the global imaginary. On considering Richards's premise in the book *So Much Nearer: Essays Toward a World English* (1968) that promotes English language learning, Phillipson (2008) argues that there is an underlying sense of benevolence and apolitical discourse that is deployed: "We of the West have somehow, out of a strangely unselfish regard, indeed a regardless impulse of benevolence, committed ourselves to universal education as well as to universal participation in government" (Richards, p. 240, as cited in Phillipson, 2008, p. 14). Phillipson's (2008) insights into the unquestioned benevolence of English language education points to the way white supremacist ideologies work to "help" and "civilize" the Other without acknowledging the past colonial histories or contemporary colonial presences. As As Phillipson (2008) notes, "Learners of English may well be motivated by a desire to become members of this imagined global community" (Ryan, 2006, as cited in Phillipson, 2008, p. 4). The observation that "English is seen as integral to the crusade of global corporatisation, which is marketed as betokening freedom and democracy" (Phillipson, 2009, p. 12) illustrates how conceptions of modernity and development ripple through Western notions of capitalism, freedom, and democracy. Why have those particular ideals been co-opted as universal? Phillipson (2001) also points out that the English-speaking world consumes 80 percent of the available resources, while the non-English-speaking world is left in poverty (p. 189). How has English become a status marker of privilege, freedom, democracy, and modernity despite this great economic disparity? Clearly, this stark reality exposes a correlation that does more than signal a disparity between language and socioeconomic transnational conditions. The disparity alludes to questions of legitimacy and power. When thinking through global language initiatives, how else is global English linked to whiteness, modernity, and development?

> Much of the celebratory literature on 'global' English analyses it exclusively in such instrumental terms. However, as a recent work on the semantics and culture embedded in the grammar and words of English stresses, publications on 'global English,' 'international English,' 'world English,' 'standard English,' and 'English as a *lingua franca*' neglect the distinctive heritage embedded in the language in its core semantic and grammatical structures, since ultimately 'in the present-day world it is Anglo English that remains the touchstone and guarantor of English-based global communication.' (Wierzbicka, 2006, pp. 13–14, as cited in Phillipson, 2008, p. 35)

We see in the foregoing that the notion of "global" English—specifically, Anglo English—is ascribed symbolic power and legitimacy. However, it is important to note that the power is not just symbolic or ideological. In fact, Mignolo and Tlostanova (2007) remind us, "Globalization, as it is understood today, goes hand in hand with coloniality, with the foundation of the colonial matrix of power" (p. 110). In the context of English language policies, Pennycook (2007) tells us that colonialism functions as a core operating system that produces material consequences. The following is a brief summary of his articulation: (1) capitalist empire requires the production of docile workers to fuel capitalist expansion; (2) the discourse of Anglicism and liberalism is built upon a civilizing notion; (3) class, ethnicity, race, and economic conditions informed the development of each colony; and (4) the discourses of Orientalism with their insistence on exotic histories, traditions, and nations are in decline (Pennycook, 2007, p. 13). By examining the function of colonialism as a capitalist system of expansion marked by a racial hierarchy, Pennycook (2007) exposes colonialism within the contemporary moment of English language education. By drawing attention to how colonialism operates today within the context of English language education, Pennycook (2007), like Phillipson (2008), gestures to the visibility of whiteness as it relates to English, modernity, and development.

ENGLISH, MODERNITY, AND DEVELOPMENT

To have real impact, the post-2015 education agenda must be clearly defined and measurable. This requires precisely defining the concepts conveyed in each target as well as a set of agreed-upon indicators based on accurate and reliable data and international standards in order to ensure valid comparisons across countries and over time. (UNESCO-UNICEF, 2014, n.p.)

The foregoing highlights the link between progress and education. More importantly, however, it magnifies a "global" aspiration to *measure, improve, test,* and *uphold standards.* The question is not simply whether the notion of progress or development is an admirable goal—the complexity lies in the epistemological questions that challenge the colonial matrix of power: whiteness. We need to ask—what kind of education, whose notions of progress, and how do such taken-for-granted notions of modernity impact the lives of people? On one hand, these education global agendas adopt a benevolent stance, claiming that "progress" is not only *possible* but also *measurable.* On the other hand, however, we also see that such strides to measure and quantify progress are at the expense and denigration of marginalized languages: "There remains no doubt that the main barrier to basic education is the forced use of English as medium of instruction" (Inga teacher, Kigali, Rwanda, UNESCO, 2014, p. 283). Despite this recognition, however, the discourse produced in the *Education for All Global Monitoring Report* (2014) is one that continues to boast a race to *progress*, a race to being *developed*. More succinctly, UNESCO's education for all (EFA) discourse produces a *race to whiteness*.

The EFA discourse embodies the notion that the "idea of people not being able to get by without Europe's theoretical or cultural achievements is one of the most definitive tenets of modernity" (Maldonado-Torres, 2004, p. 32). It exudes epistemic racism and disregards the epistemic capacity of certain groups of people (Maldonado-Torres, 2004, p. 34). What is missing in UNESCO's *EFA Global Monitoring Report* is "the full spectrum of human history, its achievements, and its failures" (Maldonado-Torres, 2004, p. 36). The focus on the disenfranchised "undeveloped" and "developing" countries is rife with orientalist notions of the Other. Some development workers may argue that there have been shifts to work with the locals and that the intentions are indeed humanitarian. However, I am reminded of Cesaire's (1972) words that no form of colonization is innocent. The new trend in development to work with the locals and use mother tongue instruction may deceptively appear to be a step forward:

> In Cameroon, children taught in their local language, Kom, showed a marked advantage in achievement in reading and comprehension compared with children taught only in English. Kom-educated children also scored twice as high on mathematics tests at the end of grade 3. However, these learning gains were not sustained when the students switched to English-only instruction in grade 4. (UNESCO, 2014, p. 33)

However, Mignolo (2009) would argue otherwise: "As an honest liberal, you would recognize that you do not want to 'impose' your knowledge and experience but to 'work with the locals.' The problem is, what agenda will be implemented, yours or theirs?" (p. 178). In the foregoing EFA quote, we see that the objective is not to value languages for their intrinsic value. The actual goal is to score high on mathematics and literacy tests. Language, then, is treated as a tool to facilitate the race to progress and, by extension, whiteness. In the current economic system, D'Angelo (2010) argues that "without real economic-based reasons to use local African languages, they will disappear" (p. 80). However, UNESCO (2014) maintains its apolitical stance by negating questions that challenge the dominant capitalist economy that privileges languages that have proximity value to whiteness. Furthermore, the politics of distraction is employed by citing problems with Other countries. "Location-related disadvantages" or teacher accountability are just two examples that exhibit the politics of distraction: (1) "Location-related disadvantages begin in the early grades and widen. In Ghana, urban students were twice as likely as rural students to reach minimum levels of English in 2011 in grade 3, and more than three times as likely by grade 6" (p. 19); (2) "In Kano state, northern Nigeria, 78% of 1,200 basic education teachers were found to have 'limited' knowledge of English when tested on their reading comprehension and ability to correct a sentence written by a 10-year-old (Education Sector Support Programme in Nigeria, 2011)" (p. 237). What we learn from these two examples is that the onus is placed on the location of the learner and on teacher accountability. There is zero colonial accountability and, not surprisingly, whiteness remains firmly intact. Despite this, some may argue that English dominance is an inevitable and necessary reality:

> With English taking up such an important position in many educational systems around the world, it has become one of the most powerful means of inclusion into or exclusion from further education, employment, or social position. (Pennycook, 2014, p. 14)

However, it would be false to assume that this is merely an inevitable circumstance of globalization. As Bauman (1995) reminds us, there is an intrinsic connection between modernity and globality:

> Modernity once deemed itself universal. Now it thinks of itself as global. Behind the change of term hides a watershed in the history of modern self-awareness and self-confidence. Universal was to be the rule of reason—the order of things that would replace the slavery to passions with the autonomy of rational beings, superstition and ignorance. … 'Globality,' in contrast, means merely that everyone everywhere may feed on McDonald's hamburgers and watch the latest made-for-TV docudrama. Universality was a proud project, a Herculean mission to perform. Globality in contrast, is a meek acquiescence to what is happening 'out there.' (Bauman, 1995, p. 24)

By displacing the concept of modernity from globality, we see how the framework of modernity—its historical, sociological, cultural, and philosophical origins—is concealed within the logic of development that aims to track progress in education (Escobar, 2004). In 2002, the first EFA report was called *Education for All—Is the World on Track?* Since then, ten other issues have been published, each taking up a different topic: from conflict and childhood to literacy and language, each issue categorizes, measures, and ranks "progress" in education in a teleological way. Clearly, these efforts to improve education quality and access also have profound implications for minority language speakers: for example, in Guatemala, Spanish speakers spend six times more years in schools than do Q'eqchi', a Mayan language, (UNESCO, 2010, p. 23). What we continue to see is that "this historical relationship of the colonizer and colonized continues to inform contemporary subject identity formation and knowledge production" (Dei & Kempf, 2006, p. 3). To challenge domination, Escobar (2004) asks us to expose modernity's underside and make it visible. By making conceptions of modernity visible, whiteness can be challenged. Mignolo and Tlostanova (2006) also offer some insights. They begin with the assertion that "the modern foundation of knowledge is territorial and imperial" and they focus on what they call an "epistemic shift" in critical border-thinking (p. 205). Mignolo and Tlostanova (2006) assert that borders are the new frontiers. "'Borders' will be in the twenty-first century what 'frontiers' were in the nineteenth. Frontiers were conceived as the line indicating the last point in the relentless march of civilization. On the one side of the frontiers was civilization; on the other, nothing; just barbarism or emptiness" (Mignolo & Tlostanova, 2006, p. 205). Mignolo and Tlostanova (2006) argue in favour of critical border thinking because, in their words, it

> denies the epistemic privilege of the humanities and the social sciences—the privilege of an observer that makes the rest of the world an object of observation (from Orientalism to Area Studies). It also moves away from the post-colonial toward the de-colonial, shifting to the geo and body-politics of knowledge. (p. 206)

This shift is crucial to anti-colonial politics. Anti-colonial thought, therefore, offers the academy a way to think through seemingly natural global phenomena such as English language education, unmap the operation of colonialism, and see the transparency of whiteness.

CONCLUSION

Using an anti-colonial lens, this chapter has revealed the racialized structure of global English language education and gestures to the possibilities of resisting the epistemic racism inherent in global English language projects that are inherently linked to a Western conception of modernity and development. In making whiteness visible and exposing conceptions of modernity that firmly sustain whiteness, anti-colonial thought offers concrete and theoretical ways to think through everyday manifestations of colonialism in the context of English language education. The purpose therefore is to offer new insights that challenge sociolinguistic and development discourses that take apolitical approaches, which treat language as purely instrumental to the process of literacy building in the context of development:

> Standard English is not the speech of exile. It is the language of conquest and domination; in the United States, it is the mask which hides the loss of so many tongues, all those sounds of diverse, native communities we will never hear, the speech of the Gullah, Yiddish, and so many other unremembered tongues. (hooks, 1994, p. 168)

As scholars, we need to challenge whiteness and break free: "Imprisoned on his island, lost in an atmosphere that offers not the slightest outlet, the Negro breathes in this appeal of Europe like pure air" (Fanon, 2008, p. 21). We need to ask, what are the alternatives to the "pure air of Europe"? And we need to do so in a way that challenges domination and epistemic racism both within and beyond the academy from multiple sites—the home, the streets, and, most importantly, our minds. We need to imagine alternative conceptions of development, and one way we can begin to do so is by legitimizing "subaltern intellectual communities"— voices which are often unheard (Escobar, 2004, p. 210). We must also be attuned to which movements uphold and perpetuate whiteness and which ones shake it up and take action to undo it. With boldness we need to remind ourselves and our communities that resistance is not only possible, it is actually happening in Indigenous communities around the world. With this view, it is important that the work of anti-colonialism continues to make the structures of whiteness visible while simultaneously attending to the ways in which racialized bodies are resisting those structures.

As a whole, each section in this chapter offers brief insights into and asks questions about the ways in which language, race, modernity, and development operate; the sections make room for further discussion and invite conversation. As a dominant English language speaker from a racialized country, I am implicated in this conversation. As an English teacher and as an academic, I acknowledge the ways in which my body has been and still is a conduit of capitalism, reproducing the language of the colonizer. However, while I do not claim innocence from being part of a colonial project to teach the Other English or reproduce work in the same dominant colonial language I contest, I grapple with the tension that English, the language of the colonizer, is really the only language I know. I grapple with the tension between speaking like a native speaker and looking like a non-native speaker. My social and epistemological locations straddle the spatial frontier of the Canadian nation (the Land in which I grew up) and Trinidad and Tobago (the Land in which I was born). As I look ahead both personally and academically, my work will continue to expose the invisibility of racial logic through the project of English language education. Ending now with Achebe's poignant sentiment, I point to transformative possibilities that reinvent and reimagine the uses of the master's tools:

> *My answer to the question* Can an African ever learn English well enough to be able to use it effectively in creative writing? *is certainly yes. If on the other hand you ask*: Can he ever learn to use it like a native speaker? *I should say, I hope not.* (Chinua Achebe, as cited in Chow, 2014, p. 35)

REFERENCES

Achebe, C. (1997). English and the African writer. *Transition* (75–76), 342–349.

Amin, N. (1997a). Race and the identity of the nonnative ESL teacher. *TESOL Quarterly, 31*(3), 580–583.

Amin, N. (1997b). South Englishes, north Englishes Pakistani immigrants in Canada. *Canadian Woman Studies, 17*(2), 139. Retrieved from http://search.proquest.com/docview/217467812?accountid=14771

Amin, N. (1999). Minority women teachers of ESL: Negotiating white English. In G. Braine (Ed.), *Non-native educators in English language teaching* (pp. 93–104). Mahwah, NJ: Lawrence Erlbaum.

Amin, N., Dei, G. J. S., & Lordan, M. (2006). *The poetics of anti-racism.* Halifax, Canada: Fernwood.

Bauman, Z. (1995). *Life in fragments: Essays in post-modern morality.* Oxford: University Blackwell.

Bourdieu, P. (1991). *Language and symbolic power.* Cambridge, MA: Harvard University Press.

Cesaire, A. (1972). *Discourse on colonialism.* New York, NY: Monthly Review Press.

Chow, R. (2014). *Not like a native speaker: On languaging as a postcolonial experience.* New York, NY: Columbia University Press.

Coulthard, G. (2007). Subjects of empire: Indigenous peoples and the "politics of recognition" in Canada. *Contemporary Political Theory, 6,* 437–460.

D'Angelo, J. (2010). Developmental world Englishes and "Phillipson continued." *Asian Englishes, 13*(1), 78–81. doi:10.1080/13488678.2010.10801274

Dei, G. J. S. (1999). The denial of difference: Reframing anti racist praxis. *Race Ethnicity and Education, 2*(1), 17–38. doi:10.1080/1361332990020103

Dei, G. J. S., & Kempf, A. (Eds.). (2006). *Anti-colonialism and education: The politics of resistance.* Rotterdam, the Netherlands: Sense.

Escobar, A. (2004). Beyond the Third World: Imperial globality, global coloniality and anti-globalisation social movements. *Third World Quarterly, 25*(1), 207–230.

Fanon, F. (2008). *Black skin, white masks.* New York, NY: Grove Press.

Hall, S. (1996). When was "the post-colonial"? Thinking at the limit. In I. Chambers & L. Curti (Eds.), *The post-colonial question* (pp. 242–259). London, England: Routledge.

hooks, b. (1994). *Teaching to transgress: education as the practice of freedom.* New York, NY: Routledge.

Kachru, B. (1996). World Englishes: Agony and ecstasy. *Journal of Aesthetic Education, 30*(2), 135–155.

Kempf, A. (Ed.). (2010). *Breaching the colonial contract: Anti-colonialism in the US and Canada.* New York, NY: Springer.

Lippi-Green, R. (1997). *English with an accent: Language, ideology, and discrimination in the United States.* New York, NY: Routledge.

Maldonado-Torres, N. (2004). The topology of being and the geopolitics of knowledge: Modernity, empire, coloniality. *City, 8*(1), 29–56.

Mignolo, W. D. (2009). Epistemic disobedience, independent thought and decolonial freedom. *Theory, Culture & Society, 26*(7–8), 159–181.

Mignolo, W. D., & Tlostanova, M. V. (2006). Theorizing from the borders shifting to geo-and body-politics of knowledge. *European Journal of Social Theory, 9*(2), 205–221.

Narkunas, J. P. (2005). Capital flows through language: Market English, biopower, and the World Bank. *Theoria: A Journal of Social and Political Theory, 52*(108), 28–55.

Pennycook, A. (2007). ELT and colonialism. In J. Cummins & C. Davison (Eds.), *International handbook of English language teaching* (pp. 13–24). New York, NY: Springer.

Pennycook, A. (2014). *The cultural politics of English as an international language.* New York, NY: Routledge.

Phillipson, R. (1992). *Linguistic imperialism.* Oxford, England: Oxford University Press.

Phillipson, R. (2001). English for globalisation or for the world's people? *International Review of Education, 47*(3–4), 185–200. Retrieved from http://dx.doi.org/10.1023/A:1017937322957

Phillipson, R. (2008). The linguistic imperialism of the neoliberal empire. *Critical Inquiry in Language Studies, 5*(1), 1–43. Retrieved from http://dx.doi.org/10.1080/15427580701696886

Phillipson, R. (2009). Disciplines of English and disciplining by English. *The Asian EFL Journal Quarterly, 11*(4), 8.

Ryan, S. (2006). Language learning motivation within the context of globalization: An L2 self within an imagined global community. *Critical Inquiry in Language Studies, 3* (1), 23–45.

Tlostanova, M., & Mignolo, W. D. (2007). The logic of coloniality and the limits of postcoloniality. In R. Krishnaswamy & J. C. Hawley (Eds.), *Post colonial and the global* (pp. 109–123). Minneapolis: University of Minnesota Press.

Tuck, E., & Yang, K. W. (2012). Decolonization is not a metaphor. *Decolonization, Indigeneity, Education and Society, 1*(1) [Online journal].

UNESCO. (2010). *Education for all global monitoring report: Reaching the marginalized*. Oxford, England: Oxford University Press. Retrieved from http://www.unesco.org/en/efareport/reports/2010-marginalization

UNESCO. (2014). *Education for all global monitoring report: Teaching and learning: achieving quality for all*. Paris, France: UNESCO. Retrieved from http://en.unesco.org/gem-report/report/2014/teaching-and-learning-achieving-quality-all

UNESCO. (2015). *Education for all 2000–2015: Achievements and challenges*. Paris: Author. Retrieved from http://en.unesco.org/gem-report/report/2015/education-all-2000-2015-achievements-and-challenges

UNESCO-UNICEF. (2014). *Beyond 2015: The education we want*. Retrieved from http://www.unesco.org/new/fileadmin/MULTIMEDIA/HQ/ED/ED_new/Beyond2015_UNESCO-UNICEF-Flyer.pdf

Wa Thiong'o, N. (1994). *Decolonising the mind: The politics of language in African literature*. Nairobi, Kenya: East African Publishers.

Wierzbicka, A. (2006). *English: Meaning and culture*. New York: Oxford University Press.

CHAPTER SIX

Unsettling THE "Failed State"

An Anti-Racist Approach to the State and State Formation— A Study of Somalia

MUNA-UDBI ABDULKADIR ALI

Take up the White Man's burden—
Send forth the best ye breed—
Go bind your sons to exile
To serve your captives' need;
To wait in heavy harness,
On fluttered folk and wild—
Your new-caught, sullen peoples,
Half-devil and half-child.

—RUDYARD KIPLING, "THE WHITE MAN'S BURDEN" (1899)

Since the 1990s (especially after 9/11), the phenomenon of state failure has taken center stage in global politics and international development discourse and has become, in dominant academic and policy reflections and debates, the outcome of nearly every form of socioeconomic distress, civil strife, and political conflict in the South.

—ZUBAIRU WAI, *EPISTEMOLOGIES OF AFRICAN CONFLICTS* (2012A, P. 129)

In dominant discourses, Somalia is constructed as a collapsed and war-torn state with a growing humanitarian crisis (Acemoglu & Robinson, 2012; Gros, 1996; Dagne, 2009). Since the early 1990s, Somalia has been labeled a "failed state" by international institutions and the international community (Gros, 1996; Acemoglu & Robinson, 2012). In the media, the country is portrayed as chaotic, dangerous, and in constant civil unrest. However, in spite of these discourses and portrayals of my home country, I worked, attended school, went to parties, and had a very active social life in this nation-state considered failed.

States can be understood as particular historical geo-political formations within the world-systems (Mongia, 2007). The phenomenon of "state failure" or "state collapse" is relatively recent, and its proponents claim it can be understood by focusing on a state's "degree of statehood," determined by its nature and capacity to achieve certain given tasks (Gros, 1996; Migdal, 1988; Wai, 2012a). In fact, since the late 1980s, there has been an increasing body of literature on failed states (Acemoglu & Robinson, 2012; Gros, 1996; Migdal, 1988). This literature includes work on "fragile," "weak," "rogue," "collapsed," and "quasi" states. All of these concepts are used to describe state forms associated with a failed state. Within this discourse there is no discussion of who is conducting this research and the methodology guiding it. States considered failed are constructed as devoid of institutions, rule of law, morality, and law and order (Hill, 2005; Wai, 2012a). However, where does the concept of state come from? What other governance structures exist other than the nation-state? How does a state become failed? And what is the relationship between state formation and state failure?

In this chapter, the phenomenon of the failed state is examined as a Euro-centric construct that privileges Western experiences, histories, boundaries, borders, and systems of governance (Hill, 2005; Wai, 2012a). Using an anti-racist methodological approach, this chapter unpacks and unsettles the discourses of failed states to situate race and colonialism into the conception of states and state formation. More specifically, this discussion uses a critical discourse analysis to explore the works of well-known state specialists and scholars Joel Migdal (1988), Jean-Germain Gros (1996), and Daron Acemoglu and James A. Robinson (2012). Discourses on failed states rely on a comparative framework that (re)produces certain states as "successful" and others as "failed." The successful state, which is understood as a developed white Western state, is constructed as the universal norm that all states must emulate (Acemoglu & Robinson, 2012; Gros, 1996; Hill, 2005; Migdal, 1988; Wai, 2012b). The successful state requires the existence of failed states as a comparison in order to know itself as developed and modern. To examine how failed state discourses emerge and operate, this chapter examines the production of the Republic of Somalia as a failed state. Discourses on failed states disregard the socio-historical and political contexts that inform state and state formation as well as obscure the complex structure and power relations that are inherent within it. Instead, these discourses blame people living in states considered failed, neglecting the past and contemporary effects of imperialism and colonialism. As a result, these states and their people are pathologized as deviant and wild. The failed state is thus reproduced as an object of Western colonial fantasy and imperial interventions.

[handwritten: colonial methodology is framework for defining the failed state.]

While this chapter considers how colonial sentiment circulates through discourses on the failed state, it also aims to delve provocatively into how "expert" knowledge on the conceptualization of states and statehood is informed by a specific colonial methodology that disregards Indigenous structures, systems, and practices. As relatively new areas of academic inquiry and literature with a troublesome method, methodology, and practice, examinations of failed state theory require careful attention given the numerous (un)intended consequences.

States and statehood are seen as universal, ahistorical, and natural productions. *[handwritten: disagree]* An anti-racist approach troubles failed state discourses and works to unsettle conceptions of state and statehood that appear settled and natural. Using race as an entry point in deconstructing failed state discourses, this chapter works to rethink and destabilize the conception of state. In my examination of Somalia, I argue that Somalia's alleged failure can be used as an example to unsettle the hegemony of the Eurocentric state model as well as rethink the state, state formation, and statehood. *[handwritten: — kinda necessary ? gotcha]*

The first section of this chapter provides an overview of anti-racist research methodology. This section examines the importance of anti-racist research in unraveling the colonial ideology and racist discourses ingrained in the conception of the failed state. The second section starts with a brief discussion of failed state theory and discourses that guide the phenomenon of state failure, specifically using the works of Migdal (1988), Gros (1996), and Acemoglu and Robinson (2012). This section also deconstructs these discourses using an anti-racist framework and anti-colonial theory to unravel the power relations that are reflected in the articulation of the failed state. Applying the analysis of the previous sections, the third section provides a case study analysis of Somalia and its journey to alleged failure. This section briefly discusses Somalia's sociopolitical history and considers how its existence disrupts conceptions of state and statehood broadly. The discussion concludes with a set of suggestions for critical educators and researchers on how to engage and intervene with literature about governance in post-colonial states.

THEORY AND METHOD: APPLYING ANTI-RACIST METHODOLOGY TO FAILED STATES

Before I engage with failed state theory and the state of Somalia, it is important to discuss my own subjective positioning and my intentions for studying this topic. The position of the researcher is key to anti-racist research (Dei, 2005) and will determine how I engage and understand the research. George J. Sefa Dei (2005) emphasizes that our identities are not innocent. They are implicated in what we see or do not see (Dei, 2005). Thus, it is the duty of an researcher working within an anti-racist framework to reflect on the effect our subject position, history, and experience have on our research.

I came to studying failed state discourses because I have heard this rhetoric used to describe my home country of Somalia. Growing up in Canada, I was always confused by the media's portrayal of Somalia as chaotic and unsafe because my family in Canada and in Somalia told a very different story. My parents and other relatives went back home many times throughout the 1990s—a period when issues in Somalia made headlines in the news media daily. Whenever they returned to Canada, they always brought treats and clothes for my siblings and me. My cousins in both rural and urban Somalia would telephone us in Canada regularly and describe their lives, school, and parties and events we were missing out on back home. However, the dominant discourse constructed Somalia as unlivable and in constant civil unrest. These conflicting narratives left me very confused.

When I went back to Somalia in my early twenties, I attended school, worked for community organizations, went shopping, and attended social events regularly in a state always demonized in dominant discourse.[1] There were and continue to be problems in Somalia, as in all places. It has always frustrated me, however, that Canada and other Western states are seen as places devoid of violence, distress, and civil unrest while Somalia is constructed as a land of dark unruly bodies without order and authority. In the media and dominant discourse, there was never any discussion of how communities and societies in Somalia and the Somali territories[2] functioned without the system of centralized authority. Instead, the state and people were demonized and pathologized. The origins of states and borders were never discussed, leaving it to appear as natural, settled, and universal.

Anti-racism challenges concepts and discourses that appear natural, universal, or common sense to expose their colonial origins. Anti-racist research is intrinsically linked to anti-colonial theory because it problematizes colonial practices (Dei, 2005). According to Dei (2005), "an anti-colonial approach theorizes colonial and neo-colonial relations and the implications of imperial structures on processes of knowledge production and validation, the understanding of indigence, and the pursuit of agency and resistance, and subjective politics" (p. 5). Anti-racist research requires a paradigm shift away from colonial research to uncover power relationships in knowledge production (Dei, 2005).

This chapter employs a critical discourse analysis alongside an anti-racist approach to reveal the workings of race and racism within discourses of the failed state. According to Michel Foucault (1972), in every society the production of discourse is controlled, selected, organized, and redistributed. Within every discourse there is always a relation of power (Foucault, 1972). Discourses are unwritten rules and structures that produce meaning through particular utterances and statements (Mills, 2003). Siegfried Jäger and Florentine Maier (2009) describe discourse analysis as being "not only about the retrospective analysis of allocations of meaning, but also about the analysis of the ongoing production of reality through discourse" (p. 37). They state that discourses make the subject (Jäger & Maier, 2009).

Unpacking failed state discourses is a project of naming and deconstructing relations of power to illuminate the workings of race, racism, and colonialism. This project requires an anti-racist method and an anti-colonial theoretical framework to unsettle the origins and hegemony of the state and state formation. Employing a critical discourse analysis of failed state literature, this chapter works to critically engage discourses and structures and systems that appear natural to expose the practices of racial domination and hegemony.

Martin Bulmer and John Solomos (2004) argue that racist discourses need to be contextualized against the background of wider social relations and political cultures that shape them and allow them to develop. Therefore, racism needs to be situated within specific social and cultural environments (Bulmer & Solomos, 2004). My examination of failed state discourses is placed within a broader discussion of the state and state formation. More specifically, this chapter examines the colonial origins of the state to point to the racist discourses guiding failed state discourses. *that's a lot of layers.*

Anti-racism as a methodology not only names and challenges colonialism, hegemony, and racism; it also opens up new ways to reimagine the world. Dei (2005) argues for the use of counter-perspectives and multicentric ways of knowing to subvert and disrupt dominant discourses, colonialism, racism, and other social oppressions. Indigenous and local knowledges can work to challenge, replace, and reimagine alternatives to colonial thinking (Dei, 2005). Using Somalia as the case study, this chapter seeks to unravel the racism ingrained in failed state discourses and challenge the colonial origins of the state, as well as reimagine communities and societies outside the structure of the state. Failed state theorists do not articulate what methodologies they employ in their analysis of Somalia or any other "failed" state—it is this unnamed methodology that I hope to unravel using an anti-racist methodology, with the goal of pointing to a critical anti-racist practice for research and education.

I get it that "states" in Africa are artificial. I get not "identifying with a state. But not living in a country?

DECONSTRUCTING THE "FAILED STATE": AN ANTI-RACIST APPROACH TO FAILED STATE DISCOURSES

bureaucracy?

Much of the literature on failed states begins with Max Weber's conceptualization of the state (Gros, 1996; Migdal, 1988; Wai, 2012b). Weber describes the state as an organization composed of several agencies led and coordinated by the state's central leadership (Migdal, 1988). The state's leadership has the ability and power to make and implement binding rules for all people, as well as the parameters of rule-making for other social organizations in a given territory, using force if

yeah. government

necessary (Gros, 1996; Migdal, 1988). For Weber, this was the ideal definition of the state (Migdal, 1988).

Migdal's (1988) work on the failed state examines the capabilities of states to achieve the kinds of changes in society their leaders have sought through state policies, planning, and actions. For him, capabilities include "capacities to *penetrate* society, *regulate* relationships, *extract* resources, and *appropriate* or use resources in determined ways" (Migdal, 1988, p. 4, emphasis in original). He establishes a binary of strong states and weak states. Strong states have large capabilities to complete these tasks, whereas weak states are on the lower end of a spectrum of capabilities (Migdal, 1988). A central theme of his book is the ineffectiveness of many developing states to accomplish what their leaders and others expected of them.

Similar to Migdal, Gros (1996) looks at the capabilities of states. He situates states along a continuum, starting with those that meet none of his criteria and capacities associated with successful statehood and ending with those that meet all of them (Gros, 1996). This method allows for distinguishing among states in terms of the severity of their alleged failure (Gros, 1996). He describes states that are at one end of the continuum as extreme cases of failed states (Gros, 1996). These states have internationally recognized borders but no centralized authority (Gros, 1996). Gros (1996) uses Somalia as an example of an extreme case of state failure, positioned at the beginning of the continuum.

In their book *Why Nations Fail: The Origins of Power, Prosperity, and Poverty* (2012), failed state theorists Acemoglu and Robinson work to answer the question plaguing many people who study state formations: Why do some nations fail and others succeed? They argue that "nations fail today because … their extractive economic institutions do not create the incentive needed for people to save, invest, and innovate" (Acemoglu & Robinson, 2012, p. 372). In addition, they argue that states fail because the power and wealth of a nation are concentrated in the hands of those controlling the state, opening the possibilities for unrest, strife, and civil war (Acemoglu & Robinson, 2012).

Much of the scholarship within failed state theory establishes Western states as models for states considered to be developing (Acemoglu & Robinson, 2012; Gros, 1996; Migdal, 1988). For failed state theorists, following the path of states considered developed will allow for successful state formation. The model of statehood used in failed state theory excludes any discussions concerning its origins. Discussions of colonization and imperialism are brushed over, dismissed, or unacknowledged. Local and Indigenous structures and practices of government are disregarded in Gros, Migdal, and Acemoglu and Robinson's work. As a result, nation-states and borders go unquestioned and are constructed as natural. Jonathan Hill (2005) argues that the model of statehood used in failed state literature is based upon European values, customs, practices, organization, and structure. He states that underpinning failed state discourses is Western universalism (Hill, 2005). The notion of failed states relies on a nation-state's capabilities based on a model of statehood established by colonial powers made to be universal (Hill, 2005).

Within failed state discourses, all sovereign states are seen to have had equal opportunity to succeed. The failed nation-states fall into the categories of formerly colonized and developing or Third World states (Hill, 2005; Wai, 2012a). However, contemporary realities of neo-colonialism, neo-imperialism, and historically influenced power dynamics are absent in explorations of statehood and state failure. In addition, the use of Weber's ideal state makes no reference to Weber's use of the history of Western societies as its conceptual and analytical backbone (Wai, 2012b).

In Acemoglu and Robinson's (2012) discussion of Zimbabwe and Sierra Leone, they argue that economic stagnation, civil wars, famines, and mass displacement of people have left these regions poorer than they were before the 1960s. However, before the 1960s these states were under the control of Britain. In other words, these authors are arguing that these states were better off when they were colonized and under European rule. The underlying logic of failed state discourse is that most formerly colonized states cannot function independently. Thus, Europe and the West are needed to guide and control the states unable to govern themselves. Acemoglu and Robinson do not name the colonial discourses at play in their arguments. Instead, the people in states considered failed are constructed as unruly and in need of the colonizer for stability and order. eew.

Dei (2005) argues, "Dominant methodologies and epistemologies are incapable (by design) of capturing the experiences of the oppressed, or of capturing oppressive relations and dynamics" (p. 19). Failed state discourses are uncritical epistemologies that deny the existence of oppression and domination. Thus, failed state theorists are notorious for ignoring the pervasive effects of colonialism in both the immediate past and the all-too-relevant present of most of the developing or underdeveloped world.

According to Zubairu Wai (2012b), failed state literature produces a history abstracted from the experience of Europe as the historical expression of the universal. He argues that notions of failed statehood and statehood as a whole are constructed on the normative orthodoxy of a Eurocentric metaphor that privileges Western historicity, cultural achievements, and forms of governance over others (Wai, 2012b). In other words, to be successful, nation-states must model the trajectories of the evolution of Western societies—"Exposure to Western civilization is the key to successful statehood, as if Western states themselves are not sites of violence, woes, distress, domination and disciplinary power and authority" (Wai, 2012b, p. 29). The expectation is that the state will "advance" and "develop" economically following the directives of the West (Lauer, 2007).

The "degree of statehood" used in discourses of the failed state is measured by the standards or expected functions of Western states. As a result, the Western state is positioned as the normative model of state rationality against which the developing state is understood (Wai, 2012b). Wai (2012b) argues that this allows Europe and the West to disregard the historical constitutive relationship between states considered developing and the colonizing states.

The transformation of colonial territories into sovereign states is central to claims that statehood and state formations are universal because all societies, whether European or non-European, participate as equal sovereign states in world-systems (Anghie, 2005). Failed state literature starts from this position. Anthony Anghie (2005) emphasizes that all states are not equally sovereign and that sovereign statehood is not universal. It is impossible to provide an adequate account of sovereignty without analyzing the constitutive effect of colonialism (Mongia, 2007). Anghie's work demonstrates how colonialism was central to defining features of sovereignty and state formation. The notion of failed states universalizes a certain kind of sovereign state and, more specifically, the criteria to be a "successful" sovereign state. Western states represent a normative and universal standard of success, and it is the inability of certain states to replicate the political, economic, social, and cultural conditions that has, according to the failed state literature, resulted in their failure (Hill, 2005).

The very notion of the failed state relies on a comparative framework to determine the success or failure of a state. For instance, Acemoglu and Robinson (2012) argue that failed states such as Somalia, Zimbabwe, and Sierra Leone must learn from the experience of Britain and the United States because power and wealth are not concentered in these states. The United States and Britain are constructed as utopian-like societies without inequitable distributions of wealth and power. As a result, they produce the universal norm to which all states must strive. Acemoglu and Robinson (2012) use Somalia and other states considered failed to determine the success of Britain and the United States. As previously stated, this approach privileges Western histories, experiences, and political organizations.

Comparative analysis requires normative categories to constitute grounds for comparison. Gros's analysis of the failed state uses this comparative approach to situate states on a continuum based on Eurocentric criteria of statehood. In other words, this method distinguishes states by hierarchizing nation-states based on categories set by Europe and the West. Migdal's (1988) work employs a comparative framework to categorize states as "strong" or "weak" based on a state's capabilities. Migdal, along with other failed state theorists, operationalizes European and Western understandings of state and statehood. Radhika Mongia (2007) argues that a frequent epistemological problem with comparative analysis has been the Eurocentricity of the normative categories that ground the analysis. These categories are produced through a relationship between similarity and difference so that "the normative categories function as the similar grounds for assessing, asserting, and indeed, presuming *difference*" (Mongia, 2007, p. 385, emphasis in original). Mongia (2007) argues that with every spectre of difference comes the possibility for hierarchies as well as relations of domination and subordination. She is concerned with the uneven ways nation-states are produced as similar yet distinct, creating comparisons between successful and unsuccessful, developed and developing. (*dialectical*)

In Lauer's (2007) work on African political culture, she argues that Africa is constantly positioned as the polar opposite of the West. She states that "Africans are repeatedly reminded of their need to make every effort to shape up, to clean up, to overcome their various inherent cultural and moral shortcomings, to discipline and control themselves and their leaders sexually, fiscally, politically" (p. 293). These fallacies establish a binary that is part of a larger function of Orientalism used to separate and differentiate the West/Occident or the developed states from the East/Orient or Third World Other. Edward Said (1978) argues that the Orient was invented by Europe and the West as a place of exotic beings, romance, and haunting landscapes. The West gains its strength and identity by setting itself against the Orient (Said, 1978). Said states that Orientalism is a Western style for dominating, restricting, and having authority over the Orient. Functioning as a form of Orientalism, failed state discourses are used to reinforce Western and European superiority and to dominate the developing world through international interventions.

The failed state is reproduced as an object of Western colonial fantasy ripe for imperial interventions (Wai, 2012a). The label of failed state is used to justify interventions in states considered too weak to function without the help of the West. Rudyard Kipling's infamous poem "The White Man's Burden" (1899) calls on the white man to civilize the uncivilized people of the Third World. This "burden" Kipling speaks of is a responsibility of the white man to save the Other. This separates the developed colonizer from the un-developed Other by using Christian paternalistic discourses of goodwill and saving those in "need" of aid. *ugh!* Despite the supposed "noble" aim, Kipling merely differentiates and divides the world into a series of binaries—civilized/savage, modern/primitive, successful/failed, and developed/developing. Kipling illustrates the colonized as childlike and violent—"wild" and "half-devil and half-child" (Kipling, 1899). He portrays the white man as founder of all rationality and savior to irrational, childlike Others. This logic permeates discourses of failed states.

States labeled as failed and their peoples then as infantilized and constructed as though there is something inherently wrong with them then require the interventions of the West. This is not a new narrative; in occluding political context and maintaining that failed states squandered their equal opportunity, failed state discourses reinscribe post-colonial states and Third World people as lazy, underachieving, dangerous, and criminal. This understanding reinforces the discursive connections between the racialization of individuals within colonizing metropolises and the necessary racialization in order to figure as a colony. This analysis reveals more in its framework than in its content. Failed state discourses underscore the ever-present connection between race and colonialism.

SOMALIA: A CASE STUDY OF A "FAILED STATE"

Somalia's collapsed state represented the literal implosion of state structures and of residual forms of authority and legitimacy. *geez.*

—ADAM, 2008 (P. 150)

In 1884, the colonial powers of Europe met in Berlin to carve out borders for the entire continent of Africa (wa Thiong'o, 1986). Africa was cut up into pieces based on the European states that colonized it. The multiplicity of people, cultures, and languages on the continent was not taken into consideration. As Ngũgĩ wa Thiong'o (1986) describes, "It seems it is the fate of Africa to have her destiny always decided around conference tables in the metropolises of the Western world" *huh* (p. 4). These forms of imperialism continue to control the economy, politics, and cultures of Africa and of other former colonies (wa Thiong'o, 1986). During this meeting, Somali communities were divided amongst three European colonizers— Italy, Britain,[3] and France.[4]

On July 1, 1960, the Somali Republic was formed, uniting parts of British Somaliland with Italian Somaliland. After nearly a century, the colonial powers left behind a centralized system of government—a system alien to the locally based structures of Somali communities. With the establishment of the National Assembly, Aden Abdulle Osman was elected as Somalia's first president (Issa-Salwe, 1994). On June 10, 1967, Osman's six-year term in office expired, and he lost the presidential position to Abdirashid Ali Sharmarke (Issa-Salwe, 1994).

During the March 1969 federal elections, sixty-four parties and a thousand candidates ran for office (Adam, 2008; Issa-Salwe, 1994) and Sharmarke was re-elected. On October 15, 1969, Sharmarke was assassinated by a member of his own police force (Issa-Salwe, 1994). The president's assassination was quickly used as an opportunity for the army to seize control of the state in a bloodless coup (Adam, 2008).[5] The military junta named General Mohamed Siyad Barre as president. The Barre regime held central authority in Somalia for more than twenty years, until 1991. *dictatorship 1967 - 1991*

Although the Barre regime had some positive social, economic, environmental, and political impacts on Somalia, it reinforced a centralized approach inherited from colonialism, specifically in its top-down export/plantation model (Adam, 1995). According to Hussein Adam (1995), "its rigid centralist, militarist approach further alienated it from the residual culture of consensus that has sustained Somali society and politics over the centuries" (p. 190). From the 1980s onwards, Barre worked to disrupt clan relations by privileging his clan in government activities as well as instigating rural clan conflicts in various parts of the country (Adam, 1995). By 1991, Barre was ousted from the presidency by both northern and southern clan-based forces (Adam, 2008). Following the collapse of central authority in Mogadishu, rival groups engaged in armed struggle for political power (Dagne, 2009).[6] I remember this...

In the absence of any central authority in Somalia during the 1990s, the UN, with the help of the United States, tried to create one. Several peacekeeping missions were sent into Somalia to attempt to administer and "stabilize" the country. At the end of 2006, the United States and Ethiopia established a Transitional Federal Government (TFG) for Somalia (Adam, 2008), lasting from 2006 to 2012.[7] The establishment of the TFG was the international community's way of grappling with the issue of administering Somalia. It is important to note that the TFG was not elected into power nor supported by the people. This intervention by the international community and accompanying institutions was viewed as a way to transform the nation-state of Somalia from "failed" to "successful." However, Hill (2005) argues that failed state analysts use the alleged deviancy of so-called failed states to promote and justify their political and economic domination by Western states and other international actors. Adding to this, Wai (2012a) states:

> Africa, which since the 1990s has been the theater of a number of armed conflicts, or "state failure" as the "experts" and strategic actors are quick to point out, has become a conceptual and theoretical staple and the guinea pig for testing the various international policy prescriptions that have developed in response to the phenomenon. (p. 129)

The TFG was one of several initiatives and policies implemented by the international community and institutions for the purpose of "developing" Somalia.

Within failed state discourses, blame is used as a way to make the people of the alleged failed state rather than the colonial systems of power and international institutions responsible for their state's failure. Failed state theorists begin from the assumption that former colonies were already formed and functioning upon independence (Wai, 2012b). In fact, Wai (2012b) argues what follows this assumption is a paternalistic diatribe that the West left these independent states with a functioning bureaucracy capable of maintaining law and order, enforcing the rule of law, and delivering social services. It is then believed that despite the West's best efforts, these states, specifically, African states, continue to be plagued with state failure, abject poverty, crippling ignorance, and crumbling infrastructure (Wai, 2012b). As a result, failed state literature and the international community and institutions attribute the alleged failure of Somalia to the Somali peoples' innate character. In conceiving Somalia as failed, the people of Somalia are constructed as inherently backwards, primitive, oppressive, devious in nature, lazy, violent, corrupt, and thus unable to govern themselves. These myths are powerful because they tap into the racializing narratives upon which the history of colonization has been built. They also absolve Western states from any complicity in the issues in Somalia. To further absolve themselves, the international community uses Somalia's alleged failure to legitimize Western imperial impulses masked under the cloaks of humanitarian aid and development.

The issue of administering Somalia has been the focus of the international community for more than two decades. Even with the establishment of a federal government in 2012, Somalia is still labeled a failed state because of civil conflicts and the government's lack of full authority and power over the entire state and territories (Acemoglu & Robinson, 2012; Adam, 2008). International institutions, including the African Union and the UN, continue to work with the federal government to further administer central authority. As mentioned earlier, centralized authority is not Indigenous to Somali communities. The alien system of centralized governance, introduced by the colonizer, worked to manipulate the traditional Somali institutions (Adam, 2008; Issa-Salwe, 1994; Little, 2003). The colonizers expected their democratic parliamentary process would complement traditional political institutions; however, this system left no room for Indigenous political practices. The 1969 federal elections with a thousand candidates running indicate that centralized authority does not have appeal in the Somali territories. The party politics of the West were too foreign. Traditionally, for many Somali communities political authority was spread through the community, as there was no centre for political control (Adam, 1995; Issa-Salwe, 1994). In other words, pre-colonial Somali communities reflected a decentralized authority.

Discourses of the failed state and state formation leave no room for societies and communities that do not have centralized structures of authority or function outside of a central government structure. The very existence of a state without centralized authority questions not only the notion of state but also the very process of state formation. Adam (1995) states when discussing the collapse of the centralized authority in 1991:

> It is as if Somali society could no longer tolerate the cultural-political pollution imposed by European colonialism, and then inflated and perpetuated by the Cold War. On the positive side, there is a glimmer of hope that Somalia might also be the first to experiment with novel principles of restructuring state/civil society relationships. (p. 193)

Adam's analysis makes way for a critical discussion of the potential of restructuring relationships and reimagining authority and structures in the Somali territories that moves beyond borders and centralized authority. Perhaps instead of viewing Somalia as a failed state, we can use the practices of the Somali territories and other states considered failed to reimagine the notion of state, statehood, and state formation.

UNSETTLING THE "STATE": THEORY AND PRAXIS

Quite intentionally and without apology, there is much more to African governance than may ever be permitted within the purview of international surveillance.

—LAUER, 2007 (P. 300)

The collapse of centralized authority in Somalia led to the reassertion of communities and territories operating beyond the nation-state borders established by Europe in 1884. "In no case, however, did modern state structures succeed in displacing the underlying clan structure of Somali society" (Adam, 2008, p. 41). These local structures demonstrate that states and borders are socially, culturally, and historically produced. As stated by Dei (2005), Indigenous knowledges and practices can replace and reimagine alternatives to colonial thinking. In the case of Somalia, local governance practices continued through the introduction of a centralized state formation during the colonial era, its eventual collapse in 1991, and its reformation by the international community in 2012.

In her discussion on Ghana, Lauer (2007) states that despite Britain's invasion and control, the Indigenous systems of governance, more specifically, the Nana institutions,[8] remain the backbone of political, economic, social, and spiritual life in Ghana. She emphasizes that Indigenous and local systems are not figments or stories of nostalgia; they are very much present in many people's public and private lives. Somali and Ghanaian communities are not the only societies that continue to embrace Indigenous systems of governance—communities throughout the world reject and/or replace colonial systems with Indigenous practices (Lauer, 2007). The concepts of states and centralized authority are relatively recent establishments for most of the world. The state, as a geopolitical formation, did not exist in Africa 150 years ago (Lauer, 2007). However, this fact is clearly forgotten by many researchers and educators working in the fields of state theory, international development, geography, and history.

According to Lauer (2007), "The international community does not regard *mechanical solidarity* the village institutions of social welfare and the system of extended family and neighborhood obligations as governmental" (p. 302). Indigenous governance and institutions are not recognized by most in the international community. The West, *organic* along with international institutions, works to administer and pathologize communities without an active central state government. However, those of us working within critical education and critical research can challenge these narratives. Critical educators and researchers must move away from the limitations and hegemony of state, statehood, and imposed colonial authority. Research that embraces narratives of state failure and state formation further makes invisible Indigenous systems and institutions.

Scholarship, research, and pedagogy operating within Western epistemologies, such as failed state theory, are inadequate for understanding the workings of local and Indigenous structures. Failed state researchers, including Gros, Migdal, and Acemoglu and Robinson, *fail* to engage the communities they label as failed. In fact, the field of failed state theory emerged without any engagement or inclusion of Indigenous people and practices within its studies. Researchers who neglect Indigenous voices and practices inevitably (re)produce colonial scholarship.

By challenging and subverting colonial systems, anti-racist research works to support Indigenous structures and knowledges. It works to replace and reimagine alternatives to colonial thinking on the state and state formation. It allows for an examination of societies and communities outside the boundaries of the state. However, this research must be grounded in community. Anti-racist research makes room for Indigenous knowledges and structures to become visible by naming, challenging, and destabilizing the colonial nature of research and Western epistemologies.

Sandy Grande (2008) states that it is important to detach and rethink the notion of sovereignty from its connection to Western understandings of power and base it on Indigenous notions of relationships and community. Adding to this, Dei (2005) states, "We must not replace the hegemonic order with one that suffocates life and does not allow each of us to flourish in ways that we may not even be able to begin to imagine" (p. 12). In order to begin to imagine, we must question and destabilize research and literature on nation-states. How has research on post-colonial states been compiled? Who receives the opportunity to do research? What are the researchers intending to do with their findings? Who benefits from the research? What are the impacts on the communities being researched? (Have the researchers considered this?) How does the research bolster or support colonial scholarship?

For those of us working within critical education and critical research, we must unsettle dominant discourses to challenge hegemony. This involves considering the long-ranging impacts of analyses on people and communities within our research and in the literature we engage. We must situate our pedagogy in anti-racism to begin to embrace and even re-imagine community systems outside the Eurocentric state structure.

NOTES

1. It is important to note that when I went back to the Somali territories, I occupied a space of privilege as a diasporic body holding both a Somali passport and a Canadian passport.
2. By Somali territories, I am pointing to the fact that the idea of Somalia as a unified nation-state and its borders is socially and historically produced by Europe and remains a site of contested

borders and border making. The term Somali territories acknowledges the Somali communities and populations that have been absorbed into other nation-states (Djibouti, Ethiopia, and Kenya) as well as the territories within *Somalia* that operate independently from the nation-state (Puntland and Somaliland). As a result, I use the term *Somalia* in this chapter strategically to deconstruct the concept of state and state formation.

3. Part of British Somaliland is now split between Ethiopia, Kenya, and Somalia (more specifically, Somaliland) (Adam, 2008).

4. French Somaliland is now the Republic of Djibouti (Adam, 2008).

5. The takeover was widely welcomed as it was seen as relieving the political tension built up by the party system (Issa-Salwe, 1994). In fact, Hussein Adam (2008) argues that the military coup succeeded as a result of backlash against the "semi-anarchy" of the multiparty era.

6. Without consulting other opposition organizations, Ali Mahdi Muhammad of the United Somali Congress became interim president on January 29, 1991 (Adam, 1995; Issa-Salwe, 1994). The rushed installation of Mahdi Muhammad as president was challenged by other leaders, particularly General Mohamed Farrah Aidid (Issa-Salwe, 1994). As a result, armed conflict between decentralized opposition groups increased, contributing to Somalia's prolonged state of civil war (Adam, 1995).

7. In August 2012, the TFG tenure ended. With the aid of the international community and international institutions a federal government of Somalia was inaugurated. However, because of political and governmental divisions as well as the continuing existence of independent Somali territories (with their own systems of government and rules of law) and the current civil conflicts, Somalia is still considered a failed state within the international community.

8. Nanas are traditional chiefs in many communities in Ghana (Lauer, 2007).

REFERENCES

Acemoglu, D., & Robinson, J. A. (2012). *Why nations fail: The origins of power, prosperity, and poverty.* New York, NY: Crown Business.

Adam, H. (2008). *From tyranny to anarchy: The Somali experience.* Trenton, NJ: Red Sea Press.

Adam, H. M. (1995). Somalia: Environmental degradation and environmental racism. In L. Westra & S. Wenz (Eds.), *Faces of environmental racism: Confronting issues of global justice* (pp. 181–205). Lanham, MD: Rowman & Littlefield.

Anghie, A. (2005). *Imperialism, sovereignty and the making of international law.* Cambridge, England: Cambridge University Press.

Bulmer, M., & Solomos, J. (2004). Introduction: Researching race and racism. In M. Bulmer & J. Solomos (Eds.), *Researching race and racism* (pp. 1–15). London, England: Routledge.

Dagne, T. (2009). Somalia: Prospects for a lasting peace. *Mediterranean Quarterly, 20*(2), 95–112.

Dei, G. J. S. (2005). Critical issues in anti-racist research methodology: An introduction. In G. J. S. Dei & G. Johal (Eds.), *Critical issues in anti-racist research methodology* (pp. 1–28). New York, NY: Peter Lang.

Foucault, M. (1972). *The archaeology of knowledge and the discourse on language.* New York, NY: Pantheon.

Grande, S. (2008). Red pedagogy: The un-methodology. In N. Denzin, Y. Lincoln, & L. T. Smith (Eds.), *Handbook of critical and Indigenous methodologies* (pp. 233–354). Los Angeles, CA: Sage.

Gros, J. G. (1996). Towards a taxonomy of failed states in the New World Order: Decaying Somalia, Liberia, Rwanda, and Haiti. *Third World Quarterly, 17*(3), 455–471.

Hill, J. (2005). Beyond the Other? A postcolonial critique of the failed state thesis. *African Identities, 3*(2), 139–154.

Issa-Salwe, A. M. (1994). *The collapse of the Somali state: The impact of the colonial legacy.* London, England: Haan Associates.

Jäger, S., & Maier, F. (2009). Theoretical and methodological aspects of Foucauldian critical discourse analysis and dispositive analysis. In R. Wodak & M. Meyer (Eds.), *Methods of critical discourse analysis* (pp. 32–62). London, England: Sage.

Kipling, R. (1899). The white man's burden: The United States & the Philippine Islands. In *Rudyard Kipling's verse: Definitive edition.* Garden City, NY: Doubleday.

Lauer, H. (2007). Depreciating African political culture. *Journal of Black Studies, 38*(2), 288–307.

Little, D. (2003). *Somalia: Economy without state.* Bloomington, IN: The International African Institute and Indiana University Press.

Migdal, J. (1988). *Strong societies and weak states: State-society relations and state capabilities in the Third World.* Princeton, NJ: Princeton University Press.

Mills, S. (2003). Discourse. In S. Mills, *Michel Foucault* (pp. 53–66). New York, NY: Routledge.

Mongia, R. (2007). Historicizing state sovereignty: Inequality and the form of equivalence. *Comparative Studies in Society and History, 49*(2), 384–411.

Said, E. (1978). *Orientalism.* New York, NY: Vintage Books.

wa Thiong'o, N. (1986). *Decolonising the mind: The politics of language in African literature.* Nairobi, Kenya: East African Educational Publishers.

Wai, Z. (2012a). *Epistemologies of African conflicts: Violence, evolutionism and the war in Sierra Leone.* New York, NY: Palgrave Macmillan.

Wai, Z. (2012b). Neopatrimonialism and the discourse of state failure in Africa. *Review of African Political Economy, 39*(131), 27–43.

CHAPTER SEVEN

Student Engagement Experiences IN Nigerian Private Secondary Schools

An Anti-Colonial and Student-Centered Analysis

CHIZOBA IMOKA

SETTING THE NIGERIAN CONTEXT

We live in a world where the ontological and human rights of young Africans and their communities have at best, become the foils of rhetoricians and, at worst, these rights are not even known or seem unrealistic to African youth and their communities. What are these rights I speak of? The rights to grow up in a centered way, to grow up in a society/home that holistically and positively grounds you in your culture and upholds the dignity, agency, interests and aspirations of your ancestors (Asante, 2003, 2007). It is the right to grow up in a society where the cultural values of your ancestors and grandparents are not up for comparison, spectacle, debate and ridicule—their difference is acknowledged, upheld and honored; the commonsense, historical and social utility of these values and knowledge systems in contemporary society are affirmed. It includes the right to know your personal history and to speak of yourself as an economic, spiritual, political, cultural and social being with a pre-colonial origin and from an anti-colonial perspective. It encompasses the right to understand, speak, write in your Indigenous language (Wa Thiong'o, 1986), wholly embody Indigeneity and participate in the Indigenous life of your heritage (Dei, 2000b). This includes the right to be a community builder and nurture the ongoing revitalization and reform of your culture. This demands the right to have the language of your culture also be the language of your education (Wa Thiong'o, 1986). It is the right to know the history of the society (global, national and local) that you live in, how it has come to be, the role that people like you have played in making the society what it is (Banks, 1997). This includes the right to know the struggles of your race, the globally marginalized communities, the injustices perpetrated by your kind and your place in the world to bring about justice (Darling-Hammond, French, & Garcia-Lopez, 2002). Sadly and dangerously, these rights and the consciousness to seek/affirm them have become privileges obtainable by chance by a small group of African elites. These elites who fall into the path of intellectually honest/courageous people are fortunate to have mentors that encourage them not to succumb to social expectations about what they should be doing because of their class/age/gender and have the resources to nurture their intellectual curiosity to a level of economic/social independence.

In Nigeria, where I was born and remain emotionally connected, many young Nigerians like myself are estranged (Wa Thiong'o, 1986) from their cultural heritage and authentic socio-historical-spiritual-cultural self (Mazama, 2002). We do not know our place in history and the place of history in our lives and the communities in which we have found ourselves. We are ill equipped to initiate, facilitate and contribute to a transformative nation-building agenda. We are decentered from the logical anti-colonial and social justice intellectual location in which we ought to be grounded (Mazama, 2003). As Wa Thiong'o (1986) explained, our colonial education, socialization experiences and the imposed norms/values/languages we are scripted into have taken us away "from ourselves to other selves, from our worlds to other worlds" (p. 12).

This discussion argues for finding our way back to "our cultural self" and "our cultural community's world." This journey is about intellectually situating and grounding young Nigerians in anti-colonial thought, humanizing and decolonizing praxis for liberation and transformative participation in nation building. For this to happen, a nationwide decolonization process will need to begin in the Nigerian state. Schools can plug into this decolonization process by engaging students through an inclusive education and anti-colonial lens.

Underpinning this discussion is the postulation that schools have an ethical responsibility to educate and engage young Nigerians in a way that humanizes them and facilitates their participation in nation building. To further elaborate and engage the education polity (especially Nigeria and Africa) in this responsibility, it is important to have an understanding of the current school system from the perspective of students. Consequently, this discussion presents the results of a qualitative research project on student engagement experiences in three Nigerian secondary schools. To synthesize the data, Dei's (2000a, 2000b; Dei, Asgharzadeh, Eblaghie-Bahador, &

Shahjahan, 2006) inclusive education framework is used to analyze the results and help to outline implications for educational change.

OUTLINING THE THEORETICAL FRAMEWORK: ENGAGING STUDENTS FOR INCLUSION AND SOCIAL TRANSFORMATION

Inclusive education is defined as education that responds to the concerns, aspirations and interests of a diverse body politic by drawing on the accumulated knowledges, creativity, and resourcefulness of local peoples. A school is inclusive to the extent that students are able to identify and connect with their school's school environment, culture, population and history.

(DEI ET AL., 2006, P. 64)

Engaging students for social transformation takes off from a premise that sees education and the schooling process as a vehicle for social change and justice. It acknowledges the many forms of exclusion and injustices that exist in the schooling/societal system and seeks to correct them. For example, it challenges the oppressive and colonial majority/minority ethnic relations in contemporary African societies (Dei et al., 2006) where the "minority" groups are sidelined in the schooling polity and their historical marginalization/underrepresentation is not squarely addressed. Within the Nigerian schooling context, this can be corrected by seeking to administer schools within a philosophical mosaic that aligns all the ethnic groups as equals. This means that the history, aspirations and experiences of marginalized groups as well as dominant groups are given equitable representation in the school curriculum, school administration and school culture. This way, schools become "inclusive" of all and encourage critical consciousness in students, especially as it relates to silent/passive oppression.

This conception of student engagement grounds itself in anti-colonial thought (Dei & Asgharzadeh, 2001, 2006; Fanon, 1963, 1967; Memmi, 1969) as well as a critical democratic conception of education which McMahon and Portelli (2004) define as "a conception of education that engenders personal empowerment, personal and social transformation guided by principles of equity, social justice and inclusion" (p. 72). The personal empowerment of students is guaranteed in a schooling environment that honors the socio-historical-political differences of every student in the school while disrupting silences and inequalities located at various social intersections such as gender, religion, class and knowledge. Students are engaged with the anti-colonial version of their history (Africa, Nigeria and their ethnic group). The colonial framing of schooling and its implication for student identity formation are implicated in the whole school. As a result, students are set forth on a journey of personal decolonization through exercises such as the Unveiling Africa's Origin Story Project that required youth to learn about their pre-colonial history and reflect on the implications for their lives and society as a whole. In this way, youth learn to be proud of their heritage and culture. They begin a process of self-redefinition by gaining knowledge about their heritage and history. In the classroom, it means teaching all subjects in a multi-centric way (Dei, 2015)—where the epistemologies of all the ethnic groups of students are centered and drawn from to show varied perspectives and valid examples of variance and similarities. It also means equipping students with the mind-set that upholds and celebrates difference while acknowledging commonalities between groups.

In envisioning and articulating student identities, students are not viewed from a deficit perspective (Portelli, Vibert & Shields, 2007) that argues that students are incapable, inexperienced and delinquent. Instead, students are seen as agents of possibility, change and social justice in their communities. As agents of possibility, they are engaged to be critically aware of the social construction and history of their world, identities, race and ethnicity. Students are acknowledged as human beings with multiple identities (social class, gender, ethnicity, spirituality) that necessitate unique social experiences in the world and mediate their school experiences/learning process. Accordingly, inclusive education argues for an acknowledgment, validation and critical interrogation of these identities in the classroom and schooling context. These identities and accompanying experiences are social junctures of differences and as a result, when critically reflected upon, are sites of social knowledge that are necessary for students to have a more inclusive understanding of their lives, their communities and responsibilities in the world. In this conception of student engagement, the purpose and process of schooling are not linear or/and economically centered. It is about self/community understanding, community building and democratic transformation.

Schooling practices, norms and values should be evolving and become a mosaic of student historical identities, social experiences and community aspirations. This is reflected throughout the school environment: the textbooks, wall paintings, teaching staff, the ethnic diversity of the student population (Dei, Zine, & James-Wilson, 2002). According to Zyngier (2008), a transformatively engaged student possesses four CORE attributes (Connected, Ownership, Responsive and Empowered):

1. They are connected to and engaged with their cultural knowledge. Therefore, they are culturally competent and see their lives and experiences as sites of and tools for learning.
2. They own their learning and are able to see themselves represented in the curriculum.
3. The curriculum and teacher are responsive to the lived experiences of students. In so doing, they equip students to critique their own experiences.
4. Students then become empowered over their own lives.

Within a transformative conception of student engagement, student success soars beyond academic excellence. It also includes critical consciousness, cultural competence and commitment to living a principled life based on values such as love, respect, humility, courage, justice, community building and solidarity.

RESEARCH METHODOLOGY AND CONTEXT

The two overarching research questions of this study are inspired by my secondary school experience in Nigeria and guided by the theorization of Gloria Ladson-Billings's scholarship on culturally responsive teaching and learning, George Dei's inclusive education framework and Portelli's scholarship on student engagement and curriculum of life:

1. To what extent are the student engagement experiences of young Nigerians transformative and inclusive? Further, what is the pattern and nature of the engagement?
2. How is the "home" culture/identities of Nigerian students understood and engaged within the Nigerian schooling context?

The study was completed in two doctoral courses that I completed in the 2014/15 academic year. In the field component of the course, I was required to conduct three in-depth interviews. The research participants are females (Adanma, Folake and Etim; to protect their privacy and safety, they have been given pseudonyms) between the ages of nineteen and twenty-three. They are alumnae of three popular private secondary schools in Nigeria. Two are university students and the other works in the youth development sector in North America. These participants were purposefully chosen from my activism network because of their strong interest in Nigerian politics and previously expressed reflections about schooling in Nigeria.

The interview instrument was divided into three sections. The first section was composed of demographic questions that were extrapolated from McGill's Student Life & Learning Student Demographic Survey. I modified the survey to emphasize Nigerian lived experiences. Questions included place of Indigenous origin versus place of domicile in Nigeria, academic stream in high school, fluency in an Indigenous language, current profession and field of study. The second section was divided into three main subsections: cognitive, behavioral and affective. I asked questions relating to leadership experience in school; schooling expectations; classroom content; their role in the classroom; the extent to which social justice issues were discussed in the classroom; relationship with teachers; relationship with students; images represented in the school; feeling of inclusion, exclusion and comfort; opportunity to speak an Indigenous language in school; and how their cultural identity, social class, religious preference and gender were engaged and enhanced in the classroom/school.

In framing the questions, I kept the anti-colonial objective of the project at the forefront. For example, in asking questions about home culture and practices, I probed students to think about their homes outside of the "urban settings." I encouraged them to think of themselves as economic, historical, cultural and spiritual beings with a pre-colonial history. I asked how their pre-colonial histories were represented and engaged in at home and then at school. Questions such as these allowed me to see how students' identities evolved. It also allowed me to identify schooling factors that enabled the nature of cultural engagement that students experienced and expected to have in school. Conversely, it gave students the opportunity to see and reflect on some of the contradictions and disconnections in their identity, history and future.

KEY FINDINGS

The research participants reported student experiences that were oppressive, colonizing and far from transformative. Adanma argued that she felt nominally included in school only when she was hanging out with the economically influential students. These influential students were often related to the owner of the school and as a result earned the respect of the teachers and other students. She was encouraged to be intellectually dependent on the school rules and textbook materials. Worse still, all the participants explained that they learnt to believe that "to be Western is to be better" (Folake) and the Nigerian way of doing things is "barbaric" (Adanma). For example, Adanma noted that students were punished for using their hands to eat Nigerian meals. Therefore, the schooling process was about undoing their Nigerianness, learning new social norms/languages and taking up a new identity that was in line with the progressive and modern (i.e., Western) way of sociality.

Regarding the schooling context and the purpose of schooling, my participants reported experiences that are reminiscent of an instrumentalist conception (Foster, 1986) of education. Through this lens, students are not viewed as dynamic beings with aspirations and knowledge that should be included in their education. Instead, they are viewed as moldable instruments of respect, compliance and economic participation in society as workers or employers. Schools had a predetermined vision of what a good citizen looks like and their job was to instill these attributes in students. When asked what they believed the purpose of their education was, the women argued that it was simply about passing their school examinations. Therefore, their success as students was measured by how well they performed on their exams, how respectful of adults they were and their compliance to school rules and regulations.

This instrumentalism in the educational experience of the research partic-ipants appeared to be strongly connected to Nigeria's effort to foster a national identity in light of the 1914 colonial amalgamation of 250 distinct cultural groups. The inherent cultural and epistemological differences among these ethnic groups created a need for a national identity/narrative based on shared values, experi-ences, ways of life and aspirations. Students are molded to internalize a new con-sciousness of self and identity that overrides their ethnicity and speaks to a "One Nigeria" community narrative. Folake described this identity as a "neo-Nigerian identity" that is based on the erasure of minority ethnic groups from polity/con-sciousness, privatization/secondarization of Indigenous cultures/ways of being and foregrounding of new ways of life that are Western based and economically cen-tered. This "One Nigeria" identity/narrative is steeped in Nigeria's colonial legacy across language, dress, religion, music, food, TV shows, social aspirations, norms and values, amongst others.

On cultural days (e.g., independence celebration), the "Nigerianness" of stu-dents is communicated by the quality of the "traditional" fabrics they wear. It is worth noting that these traditional fabrics, often called Ankara, are neither indig-enous to Nigeria in their creation (often imported from China, India and Holland) nor are the styles made out of them indigenous. English is the official language in schools and society. Pidgin English is a tolerated variation of English that is often spoken by students and staff members. Folake explains:

> F: There is a neo-Nigerian culture that we all participated in. You just wore your funky tra-ditional—whoever can sew the finest traditional—the most elegant or modern looking traditional, that was what it was about. A lot of our plays were not really cultural; it was just this generic African or Nigerian. Every once in a while, we say oh "this is an Igbo play" and we try to inject an element of Igbo culture that we read in some book. But most of our student-led productions were like in an urban setting—Lagos—and we are just speaking pidgin.

Although Christianity and Islam are recognized as the two main religions in schools, participants discussed the dominance of Christianity. Adanma shares her experiences:

> C: How was your Christian identity engaged in the school?
> A: That was the dominant religion in my school. People who were Muslims, we did not really notice them.
> C: Were the prayers always Christian?
> A: Very often. Sometimes when they remember they call out Muslims and Christians to pray. Sometimes they tried; like during parties, they ask Muslims and Christians to come and pray. But when we had people visit the school, it was always a Christian that prayed.

Interestingly, all the research participants identified more strongly with their reli-gion than with their ethnic identities. Folake explains:

C: So you identified more with your Christian faith than your Kogi identity [ethnic identity]?

F: Yes.

C: And the school reinforced that?

F: Yes, values that were not Christian, people will tell you, "it is not a Christian thing to do." Especially with my set, there was a very strong ... I do not know what to call it. We had these chapel workers and lots of us were part of this group. In many ways, there was this odd guilting—attaching a lot of the school's regulations to religion. Things were doubly bad. The people who were enforcing a lot of these rules were like leaders amongst the chapel workers. Punishment was tied to religion in a very odd way.

The absence of secularity in these schools nurtured a culture of silence (Freire, 1970a) about ethnic differences and encouraged a kind of passivity and self-censorship amongst students. In a society/school that incubates a culture of silence, citizens are self- and culturally alienated. To maintain a (colonial) "social order" that thrives on being dominated, citizens must be estranged from their history and culture, at least to the extent that is required to uphold colonial social arrangements and economic interests. From this lens, these schools play host to an oppressive consciousness (Freire, 1970a, p. 47), which normalizes cultural alienation and justifies domination.

The social inequities in Nigerian society were not discussed or disrupted in the participants' schools. By not interrogating social class, privilege, the root cause of poverty and the many ways in which poverty manifests itself in people's professions, the schools appeared to be working towards normalizing the social hierarchies along class lines. By observing which foods they ate (foreign Kellogg's Corn Flakes versus indigenous Nasco corn flakes), students in Adanma's school were able to identify the rich from the poor students and engaged with each group accordingly. In Adanma's school, students from underserved parts of Nigeria such as the Niger Delta who were on scholarship were also easily identifiable by their looks, school bag and school shoes. When poverty was taken up in the classes of all the participants, it was pathologized and the impoverished were treated as charity cases. According to Etim,

E: When you get to the final year of the program, you are required to get involved in community activities. The one for my year involved going into a rural community in Lagos. We taught them a couple of things like how to make beads and how to cook so that they could earn a living out of that. We also raised money and donated it to them. Most people just stopped at that level of community development, just to fulfill all righteousness. Some of us went a step further and did other things.

C: From what I understand, there was a whole range of activities to keep people busy. In the community service that you did, I do not gather that you were taught deeply about the issues you are going to face in those communities. Before you went into the communities—did you get to learn about the history, why there is poverty? Did you have deep conversations about the issues?

E: There was nothing like that. There was a little tour and we saw how they were living. There was not any introduction or preamble about how things became the way they are. It was just about helping them and I do not think there was a continuous process to help, which is not beneficial in the long run.

CLASSROOM AND CURRICULUM CONTENT

The three research participants described their learning experience in the classroom as a teacher centered monologue that was shallow and Eurocentric. Adanma explains:

C: What was your favorite class?
A: Government and Literature.
C: Tell me about those classes.
A: First of all, when you are in SS1, you are in the same class with the same set of people. Government class was actually a boring class. People were always sleeping. The teacher will just come and download and go. It was just like: 1990—this happened. We passed because we could just cram it and drop it.

In Etim's case, asking questions in class was often interpreted as being tricky, insulting and an attempt to shame the teacher.

E: In fact, that [asking questions] was not encouraged in school. That will be interpreted as you being tricky or you probably wanting to embarrass the teacher. Because, even the teachers, I do not think when they were growing up they were allowed to ask certain things. So if they were not allowed to ask certain things but once you ask them the things they were not allowed to ask, it will be seen as you trying to embarrass them or being rude.

As in Adanma's case, students were not expected to ask questions and when they did, teachers often deflected the question to certain students who were deemed smart. Unfortunately, Adanma was not considered smart. Conversely, Folake was deemed smart in her school. As a result, she was very involved in leading her learning journey. Her biology teacher involved her in lesson planning and gave her materials that challenged her. Class learning objectives were not clear to my research participants. They were not made or taught to draw connections between their curriculum content, the social issues in the country and their role in creating change. Teachers did not appear to care or measure student learning throughout the teaching process. Student-led discussions about current affairs or lived experiences, for example, were often sidelined and clearly demarcated from the lesson plan. Students were made to think that the "real world" is divorced from their academic pursuit. Etim noted that students were victimized for complaining or providing feedback about their classroom experiences with certain teachers. For example, when students complained to the principal about their Further Math teacher, the teacher did not change her teaching style to adjust to student feedback. Instead, she returned to class to scold the students for reporting her. Adanma noted that her textbooks were filled with culturally irrelevant images and foreign people. The images on the wall were similar. In some cases, the photos around the school were those of the school owners and their relatives. Subjects relating to Nigeria's history, Nigerian people and identity were taught in a nominal and condescending way. Social studies (taught at junior school) and government (Arts stream requirement) were taught in a facts-based way. Adanma explains:

> The only reason why I was able to learn something about Nigeria is because I was an Arts student and I did government but science students have no idea. … And in government, I only learnt about the constitution and policies but we did not even understand why we had to learn those policies. There was no history; there was nothing deep.

Nigerian history and colonization were not taught with a pre-colonial lens or from an anti-colonial perspective. Etim explains:

> Right from primary school, the history of our origin has never really being considered. I think it might do us some good to know a bit of history. I think we talked about the Badagry slave trade. Learning about Ogun state or the history of Lagos state should definitely be included in our curriculum. I think it will help. I was just watching a video about Black History Month, they keep repeating the same thing—all the bad things black people did and not the positives. This is the same in our history—it is like, oh, the white man came in and they did this and did that. I am sure there have been a few positive things in our history. It will do well for us to learn that. Also, our curriculum should incorporate how to teach the younger generation about certain political goals and how we might make things better in the future.

As of March 2016, history is not a mandatory subject in the Nigerian schooling system. Only students in the Arts stream have the option of taking either history or geography. Folake was a science student so she never learned about Nigerian history in school. Her knowledge of history was from books she read and excursions she participated in outside school hours. Even though Adanma was an Arts student, the first Nigerian book she analyzed was during her university studies. In secondary school, the required text for examination was primarily Shakespeare.

Adanma reported a hierarchy in her school based on academic fields and perceived student intelligence. Science students were deemed to be more intelligent than Arts and commercial students. Students were assigned to classes based on their grades. For example, all the A students are taught together in JSS2 A, B students in JSS2 B, and so on. Student privacy was not respected. Adanma and Folake noted that students' exam results were often publically posted.

Adanma and Folake spoke strongly about the Westernization/Whiteness project that went on in their schools. Although not communicated explicitly, all my research participants understood that Whiteness meant superiority and Nigerian/Indigenous meant being backwards, barbaric and not modern. Their schools and the schooling experience were trying to and expected to modernize them. Accordingly, every Saturday, Folake had British phonetics classes where she learnt how to "Speak Right, Sound Right" in English. Adanma's and Etim's principals were non-Nigerians (white male principal and Asian female principal). The racial superiority of Whiteness was proclaimed in Adanma's school. Adanma and friends in school observed that the white principal was fearless and got away with everything a black principal would never get away with, for example, smoking in school. Speaking an Indigenous language or pidgin English was not allowed or expected. When students in Adanma's school spoke Yoruba, they were often given a dirty look and reminded, "This is not a marketplace." Folake, who is from a minority ethnic group, was ashamed to self-identify as an ethnic minority. This was partly because her ethnic identity and heritage were not recognized in the school. The only three groups that were recognized were the Igbo, Yoruba and Hausa. Even though these groups were foregrounded, they were all treated nominally. These practices diminished the cultural identity of students and sought to disengage/estrange them from their cultural heritage.

> C: I take it that you did not learn anything about your culture [Kogi] by coming to school?
>
> F: No, not at all. I think if anything it was like if you were not part of one of the dominant groups, it was kind of a thing to be ashamed of in some way.

Students from minority ethnic groups were expected to put themselves in one of these major groups or hide in silence. Adanma reported emotional and mental health issues that she experienced but she could not receive help. For example, she was bullied for having short hair and her teacher often accused her of looking very ugly.

STUDENT VOICE, POWER AND AGENCY

> E: We did not really have a say and even prefects who are supposed to run the school government. They are just figureheads, they just read out stuff. ... When they sought out the views of the prefects, it was very little. It was certainly not to change anything radically.

The three research participants were marginally involved in curating their schooling experience and shaping school programs and policies in substantial ways. In different capacities (House Captain, Sports Prefect), Etim and Adanma were involved in school leadership. But as the opening quote to this section illustrates, students did not have real political power. Adanma notes that the school administration had a conception of how things were supposed to look and work in school. Their conception was often Western and "whitewashing." She explains:

> First of all, there was nothing cultural about the school. Being a prefect and having meetings with principals, whenever you bring up ideas of, say, how you want the field to look like, they were always trying to compare with schools outside of the country and stuff. Everything was just so whitewashed. I remember our sports teachers trying to speak phonetics.

Even though Folake was not a school prefect, she was perceived to be intelligent so she was automatically placed on the school leadership team. Folake had a strong sense of what her rights were as a learner and often demanded to be engaged on those terms. She was quite aware that she could make these demands, rebel and not be punished because of her perceived intelligence. Folake shared several instances of rebellion. On one occasion, she refused to go for prep because the stipulated time did not account for the fact that students had spent eight hours in school and needed rest time. Here is her experience:

> In addition to being engaged in class, pushing myself, challenging the curriculum in some ways and being involved by joining the clubs that were available, I also led a few initiatives with my peers. We started a few things that hadn't previously been done in the school. In addition to that, we were also politically active within the context of our school. I remember when there was no water, we marched to the VP's office with our buckets in hand.
>
> I felt like a lot of the rules were misguided. I remember once we were forced to take a WAEC [national examination] English prep course with someone who could barely speak English. So I skipped the afternoon and went to my dorm and slept. Sitting here and listening to someone that cannot speak English is not helping me. But we were punished for that—we were made to water plants and skip class in the morning to complete the punishment. We also did not attend class in the afternoon. I remember another time; I stopped going to prep because I felt it was a distraction. They integrated prep so it was boys and girls prep together. I stopped going and a few other people in my set stopped going as well. We would sleep in the time people were going for prep … when the dorm is quiet after prep, we wake up and study. But we were marched to the principal's office for that and I told them straight up!
>
> C: What did you tell them?
> F: I told the vice-principal that I did not want to go for prep. I cannot remember what the outcome was but I think they left us. I think I had a lot of leeway because I did well in school, there were certain things I could get away doing because I was already known as a good student/intelligent student.

I asked Folake if she had learnt to assert her agency and subvert the system from the curriculum.

> I don't think it was something in the curriculum. I will say that the audacity came from being certain/knowing what the goals should have been. The audacity came because my goals were aligned with what the objectives of school should be. So, I wanted to get good

grades. When things were counter to that objective, I will fight it. If something was stopping me from going to class or when a routine is not the most effective way to study was imposed, I will challenge it because it was in conflict with that goal which was supposed to be the point of school anyways.

In terms of external leadership opportunities, Etim and Adanma declared that it was the same set of intelligent students that were often given the opportunity to represent the school. Etim was only recognized by her school when she excelled at the external leadership competitions she found herself. The school did not provide these opportunities or support students in acquiring them but was quick to claim the honor when they won competitions.

TOWARDS AN ANTI-COLONIAL AND INCLUSIVE EDUCATION FRAMEWORK

Critically speaking, there is nothing new about the Nigerian student experiences presented in the foregoing. In different ways, numerous scholars have written extensively about the colonial nature of African education and poor learning conditions to which African students are subjected (Akena, 2012; Brock-Utne, 2002; Bassey, 1999; Muiu, 2002; Oluniyi, 2011; Wa Thiong'o, 1986; Woolman, 2001). After much established scholarship in this area, why has so little been produced in terms of concrete educational alternatives on the continent? Why are the African educational policies not reflecting anti-colonial imperatives for contemporary nation building? What is it about African societies that makes them a breeding ground for such dehumanizing education?

Within the context of Nigeria, to understand the education terrain and contemporary education issues, it is necessary to conduct a historical analysis of the educational change discourse and to review the historical frame of the sector. Critical questions about the country's initial purpose for education and philosophy of education need to be asked and reviewed as necessary. These questions are often sidelined or are implicitly assumed to be the appropriate education foundations. Nigeria's educational philosophy was conceived to uphold Britain's colonial economic and social interests in the country beyond independence. Gleaning from the 1967 National Curriculum Conference, the impact of colonization on Nigerian society was understood to be purely material and political in nature. As the Federal Commissioner for Education at the time, W. O. Briggs argued:

To make independence meaningful we must be able, not only to fly our own aero planes, man our own ships, drive our own cars and locomotive engines and ride our own bicycles and motor-cycles, as we do now, we must also learn to manufacture many of these things ourselves, so that those from whom we now import these essentials of our modern technological world can never hold us to ransom. ... *True independence is economic independence [emphasis mine]*. (Nigeria National Curriculum Conference, Adaralegbe, A., & Nigeria Educational Research Council, 1972, p. xviii)

Without downplaying the necessity of economic independence in any nation, I argue that true independence is much more than economic independence; it is about mental and cultural independence. Mazama's (2003) assertion is instructive:

[C]olonization was not simply an enterprise of economic exploitation and political control, as it was commonly held, but also an on-going enterprise of conceptual distortion and invasion, leading to widespread confusion and ultimately, mental incarceration. (p. 3)

This misunderstanding of the nature of colonization, its legacy, implication for education and nation building is central to the existence of the colonizing educational experiences reported here by the three young women. Instead of educational policy promoting anti-colonial education that will facilitate mental liberation amongst diverse Nigerian ethnic groups and nation building based on Indigenous epistemologies and heritage, it has facilitated policies that suppress differences and uphold the inherited socioeconomic structures from Britain. So, pursuing anti-colonial changes in the education system requires looking beyond the education system for solutions. It necessitates anti-colonial critical changes/reflection outside the education system—in the wider Nigerian society. In other words, the Nigerian society as a whole will need to begin a journey of decolonization.

The arbitrary amalgamation of the previously independent nations that currently constitute Nigeria provides the impetus for this critical reflection and subsequent action to occur. Current societal structures and the national narrative that governs and validates the educational system have emanated from a colonized/colonizing reality that discourages critical thinking, suppresses differences, upholds the dominance of certain groups/ways of being over the others and subscribes to a colonial shared national identity that is mostly economically centered. In this light, the Nigerian schooling system (especially the elite private schools which are the focus of this chapter) is just an accomplice, simply an agent of Africa's neo-colonialism.

To move towards a new social reality, Nigerians need to create a new national identity, a new national purpose and philosophy that challenges the current British economically centered identity and is based on an anti-colonial version of their ethnic histories and aspirations.

The emanating national philosophy and framework will implicate the epistemological and cultural heritage of each of the ethnic groups in the country. It will foreground justice and equity as the basis upon which a union between previously independent nations could happen. It will strive to create a radically multi-cultural nation that:

... allows each of its members to define her identity for herself, by finding the group or groups to which she has the closet affinity, and must also allow each group to formulate its own authentic set of claims and demands, reflecting its particular circumstances (Miller, 1995, p. 131).

The integration of a group's self-definition, claims and demands serves as the philosophical, knowledge and legal base of the nation. It will influence governance, economic structures and social structures, amongst others. Members of the various ethnic groups must be able to see themselves and their heritage visibly represented in the national framework. Within this context, one of the purposes of schooling is to develop citizens who will contribute to the creation and consolidation of a radically multicultural nation that is inclusive. Dei et al.'s (2002) definition of an inclusive school is instructive:

> A critical integrative approach to inclusive schooling requires schools to respond to the challenges and opportunities presented by diverse communities in ways that affirm different centers of knowledge, experiences, cultures and histories in ways that permeate the entire schooling process. Despite the disparate appearance of our histories, there are ties that bind both dominant and minority populations. Inclusive education calls for the integration of the individual/family histories, concerns and practices into the larger societal collective. Inclusive schooling practices must be both critical, culturally, socially responsive and relevant, and must seek to engender empowerment and transformation in the lives of all learners. (p. 4)

This theoretical framework on schooling intersects with the issues raised in the findings section and lends itself to comprehensive changes within the school system. In contrast to the referenced schools in the findings section, this approach to schooling will inclusively engage and empower all students by affirming their knowledge, experiences and history in the entire schooling process. Student voice and agency are nurtured because students' aspirations and experiences are solicited and will help shape the schooling agenda/governance process. In the classroom, it means that teachers are dynamic and knowledge is not trapped within the pages of a textbook. Everyday lived experiences and social issues faced by teachers and students alike serve as the source for curriculum knowledge and classroom discussions. History is also taught in a disruptive but binding way. While illustrating the differences between ethnic groups, students will also learn to see similarities between groups. The ultimate purpose of schooling is to contribute to the creation of a just nation. Therefore, power relations across gender, religion, class, sex and ethnicity are always disrupted to restore equality amongst all citizens.

REFERENCES

Akena, F. A. (2012). Critical analysis of the production of western knowledge and its implications for indigenous knowledge and decolonization. *Journal of Black Studies*, *43*(6), 599–619.

Asante, M. K. (2003). *Afrocentricity, the theory of social change*. Chicago, IL: African American Images.

Asante, M. K. (2007). *An Afrocentric manifesto: Toward an African renaissance.* Hoboken, NJ: John Wiley & Sons.

Banks, J. A. (1997). *Educating citizens in a multicultural society.* New York, NY: Teachers College Press.

Bassey, M. O. (Ed.). (1999). *Western education and political domination in Africa: A study in critical and dialogical pedagogy.* Westport, CT: Greenwood.

Brock-Utne, B. (2002). *Whose education for all? The recolonization of the African mind.* London, England: Routledge.

Curran, J. (1998). Situatedness, categorical thinking, and culture of silence in the Clinton-Lewinsky fandango. *Dear Habermas.* Retrieved from https://www.csudh.edu/dearhabermas/lawans2.htm

Darling-Hammond, L., French, J. C., & Garcia-Lopez, S. P. (2002). *Learning to teach for social justice.* New York, NY: Teachers College Press.

Dei, G. (2015). Conceptualizing indigeneity and the implications for Indigenous research and African development. *Confluence: Online Journal of World Philosophies, 2,* 52–78.

Dei, G. J. S. (2000a). *Removing the margins: The challenges and possibilities of inclusive schooling.* Toronto, Canada: Canadian Scholars' Press.

Dei, G. J. S. (2000b). African development: The relevance and implications of "Indigenousness." In G. J. S. Dei, B. L. Hall, & D. G. Rosenberg (Eds.), *Indigenous knowledges in global contexts: Multiple readings of our world* (pp. 70–86). Toronto, Canada: University of Toronto Press.

Dei, G. J. S., & Asgharzadeh, A. (2001). The power of social theory: The anti-colonial discursive framework. *The Journal of Educational Thought (JET)/Revue de la Pensée Educative,* 297–323.

Dei, G. J. S., Asgharzadeh, A., Eblaghie-Bahador, S., & Shahjahan, R. A. (2006). *Schooling and difference in Africa: Democratic challenges in a contemporary context.* Toronto, Canada: University of Toronto Press.

Dei, G. J. S., Zine, J., & James-Wilson, S. V. (2002). *Inclusive schooling: A teacher's companion to removing the margins.* Toronto, Canada: Canadian Scholars' Press.

Fanon, F. (1963). *The wretched of the earth.* New York, NY: Grove Press.

Fanon, F. (1967). *Black skin, white masks.* C. L. Markham (Trans.). New York, NY: Grove Press. Original work published 1952.

Foster, W. (1986). *Paradigms and promises: New approaches to educational administration.* Amherst, NY: Prometheus Books.

Freire, P. (1970a). Cultural freedom in Latin America. In *Human rights and the liberation of man in the Americas* (pp. 162–179). Notre Dame, IN: University of Notre Dame Press.

Freire, P. (1970b). Cultural action for freedom. *The Harvard Educational Review.* Monograph series, no. 1.

Ladson-Billings, G. (1995). Toward a theory of culturally relevant pedagogy. *American Educational Research Journal, 32*(3), 465–491. doi:10.3102/00028312032003465

Mazama, A. (2001). The Afrocentric paradigm: Contours and definitions. *Journal of Black Studies, 31*(4), 387–405.

Mazama, M. (2002). Afrocentricity and African spirituality. *Journal of Black Studies, 33*(2), 218–234. doi:10.1177/002193402237226

Mazama, A. (Ed.). (2003). *The Afrocentric paradigm.* Trenton, NJ: Africa World Press.

McMahon, B., & Portelli, J. P. (2004). Engagement for what? Beyond popular discourses of student engagement. *Leadership and Policy in Schools, 3*(1), 59–76.

Memmi, A. (1969). *The colonizer and the colonized.* Boston, MA: Beacon Press.

Miller, D. (1995). *On nationality.* Oxford: Clarendon Press.

Muiu, M. W. (2002). Fundi Wa Afrika: Toward a new paradigm of the African state. *Journal of Third World Studies, 19*(2), 23–42.

Nigeria National Curriculum Conference, Adaralegbe, A., & Nigeria Educational Research Council. (1972). *A philosophy for Nigerian education: Proceedings of the Nigeria National Curriculum Conference, 8–12 September, 1969*. Ibadan, Nigeria: Heinemann Educational.

Oluniyi, O. (2011). Country report: Citizenship education and curriculum development in Nigeria. *Online Journal of Social Science Education, 10*(4), 61–67.

Portelli, J. P., & Vibert, A. B. (2002). A curriculum of life. *Education Canada 42*(2), 36–39.

Portelli, J. P., Vibert, A., & Shields, C. (2007). *Toward an equitable education: Poverty, diversity, and students at risk: The national report*. Toronto, Canada: Ontario Institute for Studies in Education.

Wa Thiong'o, N. (1986). *Decolonising the mind: The politics of language in African literature*. Nairobi, Kenya: East African Educational Publishers.

Woolman, D. C. (2001). Educational reconstruction and post-colonial curriculum development: A comparative study of four African countries. *International Education Journal, 2*(5), 27–46.

Zyngier, D. (2008). (Re)conceptualising student engagement: Doing education not doing time. *Teaching and Teacher Education, 24*(7), 1765–1776.

CHAPTER EIGHT

Indigeneity AND Resistance IN Hip Hop AND Lived Experiences OF Youth OF African Descent IN Canada

ANNETTE BAZIRA-OKAFOR

My own journeys have shaped the framework of my analysis when it comes to studying anti-colonial thought and pedagogical challenges. As a teenager, I was exiled with my family from Uganda and granted asylum in Kenya. Four years later, my family was given refugee status in Canada. Today, I am married to a Nigerian and our children were born in Canada. As children of African parents, they claim an African heritage that is alive through their parents' cultural memories and lived experiences "back home" on our ancestral lands.

African parents in the diaspora trace their rootedness to particular ancestral homelands in Africa (Dei, 2010, p. 104). Our influences are grounded in who we are as African people. While we claim and share many commonalities with all black people in Canada, our histories, cultures, experiences and traditions are not homogeneous. As Dei points out, we cannot be seduced into amputating our past. My children, as first generation Canadians, embody many experiences different from my own. Dei proffers that the voice of the diaspora is differently inflected for the youth.

> Youthful versus Elder indigenous voices offer different insights, ones we must listen to as youth negotiate the terrains of the Diaspora, migration, and multiple located identities. (Dei, 2010, p. 104)

This chapter talks about ways in which youth[1] of African descent in Canada appropriate black popular culture, particularly through hip hop and its musical style of rap, while interrogating how they make sense of their own existence within the Canadian context of race and inequality. While not always the same for migrant youth and first generation African youth, these experiences have many similarities, largely brought about by their racialized black bodies.

In this chapter I draw from observations and experiences of my teenage son; I also compare work written on hip hop in Africa and Canada, and draw on the work and experiences of Canadian recording artists of African descent and Ugandan artist Eddy Kenzo. Narrating and focusing on lived experiences of African youth are about theorizing their social existence. bell hooks (1989) and Trinh T. Minh-Ha (1989) write about the relevance of lived experiences and how these must and can be incorporated into theory. Personal experience or naming reality through confession or memory can be a process of politicization. Personal narratives unite scientific knowledge with everyday experience, and when linked to collective reality, they create a process of historicization (hooks, 1989).

For African immigrants crossing transnational borders, "back home" is a reference to our ancestral lands. Home denotes cultural, social and political boundaries (Giroux, 2009). First generation African youth in Canada often experience their families' sense of "back home" through online African music or African music that their families, usually their parents, listen and dance to in their homes, in their cars and at African events. In cities like Toronto, they also experience "back home" through African grocery stores where their parents buy African foods and African home videos. They experience "back home" through guests, relatives and friends who visit from their African homelands and through other African immigrant families living in Canada who are, from time to time, invited to share in the food and culture, along with their African Indigenous languages. They may also experience their parents' "back home" through visitations to the Indigenous lands their parents claim. "Home" and "roots" are main features in the everyday discourses of African family members (Obeid, 2013).

Michelle Obeid's (2013) probing work in "Home-Making in the Diaspora: Bringing Palestine to London" reveals that

> an ethnographic examination of mobility requires that we look at the actual lived experiences of moving persons, as "ordinary people" (whether their migration was "forced" or not) who are agentive actors embedded in social, political, and historical contexts. (p. 368)

Obeid states that the home that one left behind features in shaping the everyday processes of creating home in a new context. Similarly within diasporic African communities, African foods, languages, music, home videos and movies viewed on the Internet are some of the efforts and strategies that are reintroduced in the Canadian society. They create spaces for the reproduction of our Africanness, and our homes and gatherings are meeting points where dispersed families are repositioned (Obeid, 2013, p. 369).

Obeid's home-making is a forward-looking process in as much as it is a longing for a lost past. Citing anthropologist Ghassan Hage (1997) in his essay "At home in the entrails of the West," she reiterates that home building as an affective construct, one entailing "the building of the *feeling* of being 'at home'" (pp. 102–103). Certain social activities are produced on an everyday level, what Obeid calls "projects of rootedness." She describes them as activities that "produce attachments that root persons in a particular place" (p. 369).

Food is very important within many African communities in Canada, and African events often feature African food. Obeid points out that food as both material and symbol (Obeid, 2013, p. 374) is well known to transport people (especially ethnic and diasporic groups) to different times and places through triggering "experience or meaning in reference to the past" (cited in Holtzman, 2006, p. 363). Food elicits feelings of nostalgia (Obeid, 2013, p. 374), proudly connected to a feeling of "being there *here*" (Hage, 1997, p. 109).

Within African communities in Canada, nostalgia also evokes memories of community and family back home that are infused with strength and oneness in which everyone looks out for everyone else. Relatives and neighbours look out for your children. Recall the African proverb "It Takes a Village to Raise a Child". Parents do not carry the burden of raising children on their own because the whole community takes part in looking out for them and making sure they are safe and have enough to eat.

For many Africans in Canada, "back home" is also seen as a place where one becomes grounded. African immigrant parents who feel their children have "lost their way" and have become unruly may send those children back home to live with relatives. Parents will take such measures, believing that the Western culture and racialized environment is to blame for the children's behaviour or lack thereof. Parents who have had difficulties managing the behaviour of their teenage children may decide to send a younger sibling back home for early grounding. African parents believe in the support system of the extended family, friends and teachers back home. The communality and social systems of African cultures create an environment in which extended family and friends play a large role in raising and disciplining children. Children are therefore answerable not only to their parents and caregivers, but also to their uncles, aunties, grandparents, teachers and family friends. Bledsoe and Sow (2011) explain this dynamic:

> Even more serious for parents may be the repercussions of an undisciplined child's involvement in gangs, violence and crime. … Forbidden to levy the kind of discipline they deem necessary to control an intransigent child who may have begun to draw attention from authorities, immigrant parents … may decide to send the child back home, whether to relatives or to boarding school, to wait for the risk to abate (p. 748).

Furthermore, Giroux (2009) states that "home" is about those cultural spaces and social locations which work hegemonically and as sites of resistance. "'[H]ome' is safe by virtue of its repressive exclusions and hegemonic location of individuals and groups outside of history" (p. 81).

Although the ever-reaching hands of imperialism in a post-colonial Africa have eroded and exploited Africa's resources and cultures, ancient African civilizations and histories have not been completely erased by a few decades of colonial rule. Rich cultures and traditions are part of and sources of pride on African Indigenous lands. Youth of African descent who visit ancestral lands on the African continent, where our bodies are not politicized and reduced to a skin color, places where the body politic changes and black is dominant while white becomes the "other," and where race becomes a political and social nonentity, are impacted and empowered by such tremendous change. Suddenly they are part of the dominant group.

When my husband who is a professor went to Nigeria on an academic sabbatical, our whole family left Toronto and spent two years in Nigeria. I remember how, prior to our move, my son had expressed concern that he was afraid to go to high school. Once we saw a group of black teenage boys walking in the suburb northwest of Toronto where we live, he asked whether they were a gang. This was despite the fact that there was no teenage gang activity in the neigbourhood and blacks were in the minority. However, it was common to see the policing of teenagers in general, at a neighbourhood cafe on Friday and Saturday nights where teenagers hang out. I knew my son's fear of going to high school had nothing to do with academics, given his strong academic abilities, but I was greatly concerned because this is how mass media and dominant culture portray young black males, and he knew this was how he would be judged.

Once in Nigeria, we enrolled our children in a school that soon felt like family. There was a sense of community at this school that I had not experienced in Canadian schools. My children's African teachers and school nurse took on responsibilities towards my children beyond their formal duties. Perhaps, as Freire wrote, "it was by travelling all over the world … it was by passing through all these different parts of the world as an exile that I came to understand my own country better" (Giroux, 2009, p. 83). Or, perhaps for me, living in a predominantly white state in Canada had made me forget what it felt like to live without all the racialized labels attached to my name and body and the stereotypes that come with them. While I grew up in Uganda, and had now lived in Canada half of my life, I had taken for granted the communality found in many African cultures that I had known as a child.

Although we regularly visited Nigeria with my husband and children, it was usually for three weeks at a time. Living there for two years had a different effect on our entire family. During our two-year stay in Nigeria my son mentioned to me that he was no longer afraid to go to high school and that he realised there was nothing to be afraid of. He completed his last year of elementary school and his first year of high school in Nigeria.

Three years after returning to Canada we find the news media filled with stories of young black unarmed males being shot and killed by police in the United States and, more recently, the arrest and death of a young black woman, Sandra Bland (Ford, 2015, n.p.). The shooting and killing of black males south of the Canadian border and the lived experiences of black youth in Canada where the criminalization of black males is also prevalent are once again realities.

A legacy of racism towards black people is embedded within the systemic workings of Canadian institutions associated with white power and privilege. Black youth have to deal with the realities of racism and discrimination on a daily basis. Hip hop culture offers a way of belonging for black youth precisely because it is a form of resistance against white supremacy and racial discrimination. Black youth of African descent take on the hip hop culture as their own and identify with its forms of resistance and struggles of black people everywhere.

A hip hop rap enthusiast, my son writes, produces and performs his own rap poetry. He first got involved with the art form during our two-year stay in Nigeria, a love which he continued to nurture long after we returned to Canada. He crossed transnational borders from North America to Indigenous land in Africa where he gained interest and learned rap, an art form most associated with American hip hop, from a group of African teenagers in his school in Nigeria. Charry (2012) states that the influence of African American music and culture on Nigerians affects the music and identity of an entire generation, even those who have never traveled overseas. "Nigerian youth are able to reinterpret and appropriate African American style and music so that they form a legitimate arm of black world culture" (p. 150).

Rap as an art form known for its messages of resistance among North American youth has been taken up among African artists and youth on the African continent and used as a tool of resistance. Hodkinson and Deicke (2007) point out that in marginalizing societies, hip hop became a means for black youth to express their discontent. Hip hop's culture and its musical expression, rap, came to be regarded as an authentic and resistant form of expression for marginalized black youth (p. 79).

That African artists have appropriated rap in African Indigenous languages is one of the major changes of the art form on the continent. With so many languages spoken in Nigeria, let alone the African continent, music sung in pidgin English has a wider audience appeal because it is understood by people from different ethnic groups. In Nigeria, my son learned to speak pidgin English, which is exemplified in contemporary Nigerian music styles. Shonekan (2012) explains that the colonial experience that "led to the creation of pidgin English as the vernacular of Anglophone West Africans reflected a duality of the internal and external, of the colonizer and the colonized, of the oppressor and the oppressed" (p. 149). He asserts that this form of language hybridity "connotes the historical merging of two or more forms that nevertheless retain sufficient resemblance to the original sources" (ibid.). An appropriation of hip hop's rap music can be found in several other African countries, including East Africa. Ntarangwi (2009), for example, describes East African hip hop as combining "elements of local and popular musical traditions with mostly American (U.S.) and Jamaican music styles of rap and raga, respectively" (p. viii).

Ngoya Kidula (2012) talks about the Kenyan rap group Kalamashaka that had previously rapped in English and imitated North American gangster ghetto rappers as it addressed the poverty and injustice in Dandora, an economically marginalized section of Nairobi. Kidula explains that the English language alienated the singers from the conditions in their Dandora "hood." Kenyan rap, however, became a national phenomenon when the group released its 1999 single in Swahili, the language of the urban middle and lower classes. The album featured street Swahili (*sheng*) associated with a section of Nairobi, carrying metaphors, hyperboles and tongue twisters. The single "Tafsiri hii" had underlying meanings and idioms familiar to insiders (p. 175).

Sheng is based on Swahili and English, but incorporates Kenyan languages such as Luo and Kikuyu. It has been linked to Kenya's colonial history since the 1900s. It began at a time during British rule when the British were building the railway in Uganda from Mombasa to Jinja (Mokaya, 2006). Mazrui (1995) suggests that Sheng may have originated in the 1930s as a Nairobi underground jargon:

> The most explicit suggestion of a Sheng-like code that was in existence as far back as the early 1930s is to be found in "Miaka 50 Katika Jela" (Fifty Years In Jail) by Michael Ngugi Karanja. … [T]he examples he gives … strongly suggest that "Sheng" emerged as an underground professional code way back in the colonial period. (p. 173)

Ngũgĩ wa Thiong'o (1986) opines that

> the choice of language and the use to which language is put is central to a people's definition of themselves in relation to their natural and social environment, indeed in relation to the entire universe. (p. 4)

When hip hop and its musical style rap were acquired by East African and West African black youth on the African continent, these styles necessitated appropriation into other languages such as Swahili, sheng and pidgin—the language forms used by the middle and lower classes. English, the language imposed on Africans during the colonial era, remains the elitist form of communication used in formal schooling in Anglophone countries. The English language connotes social upward mobility and is privileged among the African elite. As such, schools privilege the English language. It is common to find students who attend elite schools who have also been raised to speak only English at home, unable to speak their Indigenous languages. This was true of many students in my children's school in Nigeria and of several other elite schools.

Wa Thiong'o (1986) explains that African realities are affected by the great struggle between two mutually opposed forces in Africa, namely, the imperialist tradition and the resistance tradition (p. 2). This duality is also manifested in the contradiction of the popular culture scene in Africa. While there is a need for African youth/artists to resist and speak against vices in society and corrupt administrations in pidgin and Indigenous languages in hip hop culture, African youth are also caught up in an elitist formal education that rewards English as a medium of social and upward mobility.

Pidgin and Indigenous languages have been popularized by the music of African youth on the continent. Ugandan artist Eddy Kenzo's (2014) music video *Sitya Loss* went viral, and even those who do not understand what Kenzo is saying embrace the catchy beat and exuberant dancing. The song "Sitya Loss" is also an example of how Indigenous languages can be learned and popularized through hip hop music. Showing its global appeal, the Luganda song featuring a mix of slang and Swahili, has been sung by musicians in other African countries, including noted artists Elodie Amondji (2015) of Côte d'Ivoire and, an all-white male Chicago-based bluegrass band, the Henhouse Prowlers (2015). The act of taking up an Indigenous language by foreign speakers speaks volumes about the decolonizing role that hip hop can have in both continental Africa and the Western world.

Kenzo's message is to stand defiant, dance and celebrate life. The visuals bear witness to the impoverished people and land in the countryside where the video was shot. The infectious smiles and laughter of dancing children, men and women, some wearing tattered clothes, are infused with pride and defiance in the face of scarcity. Kenzo, who lost his mother at the age of four, was forced to live and survive as a homeless child for more than thirteen years because he did not know where his father was, nor did he know any relatives. Music became his safe haven. Staying true to his roots even after a breakthrough in the music industry, some of his music videos continue to portray socially conscious messages of the marginalised.

The video went viral precisely because it depicts the resilience and strength of Indigenous people happily dancing in poverty-stricken surroundings. It refused to carry overtones of doom and narratives of powerlessness and helplessness. Unlike most expectations of what of poor Africans should look like, Kenzo's work depicts a resistant culture that shows the resilience of the poor and marginalised in the countryside. The video portrays their lives as happy, despite the little that they have. Their lives are not defined by materialism but by the strength of community that culminates in their celebration of life through dance and music. Kenzo's infectious and resilient artistic renditions of the poor have been imitated by other Ugandan and African artists, including Gulu Omako Mac (see DJ Dench, 2015), and a video of children from the Mathare community in Nairobi, Kenya, dancing to "Sitya Loss" (Kenzo, 2014; see also Tahmane Music, 2014).

"Sitya Loss" not only points to the loss Kenzo suffered when his mother died, but he sings about other people who have passed on.

However, the song starts out in defiance and celebration of life. The refrain of the song *Nze sitya loss* [I'm not afraid of loss], *Nze sitya loss ndi boss* [I am the boss and I am not afraid of loss] speaks to his defiance and self-determination, and his choice to celebrate life through dance rather than be afraid of its loss. Kenzo articulates this sentiment in the first verse by putting the onus on the youth to make this change and to bring an end to quarrels, fights and materialism:

> Yefe abavubuka envumulo … [We are the vibrant/powerful youth]
> Sagala nyombo Kubanga eno sawa ya ndongo [I don't want any quarrels/fights because it's time to dance]
> … Wama sembera [Please come closer]
> Bulamu bwasoba [life is messed up]
> Jangu twetale [Come let's play/dance]
> Byansi bya kuleeka [Everything on this earth will be left behind] [4]

Kenzo's music video resists images of helpless starving children with flies crawling on their faces—images we often see in charity commercials. Defying stereotypes of the needy and poor African through strong imagery, featuring a mix of the local Indigenous language, Luganda, with *Uglish*, the Ugandan pidgin, Kenzo's defiant artistic expression reclaims the contested colonial land and inhabits it on his own terms. The audience's reading of resistance in the dancing bodies in Kenzo's music video creates new emotions in an audience used to charity driven images of helpless, poor Africans.

Charitable development agencies tend to subscribe to discourses of authority in which the body is exoticized in order to create the space of otherness. Some local groups seeking funds from the West have also been complicit in the Othering of the African body. Kenzo's video made from a space of the Other challenges this discursive authority and authorial identity. The subject positions in Kenzo's video speak to an anti-colonial narrative informed by Kenzo's Indigenous language.

Music videos, including Kenzo's work, featuring homegrown cultural per-spectives dismantle the political and philosophical standpoints of the colonial and create messages and images grounded in subaltern differences and ways of knowing. Kenzo as the voice of the marginalized, along with the dancing bodies of children, men and women as the bodies of resistance, perform from colonial spaces in the pursuit of resistance. Walcott (2003) contends that the use of the body

> echoes the various ways in which black cultural practices have always treated bodies as a canvas upon which historical and contemporary social relations may be signified, inscribed and rewritten. The body, therefore, is not only used as a biological mechanism, it also works as a site for the contestation of social relations as those relations relate to acts and actions of power on and through the body. (p. 97)

As the subject and the material come together in Kenzo's music video, they offer a critique of the colonial space in which the West is implicated in the underdevelop-ment of Africa through colonialism and imperialism. Kenzo's attempt to reclaim agency in the face of cultural obliteration and his authentic voice challenge domi-nant renditions often perpetuated in the media.

As settlers on Canadian land, African bodies have also been racialized by the dominant group of white Anglophone settlers in Canada from early colonial times to the Second World War as part of the project to create a nation and a national identity. Mackey (1998) points out that white Anglophone settlers in Canada mobilized representations of others and decided how non-British cultural groups were "managed, located, let in, excluded, made visible or invisible, represented pos-itively or negatively, assimilated or appropriated, depending on the changing needs of nation-building" (pp. 37–38). "These cultural groups," she explains, "become infinitely manageable populations as well as bit players in the nationalist imagi-nary, always dancing to someone else's tune" (p. 62). More recently, Quayson and Daswani (2013) observe that

> popular sentiments linked to a sense of nationalism created along the lines of "common blood," "dominant race" … are often used to create fear and hostility against outsiders who are seen to be "swarming" into the country and changing its moral fabric. (p. 15)

Described as an invading force unable to fully integrate into the resident soci-ety, they have become scapegoats for national distress, projecting blame onto the Other to preserve the national self (ibid.).

An ethnographic study of an immigrant refugee group of African youth attending an urban French language high school in southwestern Ontario points to the racism, human degradation and the annihilation of black people, partic-ularly youth of African descent (Ibrahim, 2008). Awad Ibrahim explains that continental African youth find themselves in a racially conscious society that "asks" them to racially fit somewhere (p. 243). He argues that African youth, prior to coming to Canada, were not black in Africa, but become black in North America where "they fall within the 'eyes of power,'" where "blackness is conceived as a performative category, a form of speech, an attitude and a social location one takes up" (p. 235).

Faced with the social imaginary that African youth are already black, this imaginary determines how and with whom they identify, what they linguistically and culturally learn and how they learn it. According to Ibrahim, what they learn is Black English as a second language that they accessed through black popular culture. "They learned by taking up and repositing the Rap linguistic and musical genre and, in different ways, acquiring and rearticulating the Hip-Hop cultural identity" (Ibrahim, 2008, p. 243). Since rap itself is a contemporary black cultural form, re/citing it by African students is in fact a performance of where they want to locate themselves politically, racially, culturally and linguistically (p. 246). Although youth of African descent often identify with black culture in Canadian society, their African backgrounds and African communities within which they function also offer unique African experiences that are different from black Canadian culture. The life experiences of immigrant youth of African descent also inform their musical styles.

Somali-Canadian hip hop artist K'naan, for instance, lived through violent experiences as a child of war in Somalia, and in Toronto's gang-ridden neighbourhood of Rexdale[5] where he spent the later years of his childhood. Although K'naan's music has been described by Welte (2006, n.p.) as "a sound that fuses Bob Marley, conscious American hip hop, and brilliant protest poetry," K'naan describes his subject matter as urgent music with a message that talks about the situation in his home country of Somalia, calling for an end to the violence and bloodshed. "Soobax," meaning "come out", was his first music video and the most famous song on his album *Dusty Foot Philosopher*. The following excerpt from "Soobax" (2009) shows K'naan's resistance and a return to the land as a protest of the colonial and imperial forces evidenced in the wars that rendered him a refugee outside his own country, ruining the once beautiful homeland of his memories.

> … Left alone, all alone
> Settle your issues on your own
> What to do? Where to go?
> I got to be a refugee damn, soobax
>
> Mogadishu used to be
> A place where the world would come to see …
>
> My skin needs to feel the sand, the sun

K'naan went to Kenya where he shot the music video against a backdrop of *matatus* (local taxis) and regular people on Nairobi's streets singing and dancing to the song. Fusing Somali traditional music, African drums, hip hop and reggae, K'naan laments his home country, Somalia, partly in his native language and partly in English.

For second generation African youth such as Canadian-born, Vancouver-based rapper HeatWave, it is the memories lived through parents that inform life experiences and music. In January 2014, HeatWave visited Uganda for the first time. The visit was a life-changing moment for the artist:

> The motherland has been a very humbling experience for me. It has brought me a new found enlightenment and it has humbled me in many ways. Drinking and bathing in clean water and never running out of water is a blessing. … These things are not very common in Uganda unless you are very, very fortunate or you come from a wealthy family.
>
> I had a chance to see where both my parents are from, where they grew up and where they took each other on their first dates before I was born. I also got a chance to see where they buried all the historic and important people in my family. …
>
> I inherited land in Uganda this year and I plan on starting a farm business out there. … Since I've had a chance to see where it all started and where it will all end, it gives me a new feeling about my life. Now I'm just living to live, every minute, every hour, every moment is pretty much a blessing to me. … I played a promo show at Sabrina's Pub downtown Kampala, and Uganda was very receptive to my art. That alone feels like a home-run for me, being able to live my dream like that and share my music with the motherland in general. … My Journey has been well worth it, I've made a lot of friends, gained new fans outside my core audience and gained wisdom from very wise people. There's not too much more in life that I think I can ask for but I will continue to keep pushing forward in whatever I decide to do in my future. But best believe, I'm already content with what life has thrown my way already.
>
> There was a time in my life where I had thoughts that maybe I wouldn't be able to see or live past 25 years as a result of my lifestyle as a youngin'. I always thought that things would creep up on me but now that I am in a different space and I'm living righteously it's easier for me to stay focused and do what I love the most—getting to the music and putting out the best art that I can possibly put out. (Kasskills, 2014, n.p.)

HeatWave's claims to his roots and ancestry became sources of healing. Reclaiming his ethnicity became his resistance to the marginalization and exclusion of his lived experiences in Canada.

For these artists, Indigenous land is a space of contestation and resistance, as well as a space of spiritual healing. This is apparent in the refrain from his song "Life Changing" (HeatWave, 2014a), and with a music video filmed during his visit to Uganda:

> … My life has changed since I returned to Africa
> knowing my roots and knowing the truth

Proud of his newfound history and relatives he did not know, HeatWave calls them out in the song and acknowledges his connection to the land and relatives as the foundation of his strength

> What's up fam, what's up *baba* [father or uncle]
> What's up to my cousins, what's up *jaja* [granny]
> Lots, lots of fam shed a lot of tears.

In his music video *Relatives* (HeatWave, 2014b), also filmed in Uganda, he proudly proclaims

> ... I got some relatives
> As a matter of fact I got culture
> I got deep roots, I got family, I represent so heavily.

Like Kenzo, HeatWave shoots his videos away from the luxurious cityscapes that depict materialism, preferring the countryside landscapes and the city in the horizon, making reference to the love and spirit of the poor in the sites of economic marginality:

Other than his newfound ancestry, however, HeatWave calls on people to share knowledge and talks about how he is gaining wisdom.

Noted artist Arami The Corrector, originally known as YogE, is an immigrant youth of Eritrean descent. He was born in Jeddah, Saudi Arabia, and moved to Canada at the age of three.

Arami The Corrector shot his music video *Signs* (Kasskills, 2013a) in Kibera, Nairobi's largest and one of its most economically marginalized communities, featuring Octopizzo, a hip hop artist from Kibera (Octopizzo, 2013, n.p.). Arami talked about his experience in Kenya, saying, "the smiles that rose on all faces I saw, it wasn't what I expected but had me on another level of energy. You ain't seen hustle and happiness until you've been to East Africa" (Kasskills, 2013a, n.p.). The video opens with an intro by Octopizzo of an insider's view of Kibera:

> We're in the real town. This is the hood that makes the hood in America look like paradise. ... This is Kibera baby, still proud, nobody is crying, everybody is poor though, but everybody is humbled just to be alive. So man, fuck poverty man, we live here.

This is followed by Arami's opening line in which he raps in the first person, although it is obvious that the message is intended for the world to see the poverty that surrounds them.

> Why can't I listen to the signs,
> they are plain and simple
> right in front of my eyes
> Act like I don't hear them ...

Asked about his music and why he changed his name from YogE, Arami responds:

> Knowing my culture and where I came from and knowing I still have a lot to learn and way more to see, I knew I didn't have to rap about the regular "ish" you hear every day. I've been back home to East Africa four times about to go on the fifth. Losing both my grandparents last year was a big influence to the change of my name. Sayin R.I.P to that brotha YogE, and taking the name my grandpa gave me. "Arami" in my language means "teacher" or "the one to correct." So it was pretty easy when I decided I was going with The Corrector. A lot of what's going on in the world today needs correcting; I'm just trying to let 'em know with my music. (Kasskills, 2013a, n.p.)

For Arami, reclaiming his Indigenous African name as his stage name was a result of soul searching, a way to reclaim who he is as an African through a spiritual awakening fostered by his visit to the motherland. His stage name recalls the significance and meanings of African Indigenous names. Ogiorumua (2015, n.p.) states that

> within the African cosmology, a name signifies one's cultural background, history and identity. African names are coded with meanings, which usually originate from any historical events or current happenings. These names are replete with literal meanings and acknowledgement, wishes, blessing, challenges, or rituals.

Hip hop artist Selekwa, born to a French Canadian mother and a Tanzanian father, goes by his African name as his stage name rather than Joseph Benac, the name given to him by his mother:

> As a youngster, he was often told that the name his mother chose for him, Joseph Benac, had a higher purpose while his father's side of the family called him "Selekwa Mtebe," or "Treasured Child," which most certainly describes this truly gifted and talented artist. (Hip Hop Canada, 2012, n.p.)

The work of African-born immigrant youth is not always focused on a social cause from back home.

Kenyan-born, Sudanese spoken-word artist Yusra Khogali roots her work in a hip hop culture that speaks mainly to the poverty and violence she saw growing up in Regent Park. A student at the University of Toronto, Khogali (2014, n.p.) calls herself a social justice advocate and humanist who uses her art to challenge "oppressive systems, institutions and practices."

In "Blood Music," for example, Khogali (2011) speaks about the plight of black men in a racist and white supremacist society, and cautions black men against being made into pawns and selling their souls for materialism and superficiality. This is a commentary on the commercialization of hip hop as it is often portrayed in mainstream media, and references the commodification of black culture by billion-dollar corporations:

> … Real men use their power and resource to create change
> Because generations are at stake, we need to stop this cycle of mistakes and go as a race.

Shad K.'s 2013 single "Fam Jam" lyrics touched on immigration policy, colonialism, oppression and First Nation rights (Wheeler, 2013, n.p). The Kenyan-born and Juno Award–winning rap artist's parents fled the Rwandan genocide, later migrating to Canada where he grew up in the suburbs and earned his undergraduate and graduate degrees from Wilfrid Laurier University and Simon Fraser University, respectively. Shad K. draws from his African background in some of his music in which he identifies as Kenyan. His self-made debut album, *When This Is Over* (Quinlan, 2005), was recognized for its lyricism and focus on social issues as heard in the track "I'll Never Understand," which examines the Rwandese genocide and features the poetry of his mother, Bernadette Kabango.

Like Arami The Corrector and Kenzo, Shad K. takes on sociopolitical issues in East Africa and how they affect us all. Shad K.'s (2006) music video is replete with the bodies, mass graves and skulls of the men, women and children killed during the Rwandan genocide. His mother's poignant voice in the background speaks of the cruel murders of her family, and the refrain "I'll never understand" punctuates her verses. The video opens with a caption of the words of Kofi Annan, Secretary General of the UN, 1997–2006: "In their greatest hour of need, the world failed the people of Rwanda." Shad K. contemplates the brutality of the genocide in the first verse, and like Arami The Corrector, questions why the rest of the world turned the other way:

> … And I'll never know what's more sad,
> the fact that they could have been spared
> or the fact that till this day nobody cares for the innocent
> victims of a full fledged holocaust …
> they always turned a blind eye
> And I'll never understand why

The closing caption of the music video reads: "We were told it would never happen again." A photo of gunmen with the word "Darfur" in the background slowly materializes on the screen, and the caption ends with "it is."

This rendition of history evokes memory through his mother to reclaim "back home," Rwanda, as he tries to come to terms with a heritage of a painful past. Not only does Shad K. use his platform as a hip hop artist to speak against the atrocities committed during the Rwandan genocide, he also uses it as a call to action, a catalyst for change and awareness so that the world will not close its eyes to the pain and suffering of African people.

Charry (2012) contends that American rap artists reference their history by going back to old sounds of black music to find new ways to make rap relevant and unique. American deejays, for example, "crate-dig-search through crates of obscure vinyl record albums for new sounds. … [A]s African rap has matured and second and third generations have emerged, both more critical and more commercial voices have emerged sometimes in the same time and place. One widespread effect has been to rekindle interests in older local traditions" (Charry, 2012, p. 18).

Rap provides access to historical narratives for black youth of African descent. Charry (2012, p. 18) makes reference to the rap music of African youth who grew up in France and the way in which they navigate their African identity, although they have not experienced Africa in the way their parents did. He says that their relationship with Africa is varied, "from a kind of love or nostalgia for the Africa of their parents, which brings them in close contact with African music, to Africa being just one symbol of their identity among others." This "meeting of generations" (p. 19) is a way for African youth to evoke their African roots and to link to their African cultures and African Indigenous knowledges.

For artists who go back home to Indigenous lands imbued with colonial intonations of Europe's underdevelopment of Africa and locus for imperialistic capitalism, the impoverished spaces and lands on which these artists make their music videos engender new meanings. Music and dance become an anti-colonial critique of colonial representations, reclaiming the land as a site of empowerment.

Through the act of going "back home" to Indigenous lands, reclaiming underdeveloped and impoverished spaces, black Canadian hip hop artists of African descent instill new meanings on the land through Indigenous bodies, Indigenous languages and anti-colonial narratives that resist dominant ideology and marginalization and bring about healing. For these African artists, decolonization and spiritual healing are attached to Indigenous land. They reclaim the past as a form of authenticity, and claim to the land grounds their beliefs in their ancestors. This is imperative for decolonization to take place.

For some artists, stage names recall the significance and meanings of traditional African names: *YogE*, for instance, felt compelled to take on the name *Arami* which was given to him by his grandfather. For my son, it was during the critical period of his teenage years that he was introduced to rap in Nigeria, learned pidgin and regained confidence as he learned and lived on African Indigenous land. Hence, youth of African descent reposition the rap linguistic and musical genre and, in different ways, acquire and rearticulate the hip hop cultural identity (Ibrahim, 2008, p. 243). By appropriating and owning hip hop culture and rap musical style, black youth of African descent are able to articulate their experiences in their physical locations and through memory. Rap is a way to reclaim their African identity and Indigeneity, and to resist the colonial and imperial position that the white dominant race imposes on them. Wa Thiong'o (1986, p. 3) has put forward that

> the oppressed and the exploited of the earth maintain their defiance: liberty from theft. But the biggest weapon wielded and actually daily unleashed by imperialism against that collective defiance is the cultural bomb. The effect of a cultural bomb is to annihilate a people's belief in their names, in their languages, in their environment, in their heritage of struggle,

in their unity, in their capacities and ultimately in themselves. It makes them see their past as one wasteland of non-achievement and it makes them want to distance themselves from that wasteland. It makes them want to identify with that which is furthest removed from themselves; for instance, with other people's languages rather than their own.

Black and African youth in Canada carry racialized identities in a society where prejudice, discrimination and intolerance are the norm. The dominant culture continuously seeks to incarcerate and violently discipline black bodies to the point of killing them, as seen in the white police shooting deaths of young black males in the United States. Mbembe's (2003) theory of necropolitics talks about biopower in which the body politic allows the control of certain bodies considered disposable. Drawing from Foucault, he posits that racism is

above all a technology aimed at permitting the exercise of biopower, "that old sovereign right of death." In the economy of biopower, the function of racism is to regulate the distribution of death and to make possible the murderous functions of the state (Mbembe 2003, p. 17).

Mbembe points out that race figures prominently in the calculus of biopower and suggests that "the politics of race is ultimately linked to the politics of death" (ibid.).

There is a need for African black youth to be grounded in an anti-colonial cultural and social system that builds them up to resist everyday racism—in the classroom, on the street, in the workplace. Decolonization is psychologically degrading and dehumanizing; ultimately, resistance is a spiritual struggle and life-changing process. It is imperative that African youth have access to cultural and social systems that ground them.

I have shown how (re)visiting their African Indigenous lands can be a form of empowerment and healing for youth of African descent. Youth programs, therefore, that invest in visits to African Indigenous lands would greatly benefit African youth. This experience gave confidence to my son and to many other youth artists discussed here. However, returning to Canada and facing racism once again can erode the benefits of a onetime visit. Repeat and long-term visitation programs that allow participants to experience Indigenous lands and acquire Indigenous knowledges, including learning Indigenous languages, are imperative in making any profound change and bringing about healing in the lives of African youth. Understanding the impact and change such visitations create in the lives of the artists and youth can go a long way to building a sense of empowerment, normalcy and confidence.

Such youth visitation programs have been proven to work. Canadian government–supported international student youth exchange programs for twelve- to eighteen-year-olds, such as the Canadian Education Exchange Foundation

(CEEF) and YES Canada Student Exchange, are in line with the outcomes put forward in this chapter for visiting Indigenous lands. The goals are listed as enhancing language proficiency, increasing awareness of other cultures, fostering global awareness and promoting personal growth and development.[7] National programs such as Exchanges Canada, facilitating youth exchanges across Canada, list their goals as enhancing knowledge and understanding of Canada among participants, connecting Canadians with one another, and developing a sense of Canadian identity and attachment to Canada by helping youth appreciate the diversity and the shared aspects of the Canadian experience.[8] The educator exchange program run through CEEF also lays out its objectives for educators as providing not only opportunities for personal and professional development, but also opportunities to foster global perspectives and to nurture respect and awareness of diverse cultures.[9] So far, there are no African countries in the destinations listed in the international Canadian programs named here. These programs recognize that personal growth, a sense of identity, language proficiency and the benefits of cultural immersion are vital to creating a better world for all. With language as a crucial tool for decolonization, learning any African Indigenous language and pidgin is a form of resistance and decolonization, embracing African languages as opposed to European languages imposed on Africans by the colonizers. Hip hop is synonymous with resistance and so is its use of language. Wa Thiong'o (1986) puts forward that the politics of language is about national, democratic and human liberation.

> The call for the rediscovery and the resumption of our language is a call for a regenerative reconnection with the millions of revolutionary tongues in Africa and the world over demanding liberation. It is a call for the rediscovery of the real language of humankind: the language of struggle. ... In struggle is our history, our language and our being. (p. 108)

The black struggle is about resistance. A study on black youth is incomplete without understanding the medium of hip hop and its musical styling, rap. Rap should be taught in schools so that its purpose is understood. A history of rap—including the ways in which rap has evolved and the appropriation of rap in African countries and by languages and pidgins—would benefit not only African youth. Incorporating rap into the mainstream curriculum would also lead to a much wider appreciation of the art form and a better understanding of its politics of resistance, its language and poetry. It would place the black struggle into perspective for the dominant culture. When youth of African descent understand and appreciate this art form and all it represents, they will create more responsible art that is imbued with political meanings that inform and empower (Henderson, 2009; Walcott, 2003).

Rap has been labeled as violent and degrading to women, and therefore given little chance to be understood, especially by mainstream institutions. A history of rap would show its development, just like any history learned in schools. A study of world wars, revolutionary wars and civil wars are acceptable forms of violence to be studied in the mainstream, yet somehow rap history as an art form of struggle and resistance does not qualify as worth studying. As much as the histories of the wars fought around the world lead to an understanding of how nation-states came to be and the politics that govern them developed, a study of rap creates a better understanding of the black struggle and resistance manifested through art forms that were very important in the black resistance movements in North America.

Rap music is a part of the legitimate history of black people. Just as all European and North American states were built on violence, the origins of rap come from the violence imposed on African and black people through slavery, racism and segregation produced by white-supremacist states. Rap is simply a response to this violence. Music was the main form of self-preservation and non-violent form of resistance that black people could undertake during slavery. Negro spirituals and other forms of music were used to tell stories—for self- and cultural preservation, to celebrate life, to mourn a life and to sustain life in hard times (Omo-Osagie, 2007). It still remains one of the main and most widely used non-violent forms of resistance today because it appeals to the masses.

Deirdre Glenn Paul (2000) argues that rap should be used in the classroom as a site of critical inquiry because it is "a vehicle through which teachers can privilege student voices … while simultaneously teaching them to interrogate those voices" (p. 247). Giroux et al. (1989) also affirm that rap can foster a "pedagogy which engages popular culture in order to affirm rather than mute the voice of the student" (p. 251). Paul asserts that through these dialogues "teachers are exposed to a new way to potentially approach students and culturally synchronize literacy instruction" (p. 251). They also can "critically explore significant issues attached to language, culture, and power through texts to which students relate in their everyday lives" (p. 251).

Paul (2000) defines cultural synchronization as a "harmony established between the cultural systems of schools, diverse groups of learners, and the communities from which those learners come" (p. 247). Black cultural manifestations identifiable through cultural norms, language, behaviours and attitudes are for the most part found in lower socioeconomic status communities where racial isolation is prevalent and assimilation into the majority culture is minimal (Irvine, 1991, p. 24). Teachers, who are often cultural outsiders in the communities they work in, tend to misunderstand or misinterpret the cultural nuances. Gay (1993) shows that poor students living in large urban areas tend to have teachers who are middle class and live in small- to medium-size suburban communities. Because many of these teachers have been classically educated they privilege Eurocentric epistemological models and high culture art forms. On the other hand, their urban-center students and communities value popular culture art forms and privilege experiential knowledge (Paul, 2000, p. 249).

In order to develop an effective pedagogical repertoire, it is imperative that there is a shared cultural synchronization between many teachers and their students. A lack of cultural continuity would result in cultural misunderstanding, resistance from students, a low teacher expectation for student success and self-fulfilling prophecies of student failure (Paul, 2000, p. 247). Popular culture is a significant part of the experiences of black youth in Toronto, especially in communities with a high demographic of black people. Black art and visual representations of blackness are all around them and hip hop and rap are part of that world.

For black people in a predominantly white state, a site where racially motivated violence is used against black people on a daily basis, especially young black males, rap music is their most accessible non-violent form of resistance. Rap holds a critical place in the study of black history. Rap's artistic delivery styles can manifest vivid raw emotions, particularly anger. Unfortunately, this anger is not viewed within the context of the history of white supremacist states exercising violence against black people. When such misrepresentations of stylistic choices are not read in context, it fosters an environment of racism that produces stereotypes and negative labels.

The portrayal of violence against women should be seen in the same light as the history of white women in any historical period of any state. The history and struggles of white women to earn as much as their male counterparts, to be fairly represented in different institutions, and to have equal rights in different affairs in life, including the right of protection from violence, are read within national histories. The history of black women and the violence and abuse of black women also ought to be read within the broader context of racism, feminism, colonialism, slavery and imperialism in the national histories of Canada, the United States and European countries. Understanding the history of rap is not only beneficial to the dominant group but also fosters a better understanding of our own history so that black and African youth are aware of the political messages they portray through their music. From a stylistic point of view, black women's voices are not silenced. Black musical cultures have played significant roles in the resistance politics of black people from time immemorial, including black women's resistances. Other genres favoured by black women as a medium of expression include rhythm and blues and soul—all are replete with songs of black women talking back to their men and "holding their own."

This chapter has explored ways in which youth of African descent, including migrant and first generation youth in Canada, appropriate rap, the musical style of hip hop, and use it as a tool of resistance as they make sense of their own identities within the context of racism and inequality in a white supremacist state. For artists who go "back home" and make music on African Indigenous lands, performing on Indigenous lands is necessarily a way for African youth to reclaim their identities and histories and bring about spiritual healing as they imbue new and different meanings on Africa's colonised lands. Local African artists who have appropriated hip hop in Indigenous languages and pidgins use it as a form of resistance to speak against the vices and injustices in society, countering racist images used by development agencies in the West. Since going "back home" to Indigenous lands is necessarily a process of healing for youth of African descent who face racism on a daily basis, it is imperative that programs, notably student and teacher exchange programs, include African countries as destinations to foster relationships in schools that create an understanding of our African cultures and languages. Mainstream curriculum that teaches rap as a history of resistance in the black struggle is another key way to connect hip hop to the identities and struggles facing African diasporic youth.

NOTES

1. The words "youth" and "artist" are used interchangeably, as the discussion focuses on youth who are hip hop or rap artists.
2. http://pancocojams.blogspot.ca/2015/08/eddy-kenzo-sitya-loss-ugandan-video.html
3. http://pancocojams.blogspot.ca/2015/08/eddy-kenzo-sitya-loss-ugandan-video.html
4. http://pancocojams.blogspot.ca/2015/08/eddy-kenzo-sitya-loss-ugandan-video.html
5. Regent Park is Canada's oldest and largest social housing project. Like Jane-Finch, it has a high demographic of children and youth eighteen years and under, and the majority of families are classified as low-income. It is one of the city's poorest and most crime-ridden areas. Regent Park residents come from diverse cultural backgrounds including many new Canadians from Africa, Asia and Latin America. There are more than sixty different first languages represented, making Regent Park one of Toronto's most culturally diverse neighborhoods. http://www.torontorealestateboard.com/about_GTA/Neighbourhood/gta/neighbourhoods/downtown/regent-park/
6. genius.com/Knaan-soobax-lyrics
7. http://www.ceef.ca/student_intro.html
8. www.exchanges.gc.ca (http://pch.gc.ca/eng/1266324590531)
9. http://www.ceef.ca/educator_intro.html

REFERENCES

Amodie, E. (2015). *Elodie Amodie performs Sitya Loss of Eddy Kenzo @ Star Karaoke, Abijan, Côte d'Ivoire* [Video file]. Retrieved from https://www.youtube.com/watch?v=NAsbcsqVFLI

Arami The Corrector. (2013). *Signs—official music video* [Video file]. Retrieved from http://www.hiphopcanada.com/2013/07/arami-the-corrector-signs-video/

Austin, J. (2014, January 31). African parenting styles we like. *AFK Insider*. Retrieved from http://afkinsider.com/40558/african-parenting-styles-like/2/

Bernard, A. (2008, May 13). K'naan interview. *RapReviews*. Retrieved from http://webcache.googleusercontent.com/search?q=cache:ykzPl2uTvBEJ:www.rapreviews.com/interview/knaan08.html+&cd=1&hl=en&ct=clnk&gl=ca

Bledsoe, C. H., & Sow, P. (2011). Back to Africa: Second chances for the children of West African immigrants. *Journal of Marriage and Family, 73*(4), 747–762.

Bosire, Mokaya. (2006). Hybrid languages: The case of Sheng. In A. F. Olaoba & P. A. Michael (Eds.), *Selected proceedings of the 36th Annual Conference on African Linguistics* (pp. 185–193). Somerville, MA: Cascadilla Proceedings Project. Retrieved from http://www.lingref.com/cpp/acal/36/chapter1423.pdf

Charry, E. (2012). *Hip hop Africa: New African music in a globalizing world.* Bloomington: Indiana University Press.

Dei, G. J. S. (2010). *Teaching Africa: Towards a transgressive pedagogy.* New York, NY: Springer.

DJ Dench. (2015). *African ghetto kids dancing best 2015! Song by Gulu Omako Mac by Acholi Rapper Lobby* [Video file]. Retrieved from https://www.youtube.com/watch?v=bC9AcprLyig

Ford, D. (2015, July 21). DA: Sandra Bland's death being treated like murder investigation. CNN. Retrieved from http://www.cnn.com/2015/07/20/us/texas-sandra-bland-jail-death/

Gay, G. (1993). Building cultural bridges: A bold proposal for teacher education. *Education and Urban Society, 25*(3), 285–299.

Giroux, H. (2009). Paulo Freire and the politics of post colonialism. In A. Kempf (Ed.), *Breaching the colonial contract: Anti-colonialism in the US and Canada.* Dordrecht, the Netherlands: Springer.

Giroux, H. A., Simon, R.I, & Contributors. (1989). *Popular culture, schooling, and everyday life.* New York: Bergin and Garvey.

Hage, G. (1997). "At home in the entrails of the West: Multiculuralism, ethnic food and migrant home-building." In H. Grace, G. Hage, L. Johnson et al. *Home/world: Space, community and marginality in Sydney's West,* pp. 99–135. Annandale, NJ: Pluto Press.

HeatWave. (2014a). *Life Changing, ft. Slim Emcee* [Video file]. Retrieved from https://www.youtube.com/watch?v=WCzSFcWvIaw

HeatWave. (2014b). *Relatives, ft. Arami The Corrector* [Video file]. Retrieved from https://www.youtube.com/watch?v=FrBOAiozf1I

Henderson. F. (2009). Successful, single, and "othered": The media and the "plight" of single black women. In Hammer, R., & Kellner, D. (Eds.), *Media/cultural studies: Critical approaches.* New York: Peter Lang.

Henhouse Prowlers. (2015). *Henhouse Prowlers playing Sitya Loss by Eddy Kenzo* [Video file]. Retrieved from https://www.youtube.com/watch?v=dsvsytVRl6I

Hip Hop Canada. (2012). Selekwa releases "Top my game" EP on iTunes; new single with Choclair. Retrieved from http://www.hiphopcanada.com/2012/10/selekwa-releases-top-my-game-ep-onitunes-new-single-with-choclair-news/

Hodkinson, P., & Deicke, W. (Eds.). (2007). *Youth cultures: Scenes, subcultures and tribes.* New York, NY: Routledge.

Holtzman, J. D. (2006). "Food and Memory." *Annual Review of Anthropology, 35:* 361–378.

Hooks, b. (1989). *Talking back: Thinking feminist, thinking black.* Boston, MA: South End Press.

Ibrahim, A. (2008, March). The new flaneur: Subaltern cultural studies, African youth in Canada and the semiology of in-betweenness. *Cultural Studies, 22*(2), 234–253.

Irvine, J. J. (1991). *Black Students and School Failure: Policies, Practices and Prescriptions.* New York: Praeger.

Kasskills. (2013a, July 29). *Arami The Corrector—Signs* [Video file]. Retrieved from http://www.canada.com/2013/07/arami-the-corrector-signs-video/

Kasskills. (2013b, August 8). From Africa to Canada: Words with Arami The Corrector[Interview]. Retrieved from http://www.hiphopcanada.com/2013/08/words-with-arami-the-corrector-africa-to-canada-interview/

Kasskills. (2014, January 15). *Heatwave—30 days in Africa: Episode 2—the soil* [Video file]. Retrieved from http://www.hiphopcanada.com/2014/01/heatwave-30-days-in-africa-episode-2-the-soil-video/

Kenzo, E. (2014). *Sitya loss* [Video file]. Retrieved from http://www.youtube.com/watch?v=ex0NwMcf8iE

Khogali, Y. (2011). *Blood music* [Video file]. Retrieved from https://www.youtube.com/watch?v=cI6jd3Zw0_c

Khogali, Y. (2014). Untitled. Retrieved from www.yusrakhogali.com

Kidula, N. (2012). East Coast (Kenya and Tanzania): The local and global in Kenyan Rap and Hip hop Culturel. In E. Charry (Ed.), *Hip hop Africa: New African music in a globalizing world.* Bloomington: Indiana University Press.

K'naan. (2009). *Soobax* [Video file]. Retrieved from https://www.youtube.com/watch?v=8mVY30buW4Q

Mackey, E. (1998). *The house of difference: Cultural politics and national identity in Canada.* London, England: Routledge.

Mazrui, Alamin. 1995. Slang and codeswitching: the case of Sheng in Kenya. *Afrikanistische Arbeitspapiere 42:* 168-179.

Mbembe, J. A. (2003). Necropolitics. *Public Culture, 15*(1), 11–40.

Mignolo, W. (2007). Delinking: The rhetoric of modernity, the logic of coloniality and the grammar of de-coloniality. *Cultural Studies, 21*(2–3), 449–514.

Minh-ha, T. T. (1989). *Woman, native, other: Writing postcoloniality and feminism.* Bloomington: Indiana University Press.

Ntarangwi, M. (2009). *East African hip hop: Youth culture and globalization.* Champaign: University of Illinois Press.

Obeid, M. (2013). Home-making in the diaspora: Bringing Palestine to London. In Q. Ato & D. Girish (Eds.), *A companion to diaspora and transnationalism.* Chichester, England: Wiley Blackwell.

Octopizzo. (2013). About Octopizzo. Retrieved from http://octopizzo.com/home/about-octopizzo/

Ogiorumua, V. (2015, April). *The significance of African names: A cultural restorative pedagogy.* Paper presented at the ninth annual "Decolonizing the Spirit" conference: Indigenous Pedagogies and Cultural Resistance in Education. OISE, University of Toronto.

Omo-Osagie, S. (2007). "Their souls made them whole": Negro spirituals and lessons in healing and atonement. *Western Journal of Black Studies, 31*(2), 34.

Oso, L., & Mateos, N. R. (Eds.). (2013). *International handbook on gender, migration and transnationalism.* Cheltenham, England: Edward Elgar.

Patrick, R. B. (2010, May 23). Shad gets it. *Exclaim!* Retrieved from http://exclaim.ca/Music/article/Shad_Gets_It

Paul, D. G. (2000). Rap and orality: Critical media literacy, pedagogy, and cultural synchronization. *Journal of Adolescent and Adult Literacy, 44* (3), 246–251.

Quayson, A., & Daswani, G. (Eds.). (2013). Introduction. In *A companion to diaspora and transnationalism.* Chichester, England: Wiley-Blackwell.

Quinlan, T. (2006, January 1). Shad: When this is over. *Exclaim!* Retrieved from http://exclaim.ca/Music/article/shad-when_this_is_over

Rexdale. (n.d.). Retrieved from http://rapdict.org/Rexdale

Ryanphoto.Flickr. (2010, December 16). Shad. *Montreal Gazette.* Retrieved from http://www.montrealgazette.com/entertainment/Shad/3992363/story.html

Shad K. (2005). *I'll never understand—official music video* [Video file]. Retrieved from https://www.youtube.com/watch?v=2r7UK3B6VWQ

Shonekan, S. (2012). Nigerian hip hop: Exploring a black world hybrid. In E. Charry (Ed.), *Hip hop Africa: New African Music in a globalizing world.* Bloomington: Indiana University Press.

Tahmane Music. (2014). *Mathane Kids (BMF) dancing to Sitya Loss—made in Mathare, Nairobi* [Video file]. Retrieved from https://www.youtube.com/watch?v=o4CX9P6GQcw.

Walcott, R. (2003). *Black like who? Writing black Canada.* Toronto, Canada: Insomniac Press.

Wa Thiong'o, N. (1986). *Decolonising the mind: The politics of language in African literature.* Nairobi, Kenya: East African Educational Publishers.

Welte, J. (2006, August 7). *K'naan breaks out* [Audio recording]. Retrieved from http://web.archive.org/web/20070929104442/http://www.mp3.com/news/stories/5720.html

Wheeler, B. (2013, October 22). Shad: Why the thoughtful rapper is at the top of his game. *The Globe and Mail.* Retrieved from http://www.theglobeandmail.com/arts/music/shad-the-thoughtful-rapper-is-at-the-top-of-his-game/article14974009/

CHAPTER NINE

Black African-Aboriginal Coalitions FOR Decolonization Struggles

The Missing Links

SULEYMAN M. DEMI

INTRODUCTION

This chapter is a personal reflection on the debates regarding settler colonialism and coalition building for anti-colonial struggles in North America. I came to Canada from Ghana having limited knowledge about Indigenous people's struggles—only to be confronted with the implications and complicities inherent in the appropriation of Indigenous land. I found myself asking many questions, each one without answers: Does returning to Ghana exonerate me from the implications or complicities of ongoing colonization and land appropriation in Canada? How does my return to Ghana impact Indigenous people's struggles for sovereignty? Whose land am I on? What responsibility do I owe to Aboriginal people? As an individual who had seen the remnants of colonization and the imposition of neo-colonization in Africa, these questions keep echoing in my mind. Although definitive answers to these questions remain elusive, the exploration of a shared sense—albeit with different experiences—of *Indigeneity* in North American and African contexts offers a common ground for coalition building and shared understanding. In problematizing the notions of settler and settlerhood within a Canadian context, this chapter seeks to explore how black Africans and Aboriginals might engage in coalition building. This chapter intends to explore the relatedness of the black Africans and Aboriginals and how their marginalization is inextricably linked to colonization. Following a literature review about coalition building and settler colonialism, the chapter contends that black Africans and Aboriginals share a strong spiritual ontology that makes them intricately connected to each other's struggle—necessitating coalition building. These coalitions should be based on "principle" and should be seen as a responsibility that every Indigenous group owes to each other as imbedded in the spirit of Indigeneity. Hence, to reference Cannon and Sunseri (2011), Indigenous struggle should aim for the politics of liberation, not just the politics of recognition.

Though I was born a few decades after Ghana had gained independence from Britain, I could feel the tension between my Indigenous Ghanaian upbringing and the Eurocentric education system, one founded on Western values and ideals. In this context, "Indigenous upbringing" is used here to refer to living in demarcated territory with distinct linguistic, cultural and social organizational structures and also where local knowledge is valued, not in the Western contexts of marginality or primitivism. The term "Indigenous people" has no single definition because of the diversity of Indigenous groups; however, "Indigeneity" begins with self-conviction and meeting criteria set by recognized Indigenous groups. To Africans, to be qualified as an Indigenous person means that one "holds a unique African language, knowledge systems and beliefs and possesses invaluable knowledge of practices for the sustainable management of natural resources" (Shizha, 2012, p. 2). This definition includes all previously colonized societies or tribes that have ancestral roots in continental Africa irrespective of their marginalization status (Kapoor & Shizha, 2010; Shizha, 2013). Africans reject the definition of Indigenous people as "societies that have remained on the margin of 'modernization'" (Shizha, 2013, p. 2).

As were other Ghanaians (see Adjei, 2007; Darko, 2014; Dei, 1996), I was educated in a system that sought to transform me into a different person—perhaps a European in thinking and an African in body. Elaborating on the divisiveness of the Western schooling system in Ghana, B. S. Kwakaw (cited by Bray et al., in Nwomonoh, 1998, p. 265), a social observer, contended that

> the effect of the Western type of education has been to produce … three nations in one country, each unable to communicate effectively with the others … the "educated" … many who do not understand the ways of the "educated" … then … a third group, the "half educated" who understand neither the ways of their own indigenous society nor those of the "highly educated."

This was the educational system I was subjected to growing up in Ghana. Having such a background allows me to appreciate the marginalization of Aboriginal forms of knowledge and cultures in North America. I must also acknowledge my limitations, saying with humility that I am not an expert on the African situation, nor do I claim to be an expert on the field of Aboriginal history or culture. Despite these differences, however, coalition building offers an important site for common purpose and struggle.

Coalition building is a political alliance mobilized around a group of people with shared interests or principles to address certain injustices and to ensure societal equity or change societal wrongs or to promote societal good. However, various attempted coalitions in decolonizing struggles in North America, and in particular Canada, have suffered numerous challenges due to the underestimation of the intensity of colonization and its modus operandi. The challenges facing coalition building among minority groups, particularly in North America, are identified as "competing marginalities" and part of a "race to innocence" (Fellows & Razack, 1998). Attempts to categorize oppression into hierarchies—what has been described as "oppression Olympics" (Sexton, 2010)—and differences in interest and objectives among groups (Trask, 1991) are questionable. Decolonization is such a broad concept that any attempt to assign a specific meaning to it and reject other meanings can reduce it to a narrow confinement.

Tuck and Yang (2012, p. 1) contend that "decolonization brings about the repatriation of Indigenous land and life; it is not a metaphor for the things we want to do to improve our societies and schools." This assertion not only limits the meaning of decolonization in regard to land but also categorizes oppression into hierarchies; these hierarchies create tiers of division, something counterproductive to coalition building. Oppressions differ in scope and magnitude; however, creating hierarchies may themselves be forms of suppression by limiting the range and breadth of experiences.

The term "decolonization" is such a broad concept that its invocation raises several questions: What are we decolonizing? How do we engage in a decolonization struggle? How far do we intend to go with our decolonization struggles? These questions are crucial if successful decolonization is to be achieved. As Dei (2014) argues, "nobody has yet been fully decolonized"—so talking decolonization must aim at specific issues. Strategies matter, as events of the past should guide our understanding of the present and plans for the future. To what extent do we intend to undertake a decolonization struggle? Decolonization should be a sustainable, continuous process—one calling for Aboriginals and non-Aboriginals to lobby each other to make their presence felt and their voices heard in the populace and government machinery.

Colonization is so pervasive that decolonization is context-bound and variable, meaning its experiences, interpretations and implications differ according to the setting. For instance, to Africans in their homeland, decolonization means restoration of African values, virtues, cultures and economic emancipation. It means weaning themselves from the dictates of the foreign influences in their governance and social and economic policies. To many Aboriginals, decolonization could refer to efforts to resolve the unresolved, including the sovereign right to self-government, to protect and preserve their cultures and to retain title to Indigenous lands (Tuck & Yang, 2012). The understandings of decolonization between Aboriginals and black Africans are not mutually exclusive, but overlapping and interlocking. When relating this to coalition building efforts of black Africans and

Aboriginals in North America, neither group can be considered "passive victims" of European exploitations, marginalization, racialization and extermination (Brands, Breen, Williams, & Gross, 2011).

The horrendous act of genocide committed against Aboriginals and inhumane treatment of black Africans as slaves on North American land could be singled out as the major catalysts through which to form an alliance for liberation struggles rather than compete for marginalities or identification within the white supremacist world. Amadahy and Lawrence (2009) noted that these acts of Indigenous genocide and black slavery have helped to shape the lives of Aboriginals and black Africans in the United States and to forge a better relationship than they have in Canada. Perhaps this may be due to Canada's claim to innocence regarding slavery. The appropriation of human and material resources from both black Africans and Native Americans by Europeans, which provided the needed capital for further exploration of Asia, could be a point of convergence for solidarity. The triangular trade of slaves and goods, spanning Africa, North America and Europe, is a shared history of particular importance to both groups.

For Aboriginal people in the Americas, as the targets for physical and cultural destruction and assumption of the role of vanquished (Amadahy & Lawrence, 2009), their successful erasure will legitimize the continuous occupation of their traditional lands and the perpetuation of long-standing land-claim disputes. Conversely, black people, those who are part of the African diaspora, continue to suffer severe forms of racism. As Amadahy and Lawrence (2009) rightly put it, "everything from standards of beauty to notions of criminality hinges on the degree of phenotypic blackness" (p. 106). There is an inverse relationship between societal acceptance and blackness in the white supremacist world; the darker your skin, the less acceptable you are to the society. The colonial legacies of slavery, resource appropriation and the recent neo-liberal economic policies of the World Bank and the International Monetary Fund (IMF) imposed on Africans have further reduced the continent to one that is hard hit with poverty and prone to conflicts. Patrick Wolfe (2006, pp. 387–388) juxtaposes the strategic positions that white supremacy places on black Africans and Aboriginals:

> Black people's enslavement produced an inclusive taxonomy that automatically enslaved the offspring of a slave and any other parent. … [T]his taxonomy became fully racialized in the "one drop rule," where any amount of African ancestry, no matter how remote, and regardless of phenotypical appearance, makes a person black. … [I]n stark contrast non-Indian ancestry compromised their indigeneity, producing "half breeds," a regime that persists in the form of blood quantum regulations. As opposed to enslaved people, whose reproduction augmented their owners' wealth, Indigenous people obstructed settlers' access to land, so their increase was counterproductive.

The manipulation by white colonialists places black Africans and Aboriginals at the opposite ends of the hegemonic dynamic, thereby creating antagonistic relationships that give credence to white supremacy.

CHANGING THE LANGUAGE OF COALITION POLITICS

As Schlosberg (2013) and Trask (1991) demonstrate, successful environmental protection coalitions reveal the power of coalition politics. However, coalition for decolonization is saddled with many drawbacks, including the peculiar nature of colonization and the resultant repercussion of decolonization. Decolonization is often met with violent resistance when it involves racialized bodies taking back occupied land. Douglas Sanderson (2011, p. 181) identifies the complexities associated with the quest to embark on a process of decolonization that is grounded solely on "giving back the land":

> … we need to think more concretely about what [it] is to give back the land. Land is not like a Matisse; it is not something that you can box up and ship off. Land is simply there, wherever that "there" is, and so we need to think more clearly about what we mean when we give back the land. One version of returning the land is clear out everyone who is there and allow another population to flow in, a sort of ethnic cleansing. This, as I said, is not what Indigenous people want and the treaty regime, especially the modern day treaty regime, is evidence that no one is looking to clear out all settler people from contested territories.

Sanderson captures some of the challenges involved in embarking on a decolonization struggle with land acquisition as its sole prerogative. The question "What does it mean to give back the land?" (Sanderson, 2011, p. 181) has been addressed by several Indigenous scholars and activists, many of whom have argued that their struggle is not about ethnic cleansing but rather restoring the land from colonial dissipation. Andrea Smith (2012, p. 83) notes that the Indigenous people's struggle is not about asking everybody (settlers) to vacate the land when she echoes their contention that

> … the goal of Indigenous struggle was not simply to fight for the survival of a particular people, but to transform the world so that it is governed through principles of participatory democracy rather than through nation-states. … [T]heir vision of nationhood requires a radical re-orientation towards land. All are welcome to live on the land; they asserted, but we must all live in a different relationship to it.

Indigenous nations all over the world are welcoming nations, nations that ensure reciprocity and mutual respect, nations that accord strangers the utmost protection and care because of the belief that the collaborative efforts of strangers and Indigenes build a nation. Some Indigenous groups in Canada expressed this willingness to share their resources if doing so improves the socioeconomic conditions of the poor and the marginalized. What they vehemently oppose is the use of their resources to oppress the poor and the marginalized. This position was clearly stated by Philip Blake, a member of the Dene Nation, during his testimony at the Berger Inquiry[1]:

> If our Indian nation is being destroyed so that poor people of the world might get a chance to share this world's riches, then as Indian people, I am sure that we would seriously

consider giving up our resources. But do you really expect us to give up our life and our land so that those few people who are the richest and most powerful in the world today can maintain their own privilege? That is not our way. (quoted in Coulthard, 2014, pp. 62–63)

These arguments by Aboriginal scholars and activists assuage the fear of ethnic cleansing associated with Indigenous struggles and further complicate the notion of land as the sole aim of decolonization. However, this approach should not downgrade the efforts of any Indigenous group that grounds its decolonization solely on land. These oversimplifications and overgeneralizations will end up perpetuating oppressions.

Racism and racialization underline the different invocations and experiences of decolonization by Aboriginals and black Africans, providing anchors for maintaining settler colonialism (Smith, 2012). A central issue in contention is not the dispute about who owns the North American land, for instance, but the settlers' notion of making better use of the land than Aboriginals. To black Africans, the history of slavery all too frequently categorizes each black person as a slave, regardless of lineage or identity within the diaspora. Andrea Smith (2012, p. 68) contends that these perspectives form the "logic of white supremacy".

Coalitions provide spaces wherein this logic may be challenged through collective social action. Turning to articles calling for coalition building, Haunani-Kay Trask (1991) traces the historical injustices meted out to the people of Hawaii and emphasizes the need for coalition between Aboriginals and non-Aboriginals within decolonization struggles. However, Trask (1991, p. 1205) contends coalition building stems from convenience rather than changing the world order:

One might ask why I bothered to work in coalitions or more accurately, why I even tried to work in coalition at all. The answer simply is that my people comprise only 20 percent of the resident population in Hawai'i. If Hawaiians were dominant numerically and culturally, that is, if we controlled our islands, we would have no need for coalitions.

While Trask may be speaking from the perspective of a person who identifies as Hawaiian, it is counterproductive to coalition building if the same argument is advanced by non-Hawaiians.

For the Native people under American control, coalitions with Non-natives must be temporally and issue-oriented. *We need to see them as immediate need to immediate end, not as long-term answers to long-term goals.* For example, sovereignty has always been and will always be the long-term goal of Natives peoples. No settlers in Hawai'i including Asians and *Haole* [Hawaiians of European descent], desire Hawaiian sovereignty as a goal since it would take *land and revenues for exclusive Hawaiian use.* (Trask, 1991, p. 1210, emphasis added, with the exception of *Haole*)

Trask explains sovereignty means that Hawaiians may control their lands and exercise their legal rights as Native people. However, the idea of imputing

Hawaiian sovereignty will translate to taking "land and revenues for exclusive Hawaiian use"—suggesting that Hawaiian sovereignty will not necessarily ensure social equity, good relationships and reciprocity. With Hawaiians having control of their resources, lateral equity does not necessarily mean equal treatment but rather a targeted response to raise the marginalized group to a certain standard of sociopolitical and economic affluence.

SETTLER AND SETTLERHOOD

Seeing the potential positive impact, as well as some of the perils, of coalition building, it is instructive to consider how these alliances might be built within the concepts of the settler and settlerhood. Lawrence and Dua (2005, p. 127) contend that critical race theorists and post-colonial theorists "fail to make Indigenous presence and ongoing colonization, particularly in the Americas, fundamental to their analyses of race and racism." The result is that "Aboriginal people cannot see themselves in [an] antiracism context, again, Aboriginal activism against settler domination takes place without people of color as allies" (Lawrence & Dua, 2005, p. 120). Conversely, Martin Cannon (2012, pp. 21–22) decries the lack of enthusiasm by Aboriginal groups to convince non-Aboriginals to consider themselves as allies in the decolonization struggle:

> … I propose that as long as we remain focused on racism and colonization as an exclusively Indigenous struggle, we [those who identify as Aboriginal] do very little in the way of encouraging non-indigenous peoples to think about what it might mean to be an "ally" of Indigenous sovereignty and education.

Cannon's argument emphasizes the need for Aboriginals not to see ongoing colonization as a problem for only Aboriginal people, but as a Canadian problem that must be addressed by the collective, encouraging and engaging non-Aboriginals to make them feel needed in decolonization struggles. Who is Aboriginal and who has the right to speak for Aboriginal people are contested matters within many Aboriginal communities (Miles & Holland, 2006; St. Denis, 2007). As Nyamnjoh (2012) cautions, non-Aboriginal scholars run the risk of being labeled as "intellectual imposter[s]" when they decide to make Aboriginal issues the core of their scholarship.

Lawrence and Dua (2005) raise some related concerns about the nature of and intention behind this critical analysis. Indeed, who benefits from such analysis? Is it white supremacy and the state? If so, then this kind of analysis shifts the focus from the state to individuals, instead of uniting racialized groups towards a common goal of decolonization, entrenching boundaries separating Aboriginals and non-Aboriginals, derailing coalition-building efforts. Histories of colonization have shown how colonial administrations have employed "divide and conquer strategies" by pitting one group against another in ways to foment disaffection. Some Indigenous scholars, including Klopotek (2009) and Hill (2009), describe how previous colonial administrations instigated anti-black racism among Indigenous communities by denying Indigenous rights to families with black relatives, creating family disunity among Indigenous people with black heritage. Also, simply categorizing every non-Aboriginal on North American land, regardless of the circumstances that resulted in their displacement, as "settlers" participates in the appropriation of Aboriginal people's land.

There is ambiguity in the use of the word "settler" in this case, especially when "Aboriginal activism against settler domination takes place without people of color as allies" (Lawrence & Dua, 2005, p. 120). When are people of color classified as "settlers," and when do they partake in ongoing land appropriation and colonization? How does one expect them to join forces with the Aboriginals to fight other settlers? We should not also forget the fact that some people of color engage in colonial projects.

The term "settler" is used politically by critical scholars and Indigenous people to invoke domineering relationships. Categorizing everybody on Indigenous land as a "settler" does not only fall into the trappings of the dominant order, but it also neutralizes the agency of the term "settlers" as used by critical scholars such as Fanon (1963), Dei (1996), Mamdani (2001), Sharma and Wright (2009) and Smith (1992/1999).

If settlerhood is solely about land, then can we logically describe Aboriginals, Africans and Asians in Europe as settlers and the Europeans as Indigenous? If the answer is affirmative, then what is wrong with settlerhood? The movement of people from place to place is part of human history. In fact, recent anthropological studies have revealed that every modern human being can trace her or his origin to Africa (Albritton, 2012; Brauer, Colland & Stringer, 2004; Stringer & McKie, 1996), thus presupposing that Africa is the only continent wherein no one can be considered a settler. However, the term "settler" must invoke discomfort and provide an impetus for coalition building towards decolonization struggles (Snelgrove, Dhamoon, & Corntassel, 2014).

How long, then, does one have to live at a location to be qualified as Indigenous to or a settler of that land? If we cannot classify, for example, Aboriginals in Europe as settlers, then why is the meaning of Aboriginal/Indigenous fixed but the meaning of settler malleable? Are we not supporting the colonial imagery of the "Native other" by attempting to fix the meaning of Aboriginal/Indigenous to specific groups when everybody is native to a particular place? Furthermore, nation-states and continental boundaries are colonial creations, hence the need to problematize the use of colonially defined territory to classify people as settlers or Aboriginal. *Terra nullius*—the law of "nobody's land"—on which states such as

Canada, the United States and Australia were founded fails to stand the test of time and the moral spirit of the law, raising problematic questions about the legitimacy of these states. In rejecting the legality or legitimacy of this legal concept, a Supreme Court of Canada decision observes:

> ... When the settlers came, the Indians were there, organized in societies and occupying the land as their fore fathers had done over centuries. This is what Indian title means and does not help ... to call it a personal or usufructuary right. (Calder, 1973, in Kulchyski, 1994, p. 65)

The case of *Calder et al. v. Attorney-General of British Columbia* (1973), from which this judgment is excerpted, was groundbreaking in that the Supreme Court of Canada recognized that Aboriginal land title can and does exist outside of colonial title. This judgment rendered illegal the racist ideology, if not the actual title, by which the lands in Canada and, by extension, the United States and Australia, were declared unoccupied. This created the conditions for appropriation and the subsequent formation of states. The goal of settlers coming to North America was to appropriate Indigenous people's land, informed by a racist colonialist ideology.

> The settlers did not go to North America with the intention of joining say Iroquois or Mohegan society or to other Aboriginal communities; they could not become "savages." They planted themselves into the New World to establish their own civil society and could do so because they were English and so already "civilized" beings. (Frederick Turner, 1893, cited in Pateman, 2007, p. 55)

Turner establishes who the settlers are and what their missions and actions were in their newly found place of abode. Patrick Wolfe (2006, p. 388) helps us to understand the settler societies when he argues that "settler colonialism destroys to replace"—supporting his argument by quoting Theodor Herzl, a founder of Zionism, "If I wish to substitute a new building for an old one, I must demolish before I construct" (Herzl, 1902/1941, p. 38). The "settler" is not an accolade bestowed on people living on foreign land, but is associated with imperialism and colonialism.

The terms "native" and "settler" are analogous to "colonized" and "colonizer" (Fanon, 1963; Smith, 1992). Historically speaking, settlers are colonizers who defied the Crown's original plan of appropriation and conveyance of resources from colonized countries to their homelands, preferring to remain on contested land and to enjoy its bounty (Brands et al., 2011; Pateman, 2007). They enacted laws and instituted structures to legitimize their stay and loosen political ties with their homelands. John Westlake, a professor of law at the University of Cambridge, justified the seizure of land as something that was sanctioned by God: "True indeed, God did not create the world to be empty. And therefore the seizure of vacant places is regarded as a law of nature" (Gentili, 1933, cited in Pateman, 2007, p. 47). In his justification of *terra nullius* and the occupation of land based on civility,

Westlake defined civilization in terms of a government that can uphold European values, concluding that no such government can be found in Africa and America, hence international laws consider such Natives to be uncivilized: "… in the absence of such government, the inflow of white race cannot be stopped where there is land to cultivate, ore to mine, commerce to be developed, sport to enjoy, and curiosity to be satisfied" (Westlake, 1894, pp. 142–143, cited in Pateman, 2007, pp. 65–66). Focusing on white settlers, wherein whiteness is inextricably linked to settlement, fails to ascribe settlerhood to any race on foreign land. Wolfe (2006, p. 389) explains how the early settlers not only attempted to limit access to their lands but also appropriated Indigeneity to make them unique as a sovereign nation:

> On the one hand, settler society required the practical elimination of the natives in order to establish itself on their territory. On the symbolic level, however, settler society subsequently sought to recuperate indigeneity in order to express its difference—and, accordingly, its independence—from the mother country.

Asserting difference from their homelands required settlers to adopt Indigenous terms and practices, not because they despise these countries but to avoid the obligation of repatriating resources to the mother countries. "Settlerhood is a process of occupation; it speaks of the activities of an imperial occupying force … denotes occupation on stolen Lands through violence, land dispossession, forced displacement, genocide and robbery" (Dei, in press). For minority groups like black Africans, whose "Canadian-ness" depends on the whims and caprices of the state, describing them with the term "settler" romanticizes the term "seller"—making the term lose its agency and sense of purpose. "Settler" is linked to power of elimination and replacement, the power to enact and enforce colonial laws held by the dominant bodies. Mamdani (2001) proposes the rejection of both "settler" and "native" since they are two opposing words having their roots in colonization. However, such a suggestion could only be considered in areas where colonization has ceased; however, a settler society like the United States re-invigorates the political meanings of both "settlers" and "natives."

Joining the debate of who is or is not a settler, Amadahy and Lawrence (2009, p. 107), inferring from the meaning of "settler" as argued by Smith (1999), assert that "for groups of peoples to be forcibly transplanted from their own lands and enslaved on other peoples' lands—as Africans were in the Americas—does not make the enslaved peoples 'true settlers.' The alternative term for "settler" is certainly not "true settler" or "pseudosettler" and the introduced term "true settler" by Amadahy and Lawrence (2009) is ambiguous and needs further clarification. Andrea Smith (2012), conversely, argues that if we focus solely on the logic of settler colonialism, without looking at how migration occurs in the first place, we may neglect how we are sometimes complicit in these processes of forced migration. Other Indigenous scholars, including Fox and Bird (cited in Smith, 2012,

p. 84), advocate for the "re-articulation of Indigenous nationhood that identifies the complicities of Indigenous people in the forced migration of people through their involvement in the military."

Andrea Smith (2012, p. 66) examines two critical issues: "how lack of attention to settler colonialism impedes the analysis of race in white supremacy as formulated by scholars who focus on race and racial formation ... and how lack of attention to race and white supremacy within Native studies and Native struggles hinders the development of a decolonization framework." Smith conceptualizes this framework through the three pillars of white supremacy:

> [W]hite supremacy should not be assumed to operate in a singular fashion but rather through separate and distinct, but still interrelated logic. The primary logics of white supremacy are (1) slaveability/anti-black racism which anchors capitalism (2) genocide, which anchored colonialism and (3) orientalism which anchors war. (Smith, 2012, p. 66)

Smith concludes by cautioning that white supremacy could shift our focus from the politics of liberation to the politics of recognition. Therefore, it is important to draw on the shared spiritual ontology between the black Africans and Indigenous people to emphasize the need for coalition building.

SHARED SPIRITUAL ONTOLOGY AND THE WAY FORWARD

The conduit that intricately links black Africans and native Americans is spirituality. Spirituality means different things to different people based on their beliefs and worldviews. Hence, spirituality has been defined differently by various authors, including Jagers and Smith (1996), Kus (1992) and Potts (1991), and therefore it is very difficult to lay claim to one particular definition. Wane (2002) argues that spirituality is something so personal, unique and individualistic that it cannot be perfectly pontificated in any immaculate definition. Dei, James, Karumanchery, James-Wilson, and Zine (2000) distinguished between spirituality and religion by arguing that the latter is often observed or articulated in sacred texts or scriptures. Spirituality is, therefore, a broad concept that contains several elements, with religion being one of the significant factors (Mattis, 2000; Shahjahan, 2005). The etiology of the word *spirituality* is derived from the Latin word *spiritus*, meaning "the breath of life" (Berdyaev, 1939; Chaffers, 1994; MacQuarrie, 1972). Among many Aboriginals spirituality is conceived as something that "evolves from exploring and coming to know and experience the nature of living energy moving in each of us, through us, and around us" (Cajete, 1994, p. 42). According to African spirituality, "being is the perpetual flow of energy among animate and inanimate things" and between the Creator, the god and ancestors (Wangoola, 2000, p. 265). Energy is the core of life; hence, all things have life (Simpson, 2000).

Therefore, in this discussion spirituality is not limited to religion; rather, it focuses on human relationships with the Creator, one another and relationships with other creations both animate and inanimate that ensure respect and reciprocity. Spirituality is our innate feeling that speaks to us at the times of joy and despair. It is the inner feeling that pricks our individual consciousness to decipher good from evil, living in relationships devoid of domination and aggrandizement while respecting authority. The inner consciousness makes humans recognize that they are a part of the environment and not superior beings provided with the accoutrements to exploit and subdue nature. Spirituality is, therefore, sound knowledge of and interactions with the environment or nature. Indigenous communities around the world place higher value on spiritual maturity—the knowledge of nature—than on material accumulation. Spiritual maturity is the ability to speak and interact with the inner self and live a life of humility, peacefulness, modesty, respect and appreciation of diversity. Acts of kindness, care and love for humanity and all creatures are seen as responsibilities of humans to nature, and nature replicates such kind gestures. Spiritual maturity also helps humans to recognize that every creature, no matter how small or big, how strong or weak, contributes to ensure cosmic balance in nature.

> Mother Earth and all her children teach us that diversity is necessary to our health and well-being. You do not see the trees insisting that they all bear the same fruit. You do not see the fish declaring war against those who do not swim. You do not see corn blocking the growth of squash and beans. What one plant puts into the soil, another takes. What one tree puts into the air another creature breathes. What one being leaves as waste another considers food. Even death and decay serve to nurture new life. Every one of Mother Earth's children co-operates so that the family survives. (Amadahy & Lawrence, 2009, p. 116)

These underlying tenets of spirituality are shared by all Indigenous communities around world, even though there are different conceptualizations of spirituality among different Indigenous groups. Despite the fact that black Africans and Aboriginals live thousands of nautical miles away from each other, they share certain commonalities in their spiritual beliefs and practices which are founded on peaceful co-existence and respect for the Earth and all of its living and non-living creatures. These beliefs were lived in their daily ways of life—their rituals, the gathering of food and the institutionalization of authority.

> At the center of African spirituality was the unshakable belief that humans were but a weak link in the vast chain of nature, which encompassed the many animals, plants, birds, insects and worms and indeed inanimate things such as stone and rocks. The world was not for conquering, but for living within adorant harmony and reverence. (Wangoola, 2000, p. 265)

This quote demonstrates how Indigenous Africans, those not Westernized, believe that humans are linked to the earth, hence their continued existence depends on respect being accorded to the earth. Mutual respect in relationships is not limited only to humans but transcends to other objects and beings—such as plants, animals (both domesticated and wild) and stones. Trask (1991, p. 1199) echoes Hawaiian beliefs when she writes, "[N]ature was not objectified, but personified, resulting in an extra-ordinary respect (when compared to Western ideas of nature) for life of the sea, the forest, and the earth."

Respect for the lives of both animals and humans is accorded the highest priority by the Indigenous communities. The killing of animals was prohibited except in self-defense, to provide food for immediate sustenance or as sacrifice (Wangoola, 2000). In traditional African hunting and gathering societies, there are rules and regulations that govern their practices to ensure sustainability and cosmic balance in nature. For instance, the African practice of totems ensures that each clan or tribe has a particular animal that is fiercely protected to prevent extinction of that animal. Also, traditional rules and regulations forbid individuals from killing pregnant animals, animals nurturing younger ones or wastage through harvesting more than required. If a hunter or an individual kills an animal mistakenly through a process that contravenes traditional values and norms, respect must be shown by first rebuking the person involved and performing rituals to appease the animal family (Wangoola, 2000). For the Nishnaabeg, for instance, respect for animals is demonstrated by having symbolic treaties with animal nations (Simpson, 2008). Concerns about the wasting of deer, moose and caribou led to one of these treaties, thus intending to return the animals to their natural habitats and make themselves available for human sustenance once again:

> Honour and respect our lives and our beings, in life and in death. Cease doing what offends our spirits. Do not waste our flesh. Preserve field and forests for our homes. To show your commitment to these things and a remembrance of the anguish you have brought upon us, always leave tobacco leaf from where you take us. Gifts are important to build our relationship once again. (Simpson, 2008, p. 34)

This is one of the treaties that was respected and obeyed until the arrival of the colonizers. Mutual respect for both the animate and inanimate is lacking in the Western discourse, and perhaps this absence helped to orchestrate the racist ideologies which propelled the colonization of Indigenous people. Western science fetishizes Indigenous knowledge and practices, all too often entrenching human domination over the earth in order to meet capitalism's quest for profits. However, momentum is recently gathering among some critical scientists, including ethno-biologists, environmentalists and social activists, on the need to re-invigorate some of the Indigenous practices to address such issues as climate change, impact of industrial agriculture, commodification and desiccation of lands, the epidemic of chronic diseases and widening of the poverty gap between the rich and poor (Shiva, 1991; Via Campesina, 2009). These are the considerations that kept Indigenous people sustainable in their approach to life, often misconstrued as a lack of ability to subdue and control nature. An elderly woman of Kenyan descent registered her disdain for corporate farming practices when she opined how industrial agricultural practices affect the earth and alter the biosphere:

> What happens when you till the land over and over again? It shows you have no respect for the land. If you have no respect for the land, would you have respect for what grows on the land or people? I believe whatever education they are giving you is good education, but it is not complete education. You need to question the validity of what you are learning in relation not only to you, but also to your people, to us, to the land, to the plants and to the soil you are standing on. When you do that that will be complete education … maybe from that knowledge, you might find a way of bringing some equilibrium between the environment, people, Creator and the universe. (Nathani, 1996, p. 138)

These remarks emphasize the importance of according respect to the land in our farming practices. Land among Indigenous groups was not a commodity, regarded as a source of life for all. Monture-Angus (1999, cited in Smith, 2012) argues that calling for Indigenous sovereignty does not mean having control over the land; instead, it is about how to live responsibly *to* and *with* the land:

> Although Aboriginal people maintain a close relationship with the land … it is not about control of the land. … Earth is mother and she nurtures us all. … It is human race that is dependent on the earth and not vice versa … Sovereignty, when defined as my right to be responsible … requires a relationship with territory (and not a relation based on control of territory). … [W]hat must be understood then is that the Aboriginal request to have our sovereignty respected is really a request to be responsible. I do not know of anywhere else in history where a group of people have had to fight so hard just to be responsible. (Monture-Angus 1999, quoted in Smith, 2012, p. 83)

This respect for the Creator, the earth and all creatures that live therein makes it a responsibility for black Africans and all Indigenous groups in Canada to join together in decolonization struggles. The Aboriginal campaigns for sovereignty and decolonization must be seen as a means of restoring the respect for the earth, which is the responsibility of all Indigenous groups regardless of where they find themselves. This is the politics of liberation, not the politics of recognition (Cannon & Sunseri, 2011).

"When two elephants fight, it is the grasses that suffer." Taking inspiration from this Ghanaian Akan proverb, let us paraphrase it to say, "When two racialized groups compete for marginality, it glorifies and gives credence to white supremacy." This does not mean to remain mute when our actions and inactions oppress each other, but we must consider the likely advantages that will accrue to white supremacy when struggles escalate. A new coalition is needed, one that is more focused on changing the social order through resisting how white supremacy, patriarchy and capitalism reproduce colonial relations in both overt and more subtle ways. Though shared oppressions can be compelling reasons to bring people together, their efforts and energies should be directed to the goals of eradicating colonialism, racism, classism, ableism and all forms of oppression. We should draw from the intersections of race, gender, class, and ableism to challenge ongoing colonization in Canada. Aboriginal studies and anti-racism studies may not start from the same entry points, but both aim to dislodge colonialism, white supremacy, patriarchy and capitalism. It will better serve the interests of society to direct our arrows to dislodge these forms of domination and oppression and their rippling effects on humanity and the environment.

CONCLUSION

This chapter explored the relationship between Aboriginals and the "settlers of color"—black Africans inhabiting North America. It is worth emphasizing that neither black Africans nor Aboriginals are passive victims of European exploitation, marginalization and racialization. The race to innocence only gives credence to white supremacy. Indigenous struggle for decolonization should focus on the politics of liberation rather than fighting for marginality and identification within a white supremacist world. However, black Africans should see it as a responsibility to help restore the respect for the earth through joining decolonization struggles in the spirit of Indigeneity. We in the academy should be cautious not to re-invigorate the antagonistic relationship that white supremacy has sought to imbue in us in the past. We should be mindful of how colonialists had pitted us against each other to develop a regrettable relationship. One such example can be found in Guyana, when Mary Noel Menezes (cited in Jackson, 2012, p. 19) troublingly recalled, "[The] Dutch respected indigenous rights to the land because of trade and defense. The Dutch established a practice of remunerating them for capturing runaway enslaved peoples which included payment of 20 fl. for the hand of a Negro killed while resisting capture." There were also reported cases in which black buffalo soldiers were used to advance settler colonialism (Billington, 1991). Both acts were regrettable, and are not acts we want to repeat. Aboriginals provided the needed home to black Africans while the black Africans lived with them as relatives who shared in their struggle and marginalization. This was captured in Red Bird Investment[2] (quoted in Miles & Holland, 2006, p. 6) when they wrote, "Reverend Jason Meyer, an officer in the African Methodist Episcopal Church stated: 'this is to certify that I have made a personal visit to Indian Territory, and know it to be the best place on earth for the Negro'" (Red Bird Investment, 1905, quoted in Miles & Holland, 2006, p. 6). We can build on this good relationship and begin to theorize how we can use our past experiences to form a workable coalition that is grounded on Indigenous sovereignty, restoring the dignity of the land we live on and ensuring social equity in terms of the law, race, gender, ability, class and culture.

NOTES

1. The Berger Inquiry, also known as the Mackenzie Valley Pipeline Inquiry, was headed by Justice Thomas Berger. This 1974 Canadian commission did not recommend the construction of a pipeline through the northern Yukon and Mackenzie Valley. Testimonies from Indigenous communities would play a key role in this decision.

2. The Red Bird Investment Company was formed in Red Bird, Oklahoma. Located along the MKT (Missouri-Kansas-Texas) railroad line north of Muskogee, the company wanted to recruit people of colour to settle in a newly created all-black town. In 1905, the company published a brochure to dispel the negative perceptions that people held about the Indian Territory and encourage people to move to Red Bird, even inviting black professionals across the Cree Nation to give testimony of their experiences living in Indian Territory. In addition to the letter from the Reverend Jason Meyer, an officer in the African Methodist Episcopal Church, as noted above, comments from a physician, Dr. J. M. Davis from Muskogee, Indian Territory, were also featured, adding: "[T]his country is the paradise for the colored man" (Red Bird Investment Company, 1905, p. 36, quoted in Miles & Holland, 2006, p. 6).

REFERENCES

Adjei, P. B. (2007). Decolonizing knowledge production: The pedagogic relevance of Gandhian Satyagraha to schooling and education in Ghana. *Canadian Journal of Education, 30*(4), 1046–1067.

Albritton, R. (2012). Two great food revolutions: The domestication of nature and the transgression of nature's limits. In M. Koc, J. Sumner, & A. Winson (Eds.), *Critical perspectives in food studies*. Toronto, Canada: Oxford University Press.

Amadahy, Z., & Lawrence, B. (2009). Indigenous people and black people in Canada: Settlers or allies? In A. Kempf (Ed.), *Breaching the colonial contract*. Rotterdam, the Netherlands: Springer.

Berdyaev, N. (1939). *Spirit and reality*. London, England: Centenary Press.

Billington, M. L. (1991). *New Mexico's buffalo soldiers, 1866–1900*. Boulder: University Press of Colorado.

Brands, H. W., Breen, T. H., Williams, R. H., & Gross, A. J. (2011). *American stories: A history of the United States* (2nd ed., Vol. 1). Upper Saddle River, NJ: Pearson.

Brauer, G., Collard, M. & Stringer, C. (2004). On the reliability of recent tests of the out of Africa hypothesis for modern human origins. *The Anatomical Record Part A, 279A*: Wiley-Liss, Inc.701–707.

Cajete, G. (1994). *Look to the mountain: An ecology of Indigenous education*. Hong Kong: Skyland Press.

Cannon, M. J. (2012). Changing the subject in teacher education: Centering Indigenous, diasporic, settler colonial relationships. *Cultural and Pedagogical Inquiry, 4*(2), 21–37.

Cannon, M. J., & Sunseri, L. (Eds.). (2011). *Racism, colonialism, and Indigeneity in Canada: A reader.* Toronto, Canada: Oxford University Press.

Chaffers, J. (1994, May 25). *Spirituality—the missing "i" in mass product(i)on: Or why "mass quality" need not be an oxymoron. Conference proceedings of the Association of Collegiate Schools of Architecture European conference* "The Urban Scene and the History of the Future," London.

Coulthard, G. C. (2014). *Red skin, white masks: Rejecting the colonial politics of recognition.* Minneapolis: University of Minnesota Press.

Darko, I. N. (2014). We need to talk, and act in solidarity: Canadian Aboriginals and African immigrants in coalition. In A. Asabere-Ameyaw, J. Anamuah-Mensah, G. J. S. Dei, & K. Raheem (Eds.), *Indigenist African development and related issues: Towards a transdisciplinary perspective* (pp. 203–216). New York, NY: Peter Lang.

Dei, G. J. S. (1996). *Anti-racism education: Theory and practice.* Halifax, Canada: Fernwood.

Dei, G. J. S. (2014, Winter). Comment made in Principles of Anti-Racism class. OISE, University of Toronto, Canada.

Dei, G. J. S. (in press). *[Re]Theorizing blackness and anti-blackness from anti-colonial and decolonial prisms.* New York, NY: Springer.

Dei, G. J. S., James, I. M., Karumanchery, L. L., James-Wilson, S., & Zine, J. (2000). *Removing the margins: The challenges and possibilities of inclusive schooling.* Toronto, Canada: Canadian Scholars' Press.

Fanon, F. (1963). *The wretched of the earth.* New York, NY: Grove.

Fellows, M. L., & Razack, S. (1998). The race to innocence: Confronting hierarchical relationships among women. *Journal of Race, Gender and Justice, 1,* 335–352.

Herzl, T. (1941). *Old–new land* [Altneuland] (p. 32). L. Levensohn (Trans.). New York, NY: M. Wiener. (Original work published 1902)

Hill, R. W. (2009). Rothihnahon:tsi and Rotinonhson: ni: Historic relationships between African Americans and the confederacy of the Six Nations. In G. Tayac (Ed.), *Indivisible: African-Native American lives in the Americas* (pp. 99–107). Washington, DC: Smithsonian Books.

Jackson, S. N. (2012). *Creole Indigeneity: Between myth and nation in the Caribbean.* Minneapolis: University of Minnesota Press.

Jagers, R., & Smith, P. (1996). Further examination of the spirituality scale. *Journal of Black Psychology, 22,* 429–442.

Kapoor, D., & Shizha, E. (Eds.). (2010). *Indigenous knowledge and learning in Asia/Pacific and Africa: Perspectives on development, education and culture.* New York, NY: Palgrave Macmillan.

Klopotek, B. (2009). Of shadows and doubts: Indigeneity and white supremacy. In G. Tayac (Ed.), *Indivisible: African-Native American lives in the Americas* (pp. 85–90). Washington, DC: Smithsonian Books.

Kulchyski, P. (Ed.). (1994). *Unjust relationships: Aboriginal rights in Canadian court.* New York, NY: Oxford University Press.

Kus, R. J. (1992). Spirituality in everyday life: Experiences of gay men of Alcoholics Anonymous [Special issue]. *Journal of Chemical Dependency Treatment, 5*(1), 49–66.

Lawrance, B., & Dua, E. (2005). Decolonization anti-racism. *Social Justice, 32*(4), 120–143.

MacQuarrie, J. (1972). *Paths in spirituality.* London, England: SCM Press.

Mamdani, M. (2001). Beyond settler and native as political identities. Overcoming the political legacy of colonialism. *Comparative Studies in Society and History, 43*(4), 651–664

Mattis, J. S. (2000). African American women's definitions of spirituality and religiosity. *Journal of Black Psychology, 26*(1), 102–122.

Miles, T., & Holland, S. (2006). *Crossing the waters, crossing worlds: The African diaspora in Indian country.* Durham, NC: Duke University Press.

Nathani, N. (1996). *Sustainable development: Indigenous forms of food processing technologies. A Kenyan case study* (Unpublished doctoral dissertation). University of Toronto, Canada.

Nwomonoh, J. (Ed.). (1998). *Education and development in Africa: A contemporary survey.* San Francisco, CA: International Scholars Publications.

Nyamnjoh, F. (2012). "Potted plants in greenhouses": A critical reflection on the resilience of colonial education in Africa. *Journal of Asian and African Studies, 47*, 129–154.

Pateman, C. (2007). The settler contract. In C. Pateman & C. Mills (Eds.), *Contract and domination.* Cambridge, England: Polity Press.

Potts, R. (1991). Spirits in the bottle: Spirituality and alcoholism treatment in African-American communities. *Journal of Training & Practice in Professional Psychology, 5*(1), 53–64.

Sanderson, D. (2011). Against supersession. *Canadian Journal of Law and Jurisprudence, 24*, 155–182.

Schlosberg, D. (2013). Theorizing environmental justice: The expanding sphere of a discourse. *Environmental Politics, 22*(1), 37–55.

Sexton, J. (2010). People-of-colour-blindness: Note on the afterlife of slavery. *Social Text 103, 28*(2), 31–56.

Shahjahan, R. A. (2005). Spirituality in the academy: Reclaiming from the margins and evoking a transformative way of knowing the world. *International Journal of Qualitative Studies in Education, 18*(6), 685–711.

Sharma, N., & Wright, C. (2009). Decolonizing resistance: Challenging colonial states. *Social Justice, 35*(3), 120–138.

Shiva, V. (1991). *The violence of the Green Revolution: Third World agriculture, ecology and politics.* London, England: Zed Books.

Shizha, E. (2012). Linguistic independence and African education and development. In H. K. Wright & A. A. Abdi (Eds.), *The dialectics of African education and Western discourses: Counter-hegemonic perspectives* (pp. 148–162). New York, NY: Peter Lang.

Shizha, E. (2013). Reclaiming our Indigenous voices: The problem with postcolonial sub-Saharan African school curriculum. *Journal of Indigenous Social Development, 2*(1), 1–18.

Simpson, L. (2000). Anishinaabe ways of knowing. In R. Oakes, R. Riewe, S. Koolage, L. Simpson, & N. Schuster (Eds.), *Aboriginal health, identity and resources* (pp. 165–185). Winnipeg, Canada: Native Studies Press.

Simpson, L. (2008). Looking after Gdoo-naaganinaa: Pre-colonial Nishnaabeg diplomatic and treaty relationships. *Wicazo Sa Review, 23*(2), 29–42.

Smith, A. (2012). Indigeneity, settler colonialism, white supremacy. In D. M. HoSang, O. LaBennett, & L. Pulido (Eds.), *Racial formation in the twenty-first century* (pp. 66–90). Berkeley: University of California Press.

Smith, L. (1992, Winter). Lost in America. *Border/Lines, 23*, 17–10.

Smith, L. (1999). *Decolonizing Methodologies: Research and Indigenous Peoples.* Dunedin: Zed Books and University of Otago Press.

Snelgrove, C., Dhamoon, R. K., & Corntassel, J. (2014). Unsettling settler colonialism: The discourse and politics of settlers, and solidarity with Indigenous nations. *Decolonization: Indigeneity, Education & Society, 3*(2), 1–32.

St. Denis, V. (2007). Aboriginal education and anti-racist education: Building alliances across cultural and racial identity. *Canadian Journal of Education, 30*(4), 1068–1092.

Stringer, C. & McKie, R. (1996). *African exodus: The origins of modern humanity.* New York: Henry Holt.

Trask, H. (1991). Coalition building between natives and non-natives. *Stanford Law Review, 43*(6), 1197–1213.

Tuck, E., & Yang, K. W. (2012). Decolonization is not a metaphor. *Decolonization, Indigeneity, Education and Society, 1*(1), 1–40.

Via Campesina. (2009). Massiva Proteta en defense de la verdera democracia en Honduras [Press release]. Retrieved from http://viacampesina.org/sp/index.php?option=com_content&view=article&rod&itemid=29

Wane, N. (2002). African women and spirituality: Connections between thought and action. In E. O'Sullivan, A. Morrell, & M. A. O'Connor (Eds.), *Expanding the boundaries of transformative learning: Essays on theory and praxis* (pp. 135–150). New York, NY: Palgrave Macmillan.

Wangoola, P. (2000). Mpambo, the African multiversity: A philosophy to rekindle the African spirit. In G. J. S. Dei, B. Hall, & D. G. Rosenberg (Eds.), *Indigenous knowledges in global contexts: Multiple readings of our world*. Toronto, Canada: University of Toronto Press.

Wolfe, P. (2006). Settler colonialism and elimination of the native. *Journal of Genocide Research, 8*(4), 387–409.

CHAPTER TEN

Objects OF Settlement

Excavating Colonial Narratives

MISCHA BERLIN[1]

Archaeological excavation has played a central role in the construction of historical narratives across various settler-colonial contexts. The 'neutral' and sanitized scientific analyses of historical artifacts produce narratives of dominance that enact and enable colonial dispossession. Anibal Quijano (2007) and Audra Simpson (2007) provide insight into the ways in which 'neutral language' is constitutive of coloniality. Coloniality, in turn, works to conceal violence by disavowing its own interest in upholding scientific discourse. This chapter looks at the ways in which archaeology and anthropology are complicit in—and constitutive of—settler-colonial narratives that obscure the presence and vitality of Indigenous communities.

Looking at archaeology in Palestine and Ontario will shed light on how scientific discourses serve colonial interests in disparate contexts. The chapter takes up the work of Nadia Abu El-Haj (2001), who analyzes the ways archaeology serves settler-colonial narratives in Palestine, looking at how Jewish histories are upheld within a teleology that is founded on the erasure of Palestinian Indigeneity. In Ontario, archaeology serves to locate Indigenous 'culture' and peoples within a past that is, as Sherene Razack (2012, p. 908) has argued, "intrinsically vulnerable." Understanding how coloniality dialectically informs archaeological discourses, this discussion looks at the politics of repatriation of Indigenous artifacts that have surfaced over the past two and a half decades. In Canada, the reconciliatory politics of recognition have recently come to define the relationship between Indigenous peoples and the federal government. This discourse continues to elide alternative epistemological and ontological systems, and to further entrench colonial sovereignty. Drawing from the insights of Dei and Kempf (2006), Simpson

(2007, 2014) and Coulthard (2007, 2009), the discussion contends that there may be space for resurgent politics within colonial institutions such as museums. The effects of resurgent politics, however, should be measured against dynamics of colonial power.

PART I: THE COLONIAL UNIVERSAL AND OBJECTS OF INDIGENEITY REPRESENTING WHITENESS

Colonial forms of domination are integrally tied to the totalizing epistemology that legitimates and naturalizes violence. Anibal Quijano (2007, p. 169) maintains that coloniality has reshaped "the modes of knowing, of producing knowledge, of producing perspectives, images and systems of images, symbols, modes of signification, over the resources, patterns, and instruments of formalized and objectivised expression, intellectual or visual." Over centuries of enacting European hegemony, Quijano (2007, p. 169) notes, "European culture became a universal cultural model."

Dichotomies between subject and object introduced during the European Enlightenment, distinguished between a knowing subject and the objects of knowing. For Quijano (2007, p. 172), this dichotomy conceals the inter-subjective "social totality as the production sites of all knowledge." Instead, the subject, an "isolated individual," was constituted "in itself and for itself, in its discourse and in its capacity of reflection." Accordingly, the object was untethered from the social processes that dynamically and dialectically produce meaning (p. 172).

These binaries are profoundly racialized. They entail a disavowal of embodied knowledge and a subordination of the object to the dominant and knowing subject. As such, European scientific epistemology was fashioned free from the constitutive and meaning-making processes of other peoples' 'traditions' and dogmas. The transcendent subjectivity is constituted against the racialized, and always marked, other. Quijano (2007, pp. 173–174) maintains that cultural "differences were admitted primarily above all as inequalities in the hierarchical sense. And such inequalities are perceived as being of nature: only European culture is rational, it can contain 'subjects'—the rest are not rational, they cannot be or harbor 'subjects.'" Hierarchies abound within this totalizing epistemology.

Representations of the static native body are necessary for the production of transcendent settler-subjects. In *Black Body: Women, Colonialism, and Space*, Radhika Mohanram (1999) takes up the violence inherent in modes of objectification—how the knowing subject represents the black body. What does the skin tell us? To answer this question, Mohanram turns to Frantz Fanon. Black skin, for Fanon, signals an 'amputation,' where "a representation of him also makes him disappear" in his skin. Fanon—imagined as the black body—is over-determined by the white subject. Mohanram (1999, p. 26) observes, "The black man is pure representation for Fanon."

Representation within fields of colonial power destroys epistemological and ontological specificity. Representation itself stands in for the lived and emplaced, erasing the singular and substituting the general. As a process of naturalization it requires a continual disavowal by the dominant subject. The dialectics of race and representation are markedly unstable. Representation, as a step toward producing the racialized other, needs to be enacted, materially and discursively. The science of cultural representation, anthropology and the sub-discipline of archaeology, that seeks to know the Indigenous other, is integral to the production of whiteness and settler-subjectivity.

THE OBJECT AND THE ANTHROPOLOGIST

Historically, anthropologists' work has been to observe and document so-called traditional cultures. These observations, Audra Simpson has argued, both flatten and reify, reducing complex human structures to that which is documentable. Simpson (2007, p. 67) contends traditional peoples were compartmentalized into "neat, ethnically-defined territorial spaces that now needed to be made sense of, to be ordered, ranked, to be governed, to be possessed." As Quijano (2007) argued, the construction of the objective observer, the scientist, obscures the dynamic production of culture by people who are historically, temporally and spatially located. In settler-colonial contexts, representations of static and superstitious cultures enable the dislocation of bodies, imagined as timeless and thus placeless.

Simpson traces the objectification of Indigenous peoples and societies in settler-colonial contexts. Observable Iroquois traditions were abstracted in anthropological writing from the bodies that performed them and the land on which they were performed. 'Traditions' and 'culture' stand in for embodied and emplaced ontology. Anthropological imaginings helped construct the colonial narrative of a 'vanishing Indian,' one relegated to the amorphous pre-history that was being overturned by European modernity. Simpson (2014, p. 73) argues that anthropologists sought to document Iroquois traditions that

> seemed to lack ... a culture unambiguously connected to the places they lived upon. The Iroquois culture that appeared to them had a wholeness and stability, patterned into ritualized practices that were both intelligible to outsiders and appeared to be in jeopardy of being lost. Anthropological work on the Iroquois has fixed upon intelligibility, cultural pattern, and persistence, that which is clearly discernible to outsiders. This tendency has led to an agenda of research that has rendered meaningless any elements of culture that appeared familiar to the Western eye, or culturally anomalous to outsiders, ignoring those processes that might be meaningful to insiders but unintelligible to outsiders.

Anthropological observations flattened and objectified Iroquois culture, enabling a discursive erasure of the complex processes that give definition to ontologies and epistemologies. As Indigenous and settler economies became increasingly inter-dependent, the 'traditions' and artifacts that the settlers valued were produced and used as currency for trade.

Anthropological representations produce the discursive and material violence indelibly linked to settler-colonial ways of knowing. Complexity, diversity and dynamism that are spatially and temporally located are erased, producing static and abstracted cultures, empty lands and pre-modern peoples. Indigenous bodies themselves were imagined to represent a 'pre-history' that could only be held on to, documented and understood by the colonial eyes of the anthropologist; Indig-enous ways of knowing, transferring and embodying knowledge were quickly and inevitably vanishing.

UNCOVERING AND RAZING

Archaeology, a sub-discipline of anthropology, has similarly produced reified Indigenous pre/histories: uncovering objects, transporting them to the lab, and asking them to tell stories of past peoples and dead traditions. In diverse contexts, objects are uncovered, analysed and 'read' as representations of the settler-colonial present. Looking at two seemingly opposing contexts, in Palestine and in Ontario, this discussion hopes to unearth the violence implicit in the act of archaeological discovery.

Nadia Abu El-Haj (2001) has documented the process of uncovering Zionist narratives in Palestine, narrating a Jewish presence, embodied and augmented by the State of Israel—a metonym for the Jewish present. Zionism, imagined as the telos of Judaism, has meant Jewish claims to the past are embodied in the present. Modernity is interwoven with historical narratives in Jerusalem, presented as a 'multi-cultural' space, with Jewish cultural hegemony and presence as its defining feature.

Abu El-Haj (2001) traces the Zionist, state-centred historiography of mod-ern Jerusalem, written atop the ongoing erasure of the indigenous Palestinian population. The spaces of the Old City engender a narrative that entangles Juda-ism and the State; the former gives a sense of legitimacy and continuity to the latter that is continually positioned as *the* manifestation of the Jewish modern. The Wailing Wall and the plaza juxtapose the ancient and the modern. Else-where, the historical plays backstage to the Jewish presence/present. As Abu El-Haj (2001, p. 185) describes, "The present inhabits the past, thereby giving one a sense that this is not merely a contemporary city, but rather one that is built upon the foundations of a past whose traditions it perpetuates and within which it remains firmly embedded. ... The past is not merely monumentalized ... it is resurrected."

The plaza adjacent to the Wailing Wall was constructed on the land of the Maghrabia (Moroccan) Quarter, razed in 1967 by Israeli forces.[2] The Maghrabia Quarter, notes Abu El-Haj (2001, p. 165), established in 1193, was "inhabited by Muslim families [and] had long stood adjacent to the wall."[3] Today, the vast open space of the plaza stands in juxtaposition to the narrow, winding alleys of Jerusalem's Old City. The erasure of indigenous spaces centres a Jewish history—and present—in Jerusalem. As Benvenisti (1996, p. 82), an Israeli historian, describes it: "the former space in front of the Wall could not have accommodated the 400,000 people who swarmed to the site [after the 1967 occupation]; the maximum number able to pray there during the period of the mandate was 12,000 per day." As both a tourist attraction and religious site, the plaza is emblematic of the Zionist narratives that take Jewish presence to be a dynamic and living force in a city punctuated by the past and emboldened by the present.

In Palestine, Zionist historiography authorizes the present. Abu El-Haj (2001, pp. 188–189) notes that particular artifacts live and tell "specific histories that the present restores and completes. ... [I]t is a story produced through the choices made regarding which historical remainders to preserve, to level, and to display and what stories they would tell." George Dei and Arlo Kempf (2006, p. 309) have urged, "for those against whom education has been used as a weapon and as a tool of dispossession, anti-colonialism calls for the invocation of one's past and thus place within the present and future." In Palestine, it is the hegemony of Zionism that entrenches the settler-colonial "place within the present and future" of Palestine.

For the many others, whose stories are subsumed under either the Jewish narrative (marginalized Jewish communities) or the narrative of the 'multicultural' and liberal Israeli-state, (non-Jewish communities, ever present in the plethora of prominent monuments, religious sites and people) their histories are immaterial, and their bodies are symbolic. They are represented as part of a narrative that meets past and present in a teleology that is structured by Zionist historiography. The multicultural city of Jerusalem represents a Zionism that is rooted in the present, as much as it is in the past. Zionism is imagined as a foundation of *the* Jewish present.

Archaeologists, like anthropologists, are not merely describing but representing history. Just as the Iroquois rehearsed traditions to satisfy and profit from settler-colonial objectification that marked their bodies for extinction, so the land of Palestine is contested to represent the inevitability of the Jewish present. The histories of settler-colonialism in both cases elide extant indigenous communities.

UNCOVERING AND RELEGATING: PRODUCING THE
PAST IN ONTARIO AND SETTLER-SUBJECTS

Archaeological excavation in Ontario has worked to inscribe colonial narratives that create a division between a variegated European history and a monolithic Indigenous pre-history. The concise, 119-page work, modestly titled *Ontario Prehistory: An Eleven-Thousand-Year Archaeological Outline*, by J. V. Wright is one such example. In it, Wright maintains that Ontario's history can be divided according to archaeological evidence into "four periods: the Palaeo-Indian period (9000 B.C.–5000 B.C.), the Archaic period (5000 B.C.–1000 B.C.), the Initial Woodland Period (1000 B.C.-1000 A.D.), and the Terminal Woodland period (1000 A.D. - to the historic period)." The latter period, Wright (1972, p. 7) notes, "Ends shortly after the appearance of the French and English who *introduce* [emphasis added] the historic period." The "historic period" does not appear in the book. Just as anthropological interest in Iroquois peoples elided the colonial conditions of their study, so too do archaeologists distinguish a pure and static pre-history from the complex historical moment that began with settler-contact. Europeans 'introduce' the complexity associated with civilization. The Indigenous past is thus constructed *of* the past, and extant Indigenous peoples and their histories are positioned outside of civilization. Archaeological tools extinguish Indigenous epistemology and ontology, relegated to objects left behind.

While Wright (1972, p. 7) acknowledges these periods are "artificial devices" that "slice up the time column," he maintains that "each period … does possess certain characteristics which differentiate it from the other periods." Accordingly, Wright (1972, p. 3) describes the work of archaeologists who "above everything else … must attempt to know and understand man." Slicing up time—by slicing up land—allows for the explanatory analysis of the archaeologist who effaces ontology in the service of objective understanding. Furthermore, 'man' as a universal category provides legitimacy for scientific man to speak authoritatively about 'his' pre-history. Artifacts and monuments narrate settler-colonial presence in Jerusalem by way of elision. In Ontario, the past is invoked as a radical other, devoid of humanity precisely where humans have left traces. In both spaces, the past is made intelligible with modern concepts and tools. The implications of objectification are immaterial.

Pre-histories in Ontario are mechanical and material. In stark contrast to the history of Jerusalem, animated by biblical figures and politics that live on in the State, archaeology in Canada takes up environmental conditions that explain perceived changes of pre-historic existence. In the case of the 'Paleo-Indian'—known as the Clovis and the Plano—who spread into North America, Wright (1972, p. 13) observes, changes in traditions and customs are "in response to local conditions and increasing population densities." While teleology is read in both Canada and Jerusalem, the story is markedly different. Indigenous histories in Canada are causally determined. Indigenous peoples, like the environment, are to be documented, categorized and tamed by the civilizing tools of modernity.

Similar conceptions are formulated in a book by a renowned archaeologist, Walter Kenyon. *Mounds of Sacred Earth: Burial Mounds of Ontario* is an investigation of the burial mounds dug up in Treaty #3 territory. Kenyon (1986, p. 76) describes, with the technical specificity of a scientist, the mounds that are integrally and "functionally related to food productions." Kenyon (p. 78) makes a connection between the mounds in Ontario to similar ones found in Europe "during the post-mesolithic period … because both groups were involved in the same social processes." The divergence—observed in found instruments and artifacts—is read as the inevitable development from the "palaeolithic hunter and gatherer to a neolithic farmer." Europe, imagined to have developed to a more 'complex' horticultural society, is positioned against "much of the world" where "the process was never completed" (p. 79). While 'man' populated both Europe and Canada, in the latter, he never did master his environment. Bodies here are stripped of their ontological specificity, depicted as objects of history for whom environmental factors shape destiny. As is exemplified in the discussion of the Clovis and Plano, pre-historic peoples are imagined as the products of nature. These pre-historic societies are depicted as stagnant and those that inhabit them are without civilization, where being is 'ritualistic' and mechanistic, devoid of the agency of civilized man.

Dei and Asgharzadeh's (2001, p. 301) critique of post-colonial discourse is instructive for decoding archaeological scientific discourse. As is the case in post-colonial critiques, for Kenyon (1986) indigenous peoples' "histories … [are] strictly in demarcated stages: that is, periodization into … epochs" (p. 301). Variation is seen only between epochs. Earnestly echoing Dei and Asgharzadeh's criticism, Kenyon (1986, p. 79) notes:

> The palaeolithic hunter and gatherer inhabited a world that was essentially static. It had been shaped by mythological forces; and its functioning from day to day, and from season to season, was sustained by a complex set of rituals and taboos that most of us would describe as mechanical.

The paleolithic hunter and gatherer is influenced, without influencing. Rituals riddled with taboos meant his world was decidedly different from our own, "in the hierarchical sense" (Quijano, 2007, p. 174). While our tools provide insight into others' worlds, pre-historic tools represent a static existence.

Kenyon (1986, p. 80) contemplates skulls uncovered from another site in Northwestern Ontario:

> Openings in their occipital regions are reasonably clear evidence of power transfer. The individuals whose skulls were opened would have had some unusual and highly valued

personal characteristics: occipital openings made it possible to remove their brains. …
[T]his would have been accomplished through a religious ceremony that included eating
the brain that was the seat of such wondrous powers.

Again, culture is read through objects, and presented objectively. That these observations provide "reasonably clear evidence" of ceremonies and traditions is a neutral and objective claim. Kenyon merely represents peoples whose 'traditions' are from an*other* time. The past tense and the fact of excavation speak to this prehistory. The imagined ceremonies speak to the cannibalistic cultures of prehistoric man—a culture that is of the past.

Europeans bring Ontario "from prehistory to history" (Wright, 1972, p. 108). The importance of uncovering and documenting a prehistory is due to the imagined inevitable destruction entailed by the colonial present. The archaeologist— described by Wright (p. 3) as a "jack of all trades"—is positioned as the only interpreter of this vanishing pre-history. He masterfully constitutes a truth of the past through his knowledge of the complicated world that is grounded in the objectivity afforded to modern men. The trained scientist is tasked with compiling the "fragmented and vague evidence left by prehistoric man" (Wright, 1972, p. 3).

The violence here is not limited to representation and objectification. Rather, archaeological digs in both Canada and Israel have been sites of dispossession and continue to be contested by Indigenous populations. The sacred space, alluded to in the title of Kenyon's work, can be traversed and excavated because those who once called them sacred are presumed to have vanished. However, one such sacred space is the site of ongoing legal battles between the Anishinaabeg of Rainy River and the town of Fort Frances. As Chief of Couchiching First Nations Sara Mainville describes it, "It's land that was considered sacred to the local First Nations because there were, in the past, people buried there. … [I]t 'has a significant spiritual value'" (Hicks, 2015, n.p.). The mounds had, according to a report drafted for the Grand Council Treaty #3, been desecrated by looters and antiquarians after they were wrested from Anishinaabeg control in the early part of the century (Grand Council Treaty #3, 2000, pp. 14–15). The report identifies Kenyon (1986, p. 15) as having uncovered some nine thousand artifacts. It does so in its attempts to establish Anishinaabeg title to the land.

Chief Mainville is asserting the Anishinaabeg title to the land. Evidently, white settlement has not succeeded in absolute dislocation or dispossession. And yet, in Kenyon's records of the mounds there is no acknowledgment of those extant peoples who hold title to the lands. On the contrary, in his acknowledgments section, Kenyon (1986, p. ix) singles out "property owners … [who] graciously permitted me to excavate burial mounds on their properties." They are evidently not the Anishinaabeg of Treaty #3.

In both Palestine and Ontario, archaeological interpretations serve projects of settler-colonial dispossession. In Jerusalem, Jewish history is made present within the logics of modernity, reified in the material destruction of bodies and objects that attest to that place as a settler-colonial project. In Palestine, discourses of Jewish re-indigenization justify the destructive project. In Canada, Indigeneity is restricted to the past. By relegating Anishinaabeg peoples to history, sovereignty is enacted by settler society. In Canada, uncovering 'objects' of history means that history is objectified. Archaeology is articulated within and is productive of settler-colonial narratives. Abu El-Haj draws our attention to the ways archaeology is dialectically constitutive of coloniality. Abu El-Haj (2001, p. 277) contends coloniality is defined by archaeological "processes and practices out of which particular configurations of settler nationhood and its territorial locales were continuously substantiated and repeatedly expanded." With the strength of scientific—objective and totalized—truth, archaeologists rewrite contested and embodied histories in the abstract—singular and absolute.

PART II: THE POLITICS OF REPATRIATION

The politics of resurgent Indigeneity is often dismissed as romantic and static, unrealistic or idealistic. Reflecting on the narratives and histories constructed by archaeology, such critiques may better be leveled against settler-colonial narratives.

The exploitative histories by which archaeologists and museums accumulated Indigenous artifacts in Canada have become a point of increasing contention. Indigenous communities have drawn attention to the complicity of Canadian museums in ongoing genocide. The Truth and Reconciliation Commission of Canada (TRC), established to examine the Residential School legacy, made numerous recommendations to address this complicity, including "e) Repatriating, on request, objects that are sacred or integral to the history and continuity of particular nations and communities; f) Returning human remains to the family, community or nation of origin, on request, or consulting with Aboriginal advisers on appropriate disposition, where remains cannot be associated with a particular nation" (TRC, 2015, pp. 247–248).

Calls for repatriation have unearthed settler anxieties, once allayed by lacquered plaques on glass cases. These anxieties play centre stage in the drama of colonial repatriation. Those who are supportive of repatriation initiatives assure museum-going populations that "none of the repatriation policies would result in the wholesale transfer of all aboriginal artifacts in museums to First Nations communities" (CBC News Online, 2006, n.p.). The TRC has taken up museums as "places where a nation's history is presented in neutral, objective terms." The TRC notes the role of museums in archiving and representing national narratives that are embedded in the "architecture of imperialism" (TRC, 2015, p. 246).

Several theorists have warned that shifting colonial dynamics may work to reconstitute and reify, not cede, power (Coulthard, 2007). Let us carefully consider the ways in which colonial dynamics continue to impact repatriation. Julia Emberley considers how changes in museum policies are part of liberal universalizing epistemologies—the ones that were at the core of Quijano's (2007) colonial critique. Emberley (2006, p. 389) argues, "Liberalism maintains the view that the institutional structures of society—be they juridical, political, social and/or cultural—should remain firmly intact while the ideology of liberal universalism demands the enfranchisement of all possible social actors who conform to its rational humanist project."

It is important, then, when considering any ostensibly progressive politics that we not take for granted the liberal "cosmopolitan values" as a signal of "emergent postcolonial power relations" (Phillips, 2011, p. 136). This is not meant to dismiss the space for resurgent politics within the parameters of repatriation. As Dei and Kempf argued, anti-colonialism does not simply seek to erase the present. Rather "it calls for a strategic approach" asking, "How might science, history and education as a whole be tools for decolonization?" (Dei & Kempf, 2006, p. 309).

Phillips (2011, p. 152) contends that repatriation in Canada allows for "the recovery of cultural knowledge … [through] access to traditional forms of material culture" which will doubtlessly play a role in resurgent politics. Furthermore, it may open up spaces for critical analyses of the privileged institutions of knowledge production. These efforts may well aid in the anti-colonial struggles that persist in Canada. Thus, by foregrounding the complicity of archaeology and museums in the maintenance of settler-colonialism, repatriation efforts may serve to de-stabilize hegemonic narratives.

Glen Coulthard has traced the emergence of reconciliatory politics. The period of social activism coinciding with the late 1970s and early 1980s saw ever more visible pressure from indigenous activists, because

> colonial power [was forced] to modify itself from a structure that was once primarily reinforced by policies, techniques, and ideologies explicitly oriented around the exclusion/assimilation double, to one that is now reproduced through a seemingly more conciliatory set of languages and practices that emphasize Indigenous recognition and accommodation. (Coulthard, 2009, pp. 9–10)

Coulthard argues present-day reconciliatory politics seek to fundamentally undercut this relationship that informs epistemologies of the land. By engaging in recognition politics, the state has strengthened settler sovereignty and pacified Indigenous resistance movements. Rather than cede land and power, "the reason the Crown agreed to get into the land claims business in the first place was to 'extinguish' the broad and undefined rights and title claims of First Nations in exchange for a limited set of rights and benefits set out in the text of the agreement itself" (Coulthard, 2009,

p. 10). To what extent do museums gain legitimacy and become sites of knowledge by virtue of their complicity in this destruction?

Centring the modes of epistemic erasure of settler-colonialism may open avenues for the de-stabilizing politics of the resurgent Indigeneity. Indeed, the important role of archaeology and anthropology in the making of settler-subjectivity and totalizing epistemologies will bring into relief entrenched modes of colonial erasure. We may ask, What would it mean for colonial narratives if all the artifacts were repatriated? That is, if Indigenous 'cultures' were not presented, and represented, in museums?

The need for museums to dispel settler anxieties and uphold reformatory rather than radical changes is instructive in understanding how the museum continues to impact and influence logics of colonialism in Canada. This is not to suggest that the repatriation of all Indigenous artifacts should be the goal of anti-colonial activists. However, our politics should draw on insights of Indigenous scholars such as Coulthard (2007) and Simpson (2007, 2014), who advocate refusing co-optation and silencing by liberal reconciliatory discourses.

Ruth Phillips's collection of essays, *Museum Pieces: Toward the Indigenization of Canadian Museums*, maps the changes that have allowed for repatriation agreements.[4] Museum policy changes follow the larger trend toward reconciliatory discourse, documented by Coulthard (2007). Coulthard urges a skeptical reading of reconciliatory politics. How might museums entrench legitimacy by engaging in discourses and acts of repatriation?

Ruth Phillips (2011, p. 134) critiques "repatriation advocates [who] argue that all Indigenous artifacts in museums … cannot be considered to have been voluntarily surrendered." These advocates champion the wholesale return of all artifacts to First Nations peoples. Phillips (pp. 134–135) argues this approach is ahistorical; it overlooks the ways "artifacts that have survived into the present because they were given, commissioned, or purchased 'put down roots' in their new places." Ostensibly, argues Phillips (p. 135), some objects, barring the complicated bureaucratic and legal task of returning them, live on in museums, and allow for new and dynamic interpretations "that offer highly effective sites for fostering the understanding and respect for diversity that is needed today, perhaps more than ever."

Phillips may be right in arguing for the legitimacy of some claims by museums. Nevertheless, thinking about the ways museums and archaeologists create space for 'understanding' that is rooted in a universalizing coloniality should not be overlooked. While Phillips (2011, pp. 92, 136) does recognize the "kinds of exclusions and inclusions historically created by the rigid separations and hierarchies of nature and culture," she highlights "a notable shift in public consciousness and emergent postcolonial power relations during the late twentieth century." Phillips's (2011, p. 99) focus on post-colonial notions of "the hybrid, transcultural, and the commodified" leads her to conclude that these "outdated notions of otherness" are being supplanted. There is a trend, she maintains (p. 154), away from "nine-teenth-century universalism" toward a "contemporary global consciousness." Who, in Phillips's account, is in need of 'understanding,' and who needs to be 'under-stood'? Either we ignore the colonial power dynamics, or we deny the lasting effects that representational politics have in the maintenance of colonial regimes.

In order to forgo teleological readings of the 'post-colony,' it is useful to exam-ine the ways repatriation is imagined by museum institutions. As is made evident in the Royal Ontario Museum's (ROM, 2012, p. 1) Board Policy on *Repatriation of Canadian Aboriginal Objects*, particular instances of malpractice continue to be abstracted and singled out. "The ROM recognizes that some objects may have been acquired in circumstances which render the ROM's title invalid." Indeed, similar sentiments are found in other museum policies across the country.[5] The ROM decides on "a case-by-case basis whether to return objects of cultural patri-mony" (ROM, 2012, p. 2). For the most part, Phillips (2011, p. 138) contends that repatriation requests are only considered for "members of the originating commu-nity and/or descendants of the original owners or makers."

The concern over genealogy and authenticity echoes the entrenched colonial logics that underwrite repatriation. Simpson (2014, p. 16) extensively analyzes the myriad effects of the "old Aristotelian problem of how to govern alterity, how to make sense of that which is not yours" that plague settler-Indigenous relationships. She looks to these technical questions that are governed by binaries of belonging and genealogy, problems that arise from the paradox of state sovereignty. As such, she uncovers the settler discourses of bloodline and blood quantum that serve to reinforce the 'atrophied representations' of Indigenous communities.

In the context of repatriation, procedural questions persist in entrenching set-tler-sovereignty by centring settler knowing. Museums present the problem of repatriation as a question of utilitarian equilibrium that "satisfied the largest num-ber of goals of both the Indigenous claimants and the archaeological researchers" (Phillips, 2011, p. 137). Questions about how museums, as objectifying spaces, themselves are served by Indigenous objects rarely surface. This equilibrium has meant some "Indigenous claimants in Canada" have been critical of "the process of repatriation" finding it "frustratingly slow and the number of returned objects disappointingly small" (Phillips, 2011, pp. 136–137).

Just as the reconciliatory politics served to circumscribe Indigenous land claims, repatriation is mired in the colonial politics of recognition. Following Coulthard's critique, discourses of repatriation may serve to circumscribe claims by avoiding questions about the multifaceted ways in which a totalizing epistemol-ogy is produced. Furthermore, questions of authenticity and legitimacy may reify representations of the vanishing Indigeneity.

Phillips is insistent that there is room in these institutions to work closely with Indigenous peoples. These institutions, as Dei and Asgharzadeh (2001) have pointed out, may allow for decolonial activism that ruptures the violent totalizing colonial epistemology. Phillips emphasizes the many ongoing projects that are currently reshaping Canadian institutions. Phillips (2011, p. 153) also recognizes the ways in which concepts of cosmopolitanism may serve "neo-imperial attempts to defend the current holdings of museums." Nevertheless, without engaging in a sustained anti-colonial critique, museums as privileged sites of knowledge will undoubtedly continue to serve colonial interests.

FROM THE LAND

Just as the state defines the discourse of land claims, and recognition, so too do institutions that maintain control over objects frame the politics of repatriation. Drawing on the insights from the work of scholars such as Coulthard (2007, 2009), Simpson (2007, 2014) and Abu El-Haj (2001), the current 'conciliatory' political climate continues to facilitate colonial sovereignty and Indigenous dispossession. Archaeology has waxed and waned in its contribution to colonial projects. Notably, the aforementioned nine thousand artifacts uncovered at the burial mounds in Northwestern Ontario have helped prove Indigenous presence and have been used as an objective basis for claims to lands—lands that had been usurped in a dubious settlement between the three levels of colonial government (Grand Council Treaty #3, 2000, p. 15). Through universalizing discourse, pasts are read through the lens of the present, constituting a present that circumscribes space for representation. Repatriation politics, like recognition politics, may continue to serve colonial interests if it is not framed within an anti-colonial discourse that is committed to the sustained critique of colonial institutions. The return of land and cultural objects, it is hoped, will serve to augment a resurgent politics that draws from the past to continue to fight ongoing colonial erasure.

NOTES

1. This chapter would have been inconceivable if it were not for the support, the guidance and the abundance of time and love donated by the author's partner, Annabel. Her insight and generosity in the face of intransigence and instability have been so important to this and all of the author's work that a simple thank you is hopelessly inadequate. Nevertheless. Thank you.
2. The war saw the withdrawal of Jordanian forces from what is today called East Jerusalem, and West Bank. Between 1948 (the year the British mandate expired) and 1967, the Kingdom of Jordan controlled the 'Old City' of Jerusalem.
3. 'The wall' refers to the 'Wailing' or 'Western' Wall as it is known in English.
4. Just as Patrick Wolfe (2006, p. 389) has commented: "[T]here is a major difference between the Australian and Israeli cases. The prospect of Israeli authorities changing the Hebrew

place-names whose invention … is almost unimaginable. In Australia, by contrast (as in many other settler societies), the erasure of indigeneity conflicts with the assertion of settler nationalism." Similarly, repatriation in the case of Palestine is unimaginable given the present conditions in which Jewish culture is asserted as exclusive and hegemonic. Furthermore, the wholesale destruction of non-Jewish artifacts speaks to the specificity of the Israeli narrative.

5. For example, the *Repatriation Policy of the Museum of Civilization*, from "The Canadian Museum of Civilization Corporation (CMCC), recognizes the need to consider from time to time the repatriation of certain objects of Aboriginal origin to Aboriginal people." http://www.historymuseum.ca/wp-content/uploads/2015/09/REPATRIATION-POLICY.pdf; University of Winnipeg Anthropology Museum's Policies and Procedures states, "The Museum recognizes and respects the historical, cultural, and traditional significance of certain artifacts in its collections for living First Nation and other Aboriginal groups." Accessed at http://uwwebpro. uwinnipeg.ca/faculty/anthropology/pdffiles/museumpolicy.pdf

REFERENCES

Abu El-Haj, N. (2001). *Facts on the ground: Archaeological practice and territorial self-fashioning in Israeli society*. Chicago, IL: University of Chicago Press.

Benvenisti, M. (1996). *City of stone: The hidden history of Jerusalem*. Berkeley: University of California Press.

CBC News Online. (2006, March 16). In depth: Aboriginal Canadians—Aboriginal artifacts repatriating the past. Retrieved from http://www.cbc.ca/news2/background/aboriginals/aboriginal_artifacts.html

Canadian Museum of Civilization Corporation. (2015). *Repatriation policy*. Retrieved from http://www.historymuseum.ca/wp-content/uploads/2015/09/REPATRIATION-POLICY.pdf

Coulthard, G. (2007). Subjects of empire: Indigenous peoples and the "politics of recognition" in Canada. *Contemporary Political Theory, 7*, 437–460.

Coulthard, G. (2009). *Subjects of empire? Indigenous peoples and the "politics of recognition" in Canada*. (Doctoral dissertation). University of Victoria, Victoria, Canada. Retrieved from https://dspace.library.uvic.ca/bitstream/handle/1828/1913/Dissertation_Formated%5b1%5d.pdf?sequence=1&isAllowed=y)

Dei, G. J. S., & Asgharzadeh, A. (2001). The power of social theory: The anti-colonial discursive framework. *The Journal of Educational Thought, 35*(3), 297–323. Retrieved from http://www.jstor.org/stable/23767242

Dei, G. J. S., & Kempf, A. (2006). Conclusion: Looking forward—the pedagogical implications of anti-colonialism. In *Anti-colonialism and education: The politics of resistance*. Rotterdam, the Netherlands: Sense.

Emberley, J. (2006). (un)Housing Aboriginal possessions in the virtual museum: Cultural practices and decolonization in civilization.ca and Reservation X. *Journal of Visual Culture, 5*(3), 387–410.

Grand Council Treaty #3. (2000). *Tim Holzkamm Consulting and Seven Oaks Consulting Inc. Agency Indian Reserve 1; Selection, use and administration*. Confidential Draft Report. By Tim Holzkamm and Leo Waisberg. Ponsford, MN, and Winnipeg, MB.

Hicks, D. (2015, February 4). Seven Oaks' sacred: Chief. *Fort Frances Times*. Retrieved from http://www.fftimes.com/news/news/'seven-oaks'-sacred-chief

Kenyon, W. (1986). *Mounds of sacred earth: Burial mounds of Ontario.* Toronto, Canada: Royal Ontario Museum.

Mohanram, R. (1999). *Black body: Women, colonialism, and space.* Minneapolis: University of Minnesota Press.

Phillips, R. (2011). *Museum pieces: Toward the Indigenization of Canadian museums.* Montreal, Canada: McGill-Queen's University Press.

Quijano, A. (2007). Coloniality and modernity/rationality. *Cultural Studies, 23*(2–3), 168–178.

Razack, S. H. (2012). Memorializing colonial power: The death of Frank Paul. *Law & Social Inquiry, 37*, 908–932. doi:10.1111/j.1747-4469.2012.01291. 901

Royal Ontario Museum (ROM). (2012). *Repatriation of Canadian Aboriginal objects.* Retrieved from https://www.rom.on.ca/sites/default/files/imce/RepatriationCAOREV2012_0.pdf

Simpson, A. (2007). On ethnographic refusal: Indigeneity, "voice" and colonial citizenship. *Junctures: The Journal for Thematic Dialogue, 9*, 67–80.

Simpson. A. (2014). *Mohawk interruptus: Political life across the borders of settler states.* Durham, NC: Duke University Press.

Truth and Reconciliation Commission of Canada (TRC). (2015). *Honouring the truth, reconciling for the future: Summary of the final report of the Truth and Reconciliation Commission of Canada.* Ottawa: Government of Canada.

University of Winnipeg Anthropology Museum. (2007). *Policies and procedures revised.* Retrieved from http://uwwebpro.uwinnipeg.ca/faculty/anthropology/pdffiles/museumpolicy.pdf

Wolfe, P. (2006). Settler colonialism and the elimination of the native. *Journal of Genocide Research, 8*(4), 387–409. Retrieved from http://resolver.scholarsportal.info/resolve/14623528/v08i0004/387_scateotn

Wright, J. (1972). *Ontario prehistory: An eleven-thousand-year archaeological outline.* Ottawa: National Museum of Canada.

CHAPTER ELEVEN

Understanding Ideological AND Structural Forms OF Colonial Dominance

Jamaican Migrant Farmworkers Within Global Capitalism

STACEY PAPERNICK

SETTING THE CONTEXT

Annually, five to six thousand temporary migrant workers come to work and live in Leamington, Ontario, an agricultural community southwest of Toronto, and home to twenty-eight thousand year-round residents (Boesveld, 2013). The workers' migration is orchestrated through the Canadian Seasonal Agricultural Workers Program (CSAWP). Since its inception in 1966, the Canadian government has used this program to supply the Canadian agricultural sector with temporary foreign workers (United Food and Commercial Workers, 2011). CSAWP was created in direct response to the agricultural lobby in Canada to establish a cheap pool of farm labour with minimally regulated working conditions. This program is part of a global economic system, legislated though bilateral labour agreements between the Canadian government and participating countries. Eighty percent of the workers who come to Leamington are from Mexico and 20 percent are from Jamaica and other countries in the Eastern Caribbean (Boesveld, 2013). Leamington has the largest temporary foreign worker population in Canada (Myrie, 2013). The labour of migrant farmworkers from these countries has created a multimillion-dollar agricultural industry making Leamington the Greenhouse Capital of

North America (Leamington, 2015). Migrant farmworkers are forced to secure employment through the program as a result of the economic effects of colonialism in their countries. The impact of involuntary relocation for farmworkers to this foreign land is a separation from family, community and culture. Their labour sustains the largely white citizenry in Leamington. Migrant farmworkers have been coming there for more than fifty years but continue to be treated as the "other" and made invisible by the community.

Using anti-colonial perspectives to analyze selected media reports surrounding the events that occurred in the summer of 2013 in Leamington involving Jamaican migrant farmworkers, white citizens and local government officials and representatives of the Jamaican government, this chapter seeks to understand how global capitalism functions in Ontario. Anti-colonial concepts of dominance created by Eurocentric ideology subordinate the social and economic position of the Jamaican migrant farmworkers. Race and class are interlocking systems of oppression and, most potently, impact these workers as black bodies and the implications of the post-colonial concept of hybridity on their location in global capitalism.

In July 2013, Leamington mayor John Patterson accused Jamaican migrant workers of making alleged "lewd comments" about his daughter's "body parts" as she was walking in town (CBC, 2013). On August 28, 2013, he raised his concerns at the Police Services Board regarding the ongoing sexual harassment in the form of inappropriate comments towards women. He said, "Not to be bigoted, not to be racist, not to be anything, it is directly related to some of the Jamaican migrant workers that are here" (CBC, 2013). He also said at the meeting that they were like a "cancer" in his community (Myrie, 2013). He called for the board to consider a no-loitering bylaw to prohibit migrant workers from congregating in the downtown area (Balford, 2013). Justicia (2013), a community group advocating for migrant workers, wrote an open letter to the mayor of Leamington:

> Recent comments in the media have disparaged the use of public library facilities by migrant workers; made allegations that there are too many migrant workers "loitering" downtown; and criticized the presence of too many "ethnic" businesses serving the migrant worker community. In each instance "cultural differences" have been used to justify the wider community's adverse reaction to the presence of large groups of migrant workers in visible local spaces. To pass off this tension as a matter of difference based on one's place of origin is disingenuous at best. It alludes to there being an equal and level playing field between migrant workers and Canadians.

This excerpt of Justicia's letter encapsulates the ongoing and historical ideological and structural forms of colonial domination that are perpetuated by global capitalism. Global capitalism is an economic system that maintains inequality in social relations and material conditions regardless of location. Dirlik (1997, p. 68) noted,

Without capitalism as the foundation for European power and the motive force of its globalization, Eurocentrism would have been just another ethnocentrism. An exclusive focus on Eurocentrism as a cultural or ideological problem, that blurs the power relations that dynamized it and endowed it with hegemonic persuasiveness, fails to explain why this particular ethnocentrism was able to define modern global history, and itself as the universal aspiration and end of that history, in contrast to regionalism or localism of other ethnocentrisms.

This quotation describes the totalizing nature of social and economic relationships under capitalist structures and their origins in the history of Western European industrialization. These structures enabled global imperialism, which was not a stage in capitalist development but rather a building block for capitalist expansion, to lay the foundation for global capitalism. Samir Amin (2003) describes the two stages of European imperial conquest starting with the conquest of the Americas, attempted genocide of Indian civilizations, and enslavement of black Africans in order to establish a mercantilist system that would provide its ruling class with political and economic supremacy over other nations while increasing its own material wealth (Amin, 2003, p. 57). The totalizing nature of capitalism in this stage was conveyed in Christianity and spread by proselytization, espousing the extermination of peoples who did not comply. Anti-black racism underpinned missionary work, and Eurocentric ideology justified the atrocities committed under the guise of modern economic growth and prosperity. According to Amin (2003, p. 58), the second stage of imperialism was built around the Industrial Revolution and the colonial subjugation of Asia and Africa:

> The opening of markets (such as the opium market imposed on the Chinese by English Puritans) and the grabbing of natural resources were, as everyone knows, the real reasons for this. But once again European public opinion did not see the realities and (even in the case of the Second International) accepted the new legitimizing discourse of capital, and its references to a "civilizing mission."

The purpose of colonialism was to entrench inequality between nations. Imperial expansion created economic and social relations of dependency, controlling non-European nations through captive labour and markets for European industry (Loomba, 1998, p. 6). Without the foundation of an ideology that privileges white racial dominance, capitalism would not have been an effective tool for establishing and maintaining economic power globally. It established the binaries of European "self" and "other," Third World and First World, developed and undeveloped countries, modern and primitive economies. It circulated powerful ideas that reinforce the subject position of white bodies as superior in social relations. It is because of these ideological underpinnings that colonization and capitalism justified the violence and attempted genocide of Indigenous peoples globally and established settler colonies in the continents of Africa, Asia, Australia and the Americas as economic bases from which to spread European capitalist modernity. The social construct that imbues power into colonialism and capitalism is whiteness. Henry and Tator (2006, pp. 46–47) defined it in the following manner:

> 'Whiteness,' like 'colour' and '"Blackness,' are essentially social constructs applied to human beings rather than veritable truths that have universal validity. The power of Whiteness, however, is manifested by the ways in which racialized Whiteness becomes transformed into social, political, economic, and cultural behaviour. White culture, norms, and values in all these areas become normative natural. They become the standard against which all other cultures, groups, and individuals are measured and usually found to be inferior.

European and North American history and current realities demonstrate the impacts of interlocking systematic forms of oppression, specifically focusing on race, class and gender, which are most saliently experienced by black bodies as a result of white supremacy, and not based on cultural differences. Those committed to anti-colonial knowledge and practices understand that power operates in the structures of domination that function within capitalism. We recognize the interconnectivity between race, class and gender to understand the particular experiences of social and material oppression experienced by black men and women and the unearned social and economic power attributed to white people to allow us to subvert practices that reinforce economic hierarchies.

LOCATING MYSELF

In this discussion, I learned about the experiences of Jamaican migrant farmworkers as depicted in the media. The powerful ideas that are circulated are based on the ideology of white supremacy that I interrogated to gain an understanding of the role of global capitalism in settler colonialism. As a white body I am considering what it means to develop my anti-colonial understandings by theorizing about the experiences of black workers. By investigating the social and economic relationships of the people engaged in this situation, it was my intention to unveil how the power of colonial domination continues to operate in current relationships. It is my unearned white advantage and privileged class position as a student in the Western academy that provided me with the opportunity to look in on this reality and benefit from it. My actions are not any less oppressive as a result of this recognition and as George J. Sefa Dei (2015, n.p.) stated, "Critiquing makes our scholarship critical but there are limits to the critical." I believe this means I need to understand how my everyday practices are connected to the material implications of colonialism as a white person. As Peggy McIntosh (1989, p. 31) said, "Having described it, what will I do to lessen or end it?" The white community members of Leamington have made invisible the contributions of migrant workers in the local economy and made me aware of the politics of my food choices and how I am implicated in the "buy local" food movement (Movement for the Survival of the Ogoni People Canada, 2015, n.p.). The anti-colonial is about our different relationships to land that make anti-colonial readings complex and rife with individual complicities. The implications of my actions not to buy local will impact the workers who depend on annual employment. The land that sustains these workers is unceded territory of the Chippewas of Point Pelee, the Caldwell Nation, the only federally recognized band without a reserve of their own in Southern Ontario (Caldwell, 2012). There is the reality of wage labour of Jamaican migrant farmworkers on this land and the white growers profiting from this land, compelled by race, colonial legacies and global capitalism. The reality that peoples indigenous to this land are denied land rights demonstrates the webs of complicity that operate in colonialism through capitalism. The active component this knowledge brings to my pedagogy is an awareness of the conjoined nature of colonialism to broader systems of power and privilege (Dei, 2015, n.p.). I more clearly understand the historical reasons for unsafe working conditions, subsistence wages and limitations on migrant workers' ability to assert labour rights. I see how the immigration system is connected to the operation of global capitalism. Permanent residency would create stability and improve the work life of migrant workers and directly conflict with the goals of capital to control labour and its costs.

Beyond my own critical analysis I look for ways to see my place in allowing colonial systems of power to function and the actions I can take to make political and social change. I am a staff person in a trade union. Together, workers and I challenge the economic and social relationships they face within their workplaces. In my role as a legal representative advocating for the rights of workers with their employers, I witness the impacts of race and class oppression. By engaging an intersectional analysis that is centered on race, I complicate the metanarrative of global colonialism and capitalism that defines workers in my dealings with employers as we seek opportunities for systemic change. Transforming the economic balance of power with capital by engaging an anti-colonial lens allows me to understand that I can take action by supporting the broader struggles of migrant workers to attain permanent residency status. Permanent residency status provides the economic and social benefits of citizenship. This paper was written in the context of one of the largest national discussions about the deportation of migrants from Canada. On April 1, 2015, former prime minister Stephen Harper outlined the new "four and four" rule—stating that migrant workers who have been employed in Canada for more than four years must leave the country and cannot return for another four years. The Campaign Against the Four Year Limit on Migrant Workers (Patterson, 2015, n.p.) stated,

> Working in Canada for four years proves that the workers are needed, and that their work is permanent. These friends and community members deserve permanent residence, not

deportation. This 4 and 4 rule entrenched a revolving door immigration policy, employers can simply replace current with new workers.

The status of migrant workers remains in question following the election of Prime Minister Justin Trudeau in October 2015.

Acknowledging my own (white) privilege as a staff person in a trade union, there is social power to influence the political direction of a union. I can make the links for union leadership between the experiences of nurses in the Temporary Foreign Workers Program (TFWP) and CSAWP to leverage political and material support for migrant worker campaigns that resist ongoing colonial practices and global capitalism. I believe we have taken a protectionist approach, limiting engagement in social justice issues to the direct economic interests of our members. For example, we do not have an integrated understanding of the complex identities of nurses and their location in the global economy as a result of their histories of colonialism. Many nurses are here because of forced economic migration from their home countries. I believe we can be decentered on this issue by supporting nurses in the TFWP. Anti-colonial thought and practice require me to ask new questions before engaging in action and at this juncture I am reflecting on political transformations within the union I work for and within myself.

EUROCENTRISM: THE BASIS OF POWER IN CAPITALISM

As a result of the mayor's comments, Minister of Labour Derrik Kellier of Jamaica met with him to "improve social and cultural relationships between Jamaican farmworkers and the residents of the city" (Balford, 2013, n.p.). Kellier emphasized the importance of the program to both countries stating that "improving relationships between Jamaicans and Canadians is a high priority for the Jamaican government and, as such, there are discussions on practical steps to improve the current situation" (Balford, 2013). During the meeting, the mayor said that his comments were "overstated" in the media and did not reflect his true feelings regarding the presence of Jamaican migrant farmworkers in Leamington. He said, "This proactive action taken by the Jamaican Government to ensure that the migrant worker program continues to prosper and to address negative issues, speaks volumes to the commitment and sincerity of the Jamaican people" (Balford, 2013). He reassured the minister and other high-ranking Jamaican government officials that his council would work with residents of Leamington towards a better understanding of cultural differences and "facilitate the integration of Jamaican migrant workers, who are providing valuable service and making a significant contribution to the local economy" (Balford, 2013). In this series of statements it is evident that Eurocentrism gives global capitalism the ideological and structural power it requires to dominate black bodies. The relationship of Eurocentrism to capitalism provides the master narrative that permits the social and economic subordination of black bodies that maintains the structural power within global capitalism to control and exploit black labour. This exploitation creates dominant white bodies, even within the same class, sharing social, economic and political power. Although not all of those with white privilege seek to maintain this socio-racial and economic imbalance, they do benefit from this hierarchy. Global capitalism, as an extension of colonialism and imperialism, is a system of dominance and control that shapes economic relationships. It does not cease and has a history that defines the lives of the colonizer and colonized. Loomba (1998, p. 2) commented on the foundational role of colonialism in capitalist history:

> So colonialism can be defined as the conquest and control of other people's land and goods. But colonialism in this sense is not merely an expansion of various European powers into Asia, Africa or the Americas from the sixteenth century onwards; it has been a recurrent and widespread feature of human history.

Marxists believe that modern colonialism was established alongside capitalism in Western Europe and worked in tandem to assert European control of the economies and location of colonized peoples in these systems. Loomba (1998, p. 3) stated,

> Modern colonialism did more than extract tribute, goods and wealth from the countries that it conquered—it restructured the economies of the latter, drawing them into complex relationship with their own, so there was a flow of human and natural resources between colonized and colonial countries. This flow worked in both directions—slaves and indentured labour as well as raw materials were transported to manufacture goods in the metropolis, or in other locations for metropolitan consumption, but the colonies provided captive markets for European goods.

By establishing the connection of colonialism to capitalism, Cedric Robinson demonstrates the emergence of racial hierarchy in feudal Europe and how it shaped the hierarchy of labour under worldwide capitalism. Central to this labour hierarchy is the Eurocentric knowledge claim of white racial superiority. Robinson (1983, p. 2) explained,

> Racism, I maintain, was not simply a convention for ordering the relations of European to non-European peoples but has its genesis in the "internal" relations of European peoples. As part of the inventory of Western civilization it would reverberate within and without, transferring its toll from the past to the present.

CSAWP is a program that maintains the legacy of colonialism in global capitalism. Robinson commented, "The poverty and deteriorating well-being of Caribbean Blacks were the direct legacies of colonialism. Tens of thousands of West Indians came to the U.S. during the first decades of the 20th century" (Robinson, 1983,

p. 213). As a result of the social and economic conditions described by Robinson, it can be understood that participation in this program is one of the ways the Jamaican government is addressing its working-class poverty and unemployment stemming from colonialism. After 1655, white British colonizers and capitalists began transporting slaves to Jamaica from Africa, forcing them into a plantation system for sugarcane production (Persaud, 2001, p. 74). Although Jamaica gained independence from Britain in 1962, it continues to remain economically controlled by Britain and the United States (Nicholas, 1996, p. 18). Foreign investment is concentrated in the bauxite industry, with open-pit mining operations displacing farmers from their land and creating an economy without any other developed industries (Campbell, 1987, p. 86). The Jamaican government's response is an attempt to diffuse any of the mayor of Leamington's concerns, the result of an ongoing dependent economic relationship with the colonizer and its previous colonies. The pledge to improve social and cultural relationships is tacit agreement that black Jamaican migrant farmworkers have engaged in uncivilized behavior. This as a form of colonial mimicry wherein the mayor wants the Jamaican government to be a recognizable "other" by agreeing with his view that Jamaican men bring "negative issues" to the community. Colonial mimicry as described by Homi Bhabha (1994, p. 86) occurs when the colonizer wants to see the previously colonized "as a subject of a difference that is almost the same, but not quite." As a result of their actions, Jamaican government officials are legitimized by the white government and viewed as a "good" business partner. The failure to refute the stereotypes of black Jamaican farmworkers and the unfounded allegations of harassment raise questions regarding their implication into the subordinating ideology of the colonizer. Eurocentric knowledge defines the black body as a homogeneous object with a particular human nature. It creates a mythology of inferiority that is labeled as cultural difference but is based on anti-black racism. Both parties in their interaction impose this definition, as illustrated by Robinson (1983, p. 81):

> The "Negro," that is the colour black, was both a negation of African and a unit of opposition to white. The construct of Negro, unlike the terms African, Moor, or "Ethiope" suggested no situatedness in time, that is history or space, that is ethno- or politico-geography. The Negro had no civilization, no cultures, no religions, no history, no place, and finally no humanity which might command consideration. ... [T]he Negro constituted a marginally human group, a collection of things of convenience for use and/or eradication. This was, of course, no idle exercise in racial and moral schemata since it directly related to a most sizable quantum of labour disciplined and applied in a most extraordinary way.

When the mayor told the media that there were more complaints than usual flooding into the council regarding the "sexual comments and aggressive tendencies," he was drawing from racial stereotypes and essentialisms that define the black male as uncivilized in relation to the white male. As Justicia (2013) wrote, "Instead of dealing with sexual harassment on an individual basis, you skip right to racialized stereotypes; drawing from some of the worst parts of Canadian history. It does not escape us that the community of Leamington once supported 'sundown laws' which made it illegal for Black Canadians to walk freely in the community after sunset." bell hooks (2004, pp. 74–75) explained the basis for the dominant paradigm of the black male as hypersexual, an intersection of black racial and gender oppression:

> Within neo-colonial white-supremacist capitalist patriarchy, the black male body contin-
> ues to be perceived as the embodiment of bestial, violent, penis-as-weapon hypermascu-
> line assertion. Psychohistories of white racism have always called attention to the tension
> between the construction of the black male body as danger and the underlying eroticization
> that always then imagines that body as a location for transgressive pleasure. It has taken
> contemporary commodification of the blackness to teach the world that this perceived
> threat, whether real or symbolic, can be diffused by a process of fetishization that renders
> the black masculine 'menace' feminine through a process of patriarchal objectification.

The complicities of the Jamaican government supporting the prevailing views of black men are a result of the broader system of Euro-American patriarchy and sexism manufactured by the dominant to maintain privilege. The significance of examining Eurocentrism in this interaction is to see that colonial relations are reproduced in capitalism. Colonialism required the creation of knowledge of the "other" to establish its power as white and male. Loomba referenced Edward Said's work *Orientalism* to illustrate this point: "European literary texts, travelogues and other writings contributed to the creation of a dichotomy between Europe and its 'others', a dichotomy that was central to the creation of European culture as well as to the maintenance and extension of European hegemony over other lands" (Loomba, 1998, p. 44). The colonial project was based on establishing an ideology about non-Europeans in order to maintain power over them, and this ideology underpins capitalism in establishing racial hierarchies within social class. In order for global capitalism to maintain its ideological and economic power, it must be able to repurpose itself in Western contexts. Robinson (1983, p. 66) spoke of the ability of capitalism to adapt its structures based on white supremacy:

> Racialism insinuated not only medieval, feudal, and capitalist social structures, forms
> of property, and modes of production, but as well the very values and traditions of con-
> sciousness through which the peoples of these ages came to understand their worlds and
> their experiences. Western culture, constituting the structure from which European con-
> sciousness was appropriated, the structure in which social identities and perceptions were
> grounded in the past, transmitted a racialism that adapted to the political and material
> exigencies of the moment. ... [R]acialism was substantiated by specific sets of exploitation
> through which particular caste or classes exploited and expropriated disparate peoples.

The Jamaican Observer reported that the minister met with Jamaican farmworkers, "urging them to adapt to their new environment as best as possible and respect

Canadian cultural values and practices" (Balford, 2013). There is no Canadian identity that can be defined as the norm, but there is lurking behind this statement the power of whiteness to define black racial identity as compared with white racial identity. It reinforces the inferiority of black bodies under capitalism. As George J. Sefa Dei (2015, n.p.) observed, the "historical relationship of the colonizer with the colonized informs the contemporary subject identity formation and knowledge production." In fabricating the identity of the Jamaican migrant farmworker, the mayor is justified in his expectations that they change their behavior to "act white." Robinson (1983, p. 82) articulated this identity that justifies subordination to white bodies:

> Where previously the Blacks were a fearful phenomenon to Europeans because of their historical association with civilizations superior, dominant and/or antagonistic to Western societies (the most recent of that being Islam), now the ideograph of Blacks came to signify a difference of species, an exploitable source of energy (labour power) both mindless to the organizational requirements of production and insensitive to the sub-human conditions of work.

The goal of colonial ideology as it is practiced within capitalism is to construct the colonized as a "racially degenerate population in order to justify conquest and rule" (Parry, 1995, p. 41). The connection between systems of knowledge and structures creates social and economic inequality for Jamaican migrant farmworkers. From an anti-colonial lens, it is understood that social constructions of race produce knowledge to create the colonized "other" and in order to resist capitalism and colonialism we must decenter these identities through politics of change through action.

INTERLOCKING FORMS OF OPPRESSION: RACE MEDIATES CLASS

In order to bring an anti-colonial perspective to an analysis of the dominance of white supremacy that works within the structures of global capitalism within CSAWP in Leamington, let us consider the interlocking forms of oppression, race and class that originate in colonialism. Although the focus is on race and class, gender provides a further location of oppression in this context, as it is anchored in the mayor's comment on male Jamaican migrant farmworkers and sexual harassment. Class is mediated by race to explain the disproportionate negative impacts of capitalism on Jamaican migrant farmworkers. "The anti-colonial framework situates the implications of race in the production and dissemination of knowledge about the colonized 'others' and their social development" (Dei, 2015, n.p.). In order to understand the social and material conditions of Jamaican migrant farmworkers, race must be considered. Their historically constructed black racial identity determines their class position. Marxism asserts that control over the means and relations of productions determines class in capitalism. Jamaican migrant farmworkers have no control over either; they are indentured wage labourers bound to their employers as a result of an intergovernmental agreement. During their work placements in Ontario they have no social or economic mobility. To make this situation further exploitative, they cannot contest their working conditions without fear of deportation or failing to be allowed to return to Canada for future employment. Jamaican migrant farmworkers can be compared with the enslaved peasantry originating in feudalism and industrial capitalism. Their class position is fixed as a result of white racial dominance within working-class structures. Marxist theory of capitalist development viewed black slavery as a stage in the "primitive accumulation" of wealth, although it recurred throughout European history and was invisible as the dominant mode of production. Black bodies were not the proletariats; they were subordinate, like women and children, viewed as unnecessary to the developing economy. Gender must be considered as part of an intersectional analysis of the class position of black males because they are equated to the female gender that is rendered invisible and without value in capitalism. Robinson (1983, p. xxix) described this view:

> Driven, however, by the need to achieve the scientific elegance and interpretive economy demanded by theory, Marx consigned race, gender, culture, and history to the dustbin. Fully aware of the constant place women and children held in the workforce, Marx still deemed them so unimportant as a proportion of wage labor that he tossed them, with slave labor and peasants, into the imagined abyss signified by precapitalist, noncapitalist, and primitive accumulation.

The European colonial gaze scripts the class position of male Jamaican migrant farmworkers. Marxist theory of historical materialism is part of Eurocentric hegemony. In not acknowledging that black bodies experience class differently, resistance to capitalism solely based on class will not facilitate black working-class liberation. Fanon (1963, p. 40) articulated this point:

> The originality of the colonial context is that economic reality, inequality, and the immense difference of ways of life never come to mask the human realities. When you examine at close quarters the colonial context, it is evident that what parcels out the world is to begin with the fact of belonging to or not belonging to a given race, a given species. In the colonies the economic substructure is also a super structure. The cause is the consequence; you are rich because you are white, you are white because you are rich. This is why Marxist analysis should always be slightly stretched every time we have to do with the colonial problem.

Fanon's view indicates that not all forms of oppression are the same and that one source of oppression cannot subsume all others. In order to resist colonial inequality, we must address the interlocking nature of race and class. Anti-colonial perspectives teach us to resist all forms of Eurocentric hegemony and structural domination. In "The Power of Social Theory: Towards an Anti-Colonial Discursive Framework,"

Dei and Asgharzadeh explain that we cannot privilege one site of oppression over another because they are interconnected. "Such a realization comes from the acknowledgement that our social lives are profoundly affected by relations of power and domination, which are oppressive and colonial by nature and which are products of multiplicity of forces, structures, actions, ideologies, and beliefs" (Dei & Asgharzadeh, 2001, p. 311). Jamaican migrant farmworkers' class position is a result of racist and patriarchal ideologies that place them in a subordinated position within social class relative to white working-class males. This could be a possible explanation for why there were no members of the white working class challenging the mayor's racist views and proposed segregation laws. Robinson (1983, p. 42) reiterated these historical divisions between races within European capitalism and imperialism:

> But even more to the point, we have seen that the generic terms "the English working class" or "the English proletariat" mask the social and historical realities that accompanied the introduction of industrial capitalism in England and its Empire. Social divisions and habits of life and attitude that predated capitalist production continued into the modern era and extended to the working classes located in Britain specific social sensibilities and consciousness. The English working class was never the singular social and historical entity suggested by the phrase. … The negations resultant from capitalist modes of production, relations of production, and ideology did not manifest themselves as an eradication of oppositions among the working classes. Instead, the dialectic of proletarianization disciplined the working classes to the importance of distinctions: between ethnics and nationalities; between skilled and unskilled workers; and, as we shall see later in even more dramatic terms, between races. The persistence and creation of such oppositions within the working classes were a critical aspect of the triumph of capitalism in the nineteenth century.

Again, the complicities and tensions of colonialism within global capitalism reveal that the failure of the white working class to oppose relations of power implicates them in the web of racial, class and gender-based oppression of Jamaican migrant farmworkers.

From an anti-colonial perspective, race is centered but all sites of domination are resisted because colonial capitalist forces are complex and are meant to impact bodies differently to sustain capitalism. There are parallels between the interlocking nature of race and class for black bodies In migrant farmwork and slavery Smith contends one of the pillars of white supremacy is the logic of slavery, "As Sora Han, Jared Sexton, and Angela P. Harris note, this logic renders Black people as inherently slaveable—as nothing more than property. That is, in this logic of white supremacy, Blackness becomes equated with slaveability" (Smith, 2006, p. 67). Smith explained that this logic is the basis of class positions within capitalism. Inherent in that system, white bodies can sell their labour as commodities but anti-black racism attributes a slave status to black bodies, creating racial hierarchy. Although Jamaican farmworkers are paid wages, their terms and conditions of work place them in a disadvantageous position within the socioeconomic hierarchy.

Working at the pleasure of governments and growers, they have no ability to access permanent resident status, which would provide them with social and economic independence and enable them to seek other employment and access government support to improve their material conditions. The hierarchy discussed by Smith is also discussed by Cesaire (1972, p. 21) in *Discourse on Colonialism*. Cesaire places this hegemony within the framework of colonialism. He described the concept of colonization as "thingification" which equates black bodies with objects, placing them outside the class system. Justicia (2013) referenced the application of this view when they noted in their letter that the voice of Jamaican migrant workers is absent in the discussion: "You and your council are free to condemn and stigmatize migrant workers without any real and significant response from workers themselves; a population who has lived and worked in Leamington for fifty years, but continue to be considered temporary." They are essentialized as objects and misrepresented as subjects without agency. Racial constructions define the class position of Jamaican migrant farmworkers within global capitalism, but it is the power of Eurocentricity translated into anti-black racism that demonstrates that capitalism is not experienced in the same way by all bodies. For this reason their class is mediated by race. As described by Dirlik (1997, p. 71):

> I think it is arguable that the apparent end of Eurocentrism is an illusion, because capitalist culture as it has taken shape has Eurocentrism built into the very structure of its narrative, which may explain why even Europe and the United States lose their domination of the capitalist world economy, culturally European and American values retain their domination.

Dirlik is illustrating that race is a potent marker on black bodies so much so that the constructions of racial difference subordinate their existence to serve capitalism's economic and political purpose. Black lives are affected by the power of the colonial dominant with or without structures of economic control. Situating race within anti-colonialism is to help us resist all that is dominating, imposing and dehumanizing (Dei & Asgharzadeh, 2001, p. 312). Quijano's concept of the "colonial power matrix" and Grosfuguel's (2007, p. 217) interpretation articulates the idea that through the "coloniality of power" the interlocking nature of race and class, as sites of domination and exploitation, when mediated by racism, will structure social and economic hierarchies in global capitalism that result in black racial inequality.

HYBRIDITY: POSITIONING SOCIAL AND ECONOMIC INEQUALITY

To fully interrogate the events that occurred and continue to evolve in Leamington, let us consider the location and the subjectivities imposed on Jamaican migrant farmworkers. These realities are unique to their role in the economic system and have significant impacts on them within global capitalism. One of the key operating features of global capitalism is the transnationalization of production (Dirlik, 1997, p. 68). Capital and labour are mobile with minimal political restrictions. Growers benefit from cheap labour to maximize profit while migrant farmworkers are alienated from the means of production, their land, culture, family and community. The Jamaican government is unable to rebuild its own agricultural economy because it is forced into a relationship of expedience to address unemployment, part of the legacy of imperialism and transnational corporations. Global capitalism claims it produces a thriving global economy by facilitating labour mobility, viewed as an economic benefit for workers. However, from an anti-colonial frame I want to understand why it is repeatedly experienced as material inequality by black bodies. This experience is salient to the complexities, tensions and ambiguities of lives and colonial experiences in global capitalism after the colonial encounter (Dei, 2015, n.p.). Jamaican migrant farmworkers move across borders not by choice but as a result of material need and legislated passage. Once here, they are prevented from attaining social and economic mobility. From their hybrid location, an anti-colonial critique of capitalism may be raised to explain their marginalization as a group in Canada. Hybridity as a concept can help us to understand the connections between imperial colonial cultures and colonized cultural practices (Dei, 2015, n.p.).

Hybridity is explained by Homi Bhabha (1994, p. 36) as formerly colonized peoples occupying a space neither inside nor outside the history of Western domination but rather in a third space. He believed that this in-between post-colonial and First World position ignored the ideological and institutional structures operating in global capitalism that re-locate people in the third space. Upon arrival in Canada, Jamaican migrant farmworkers are ascribed a class position at the bottom of the socioeconomic hierarchy that provides for differences in power. This identity is determined by Eurocentrism and the social construction of race therein to assign an identity to black bodies that justifies subordination and their forced migration. Justicia's (2013) letter described the subject location of the workers as defined by the white community: "It is apparent that your council would rather have migrant workers 'out of sight and out of mind'; segregated from the white citizens of your community as much as possible." The anti-loitering laws that were proposed by the mayor were directed to control migrant workers, physically and socially, perpetuating the colonial as defined by Dei (2006, p. 3) as "anything imposed and dominating rather than that which is simply foreign and alien." Colonialism in global capitalism places Jamaican migrant farmworkers "outside" of the community and in an inferior location. The inferiority of their location is illustrated by the attempt to limit mobility and the ability to gather as a group of Jamaicans. Their subordinate location within the third space is augmented by the failure of the local government to provide them with social services like those available to any other resident—an example of material inequality in the form of resource allocation. Justicia (2013) described this locally pervasive view as "a consistent line of argument that migrant workers should be the sole responsibility of employers and that employers should be financially responsible for any form of municipal services rendered to migrants." Global capital and governments create this third space for their economic advantage. The location of migrant farmworkers appears transient; however, this is a misrepresentation of their location because they return to work on an annual basis. Employers have no financial burdens associated with labour rights because they are legislatively prohibited from collective bargaining. Further, there is minimal government enforcement of health and safety standards, ensuring they can employ migrant labour at low costs. An injured worker may be deported without compensation. Because of the state's denial to them of permanent residency status, they will never have the entitlements of a Canadian citizen and thus impose minimal cost on the social safety net. The local (predominantly white) community will not reject the economic benefits their labour brings to the area because they are "outside" local social and economic structures, and citizens can maintain their dominant views and oppressive behaviors without repercussions. Hybridity provides distance because of the subjectivities it produces and by placing Jamaican migrant farmworkers in the third space. Location in the Canadian context is significant because it will always mean unequal social and economic conditions for black bodies.

> Different colonial regimes tried (to varying extents) to maintain cultural and racial segregation precisely because, in practice, the interactions between colonising and colonised peoples constantly challenged any neat division between races and cultures The result was a mixing, a "hybridity" which became an important theme within colonial discourse theories. ... We need to remember that large sections of colonised peoples in many parts of the world had no or little direct 'contact' with foreign oppressors. Yet of course their lives were materially and ideologically reshaped by the latter. (Loomba, 1998, p. 69)

Loomba demonstrates that even without a fixed structure, global capitalism's impact, such as placement in a hybrid space, aligns its practices with colonialism as imposing and dominating.

> Colonial images continually uphold the colonizers' sense of reason, authority and control. It scripts and violates the colonized as the violent "other," while, in contrast, the colonizer is pitted as an innocent, benevolent and (imperial) savior (see also Principe, 2004). This historical relationship of the colonizer and the colonized continues to inform contemporary subject identity formation and knowledge production. It shapes and informs identities by recreating colonial ideologies and mythologies. (Dei, 2006, p. 3)

The mayor's comments regarding the Jamaican migrant workers making "lewd comments" attributed to them as a group a totalizing identity as sexual predators, evoking stereotypes of black males as comparable to savages. This subjectivity reinforces differences in identity, separating black migrants as "bad" and white citizens as "good." At the same time, it highlights their interlocking forms of identity derived from race, class and gender, identities contributing to their subordination in a location outside the dominant group. Working with their imposed identities the mayor has reinforced their subject location with the dichotomy of "us" and "them." He stated, "Maybe it's appropriate back in your home town, but here it's not" (CBC, 2013). Their in-betweenness is evident—they are not part of Jamaica and do not belong in Leamington. White women in this context also continue to essentialize black Jamaican men as predators who make them unsafe because of their black racial identity and male gender. Linda Tessier, a Leamington resident, commented, "They sometimes ask me if I'm free or single, if I want to go home with them. I get nervous, I refuse to go shopping Friday nights" (CBC, 2013; see also Boesveld, 2013). Her comments equate male blackness with violence, instilling white anxiety and fear. Both the mayor's and the woman's comments demonstrate how hybridity homogenizes Jamaican migrant farmworkers, further scripting their external location by subjectifying their identities. Anti-colonial perspectives recognize that subjectivities are maintained by the structures and relationships in global capitalism to impose social and economic inequality. When subjectivities are critiqued, there is power in the third space for these workers to self-determine how they want to use their knowledge of their marginalized position in Canada as blacks, as men, as Jamaicans, as migrants, as farmworkers to define their own representations, meanings and politics of their identity. This power can be used to resist Eurocentric colonial hegemonies that live in global capitalism.

Hybridity is critiqued by anti-colonial theorists for its failure to explain the differences in power and material conditions of inequality between groups and people.

> The positing of false binaries in understanding histories and Western historicism (e.g., colonial–post-colonial), subordinates the world's diverse histories and cultures to the grand march of a monolithic, undifferentiated colonialism of European time. … [I]nequalities of power and privilege within and among nations, regions, classes and genders are vaporized before the dazzling glare of a homogenizing postcolonialism. (Zeleza, 1997, p. 16)

The identity and location of the Jamaican migrant farmworker in modern capitalism are derived from European colonial history that demarcates their position in the white working class. Robinson (1983, p. 23) provided examples of racialized migrant labour as the backbone of colonial and global capitalism:

> The important meaning is that this form of enlisting human reserves was not peculiar to military apparatus but extended throughout Europe to domestic service, handicrafts, industrial labor, the ship- and dock-workers of merchant capitalism, and the field laborers of agrarian capitalism. There has never been a moment in modern European history (if

before) that migratory and/or immigrant labor was not a significant aspect of European economies.

Black bodies have been drafted into jobs in the economy that have particular social and economic implications. This establishes hierarchies in the working class based on race, ethnicity and culture, translating into material inequality. The colonial histories of Jamaican farmworkers have given them few choices other than to enter programs like CSAWP. Their land has been annexed by transnationals and jobs are scarce. According to Hall (1996, p. 252), it is this history that has laid the foundation for their location in the third space, fragmenting their identity from past processes that have been shaped by the practices and social representations of the dominant. Dei (2015, n.p.) explained that anti-colonial perspectives tell us that "ignoring history furthers oppression, exploitation and marginality." This is illustrated by the failure of the dominant group to challenge the views of the women and the mayor. Dirlik (1997, p. 66) maintained that not recognizing group or individual historical experiences causes "universalizing historicism" that reproduces colonialism. Despite its conceptual limitations, hybridity can help us to see how representations are manifested by the dominant over time and how they operate in the modern economy within new relations of power. This understanding can assist in resisting their epistemologies and practices.

Hybridity is a result of labour mobility celebrated under global capitalism as an opportunity for people of developing countries to commodify their labour; however, the flow of labour and capital post-colonial independence disadvantages black bodies. Dirlik (1997, p. 65) noted that although "postcolonial intellectuals may insist on hybridity, and the transposability of locations, it is also necessary to insist that not all positions are equal in power." The hybrid location creates challenges for migrant farmworkers to resist the impacts of global capitalism because of their forced dislocation from their original space. Anti-colonial resistance grounded in their communities and cultures is a position of power. In Canada, migrant farmworkers have relationships to the land different from those of white settlers. They do not have an Indigenous connection to the land, thus denying them the ability to engage in decolonizing economic resurgences. Regardless, their position creates possibilities for organizing solidarities with Indigenous peoples such as the Chippewas of Point Pelee, Caldwell Nation, who also live on this unceded territory and have been denied reserve rights which would bring their community social and economic benefits. Both are displaced peoples as a result of global capitalism and settler colonialism, coextensive of European colonialism. Hybridity as a concept emerging from the anti-colonial asks what is possible for Jamaican migrant farmworkers in this location and how organized farmwork includes locations for change.

There are several examples of successful forms of resistance that migrant farmworkers have taken as racialized immigrant groups organizing disruptively for economic change that do not leave them scripted by global capitalism. In British

Columbia's Fraser Valley in April 1980, South Asian migrant farmworkers, mostly immigrants from Punjab, India, and primarily women, self-organized and founded the first farmworkers union in the history of Canada, the Canadian Farmworkers Union (Bush, 1995, n.p.). Their organizing was in response to working in the third most hazardous industry in their province behind logging and mining. They were subjected to unsafe working conditions while simultaneously being excluded from the protection of provincial health and safety laws, leaving them exposed to unguarded machinery and toxic pesticides (Bush, 1995). They were required by the growers to live in substandard housing without potable water or toilets. In addition to unsafe working and living conditions, they faced low-wage piecework and were made to pay a portion of their earnings to labour contractors for ongoing access to employment. Further, they were often paid their wages only at the end of the growing season (Bush, 1995). Recalling the founding meeting of more than two hundred delegates, Patwardhan and Munro (1982, n.p.) feature a farmworker who shared recollections about the catalysts for collective representation:

> From India, from pre-liberated China and from other colonized countries our people came to this land at the beginning of the century. Many were denied entry because of the colour of their skin but some of us got in. We ask for work, we were given slave wages, we ask for dignity, we were racially abused. To this day the government has broken every promise to cover us under the minimum wage and other such acts. Today we have an opportunity to advance our struggle.

In their hybrid location, they understand that as farmworkers they are considered second-class workers and as immigrants of colour, as second-class citizens (Bush, 1995). Their anti-colonial understanding was channeled into action for economic change. Raj Chouhan, founding president of the Canadian Farmworkers Union, summed up the conditions that spawned the union:

> It is indeed incredible that in this day and age and in a country like Canada, a whole section of workers should be compelled to earn their living in such deplorable and discriminatory conditions as farmworkers face. It is clear that if farmworkers are not considered to be like other workers—that they are denied the status of workers in Canadian society. The law says that workers should not be expected to work more than a certain number of hours per day, and if they do, they should be entitled to overtime rates of pay ... that the conditions of work should be such that the workers do not face undue hazards and risks to their lives. The law says that if a worker gets injured while at work, he or she should be entitled to compensation. ... All of these and other similar laws are there to protect the working people from the unbridled and pernicious exploitation by owners. None of this applies to farmworkers in B.C. They have simply left us at the mercy of the contractors and farmers. ... The thousands of workingmen, women and children who provide the hard labour to produce the necessary food for the society have in fact been excluded from the category of working people. But there has to be an end to all of this. The farmworkers of this province have realized that these conditions will not change until they organize themselves. (Bush, 1995, n.p.)

The workers' goals were to abolish the labour contractor system, achieve minimum wages and maximum hours of work, and secure unemployment insurance coverage and protection against pesticide exposure and dangerous machinery. After picketing during a fifteen-month strike at Jensen Mushroom Farms, the union achieved its first contract on July 30, 1983, giving workers a $2.00 per hour raise to $7.00 per hour and full medical and dental benefits (Bush, 1995, n.p.). Although Jensen resumed operations under the new contract, it then launched a campaign to decertify the union and the farm closed in November 1983 (Bush, n.p.). On July 31, 1983, their struggle to attain unemployment insurance coverage for farmworkers resulted in reducing the twenty-five days with one employer rule to seven days—entitling more farmworkers to have coverage (Bush, 1995, n.p.). These farmworkers achieved bargaining unit recognition and labour contracts that changed the material conditions of their lives as racialized immigrants, reframing their economic relationship with capital that was scripted by global capitalism. They were also successful in altering the legislative system by changing laws affecting farmworkers at the federal level, which transformed their social relationships within the economy.

In the United States, the Coalition of Immokalee Workers arose from racialized migrant farmworkers who resisted the structures of global capitalism. Many of these workers had been forced into hidden neo-liberal slave labour markets as undocumented immigrants, hired by tomato growers in Florida to make it the leading state producer of the crop in a billion-dollar industry (Rios, 2011). Mexican and Guatemalan migrant labourers drew on their histories of colonization by taking action to shape their future through the formation of the coalition (Cox, 2012). Over a twenty-year period, they have engaged in an anti-slavery campaign to ensure colonial practices are not re-instituted by successfully ensuring that more than a thousand Florida farmworkers were released from captivity and forced labour (Burkhalter, 2012). In 1993, they instituted community work stoppages and in 1998 held a month-long hunger strike ("About CIW," n.d.). In 2000, they marched from Ft. Myers to Orlando to win industry-wide wage increases and public support for farmworkers ("About CIW," n.d.). In 2005, they changed their tactics to boycott fast-food giant Taco Bell with the goal of requiring the company to take responsibility for the human rights abuses occurring in the fields ("About CIW," n.d.). The coalition has succeeded in pressuring other fast-food companies, food-service providers and supermarket chains to join the Fair Food Campaign (Cox, 2012). In 2010, the coalition signed an agreement with the Tomato Growers Exchange to extend the fair food principles to a Fair Food Program, a groundbreaking model of worker-driven social responsibility, based on a partnership of farmworkers, growers and retail buyers (Cox, 2012). It included a worker complaint resolution system, health and safety program and a fair food premium in the form of an additional $0.01 per pound to increase wages (Cox, 2012, n.p.).

This program resulted in wages being increased from $10,000 to $17,000 per year (Rios, 2011, n.p.). Caroline Bettinger-Lopez, Director of the Human Rights Clinic at the University of Miami School of Law, remarked on the monumental nature of this achievement:

> The agreement between labourers, growers and buyers is unique because it resembles a legally binding contract that includes an accountability mechanism to ensure the tomato pickers will be treated and paid fairly. (Rios, 2011, n.p.)

The Fair Food Program has changed Immokalee, Florida, from one of the poorest, most politically powerless communities in the United States to a national and state presence with migrant workers as community leaders who have achieved livable wages, eradicated slavery and created a new model for labour relations in agriculture ("About CIW," n.d.).

In Leamington, Ontario, Canada, Jamaican migrant farmworkers could discover common ground with Indigenous peoples for organizing economic, political and social change based on their exclusions scripted by the Canadian government and local community. There is an on-going opportunity for Jamaican migrant farmworkers and Mexican migrant farmworkers to form alliances to effect change. Mexican migrant farmworkers are the largest group of agricultural workers admitted through CSAWP in Leamington (Boesveld, 2013). Although both groups have different colonial histories and identities, they continue to build alliances for economic, social and political transformation on the basis of being cast as the "other" in Western settler colonialism. Their alliances could engage a counter-hegemonic movement as described by Escobar (2004, pp. 223–224), allowing for "new horizons of meaning" and "alternative conceptions of the economy, nature, development." Jamaican migrant farmworkers can use their knowledge of their hybrid location, subjectivities, histories and heterogeneity to change their economic and social conditions in the diaspora.

POSSIBILITIES BEYOND GLOBAL CAPITALISM

In this discussion, I have tried to address the complexities, tensions and ambiguities Jamaican migrant farmworkers face as a result of their colonial experience in global capitalism. In order to explain this experience and the social and economic inequalities they endure under CSAWP, I have considered their colonial capitalist history that continues to operate in global capitalism. I have used the anti-colonial concepts of Eurocentric ideology, the interlocking nature of race, class, gender and the post-colonial concept of hybridity to expose colonial epistemologies and practices that continue to impose and dominate Jamaican migrant farmworkers in Leamington.

The strategies used by migrant farmworkers in British Columbia and Florida demonstrate that they have agency as workers and that there are forms of resistance taken by farmworkers on a daily basis to resist colonialism. Migrant farmworkers in Leamington have also engaged in transforming their economic, social and political reality. In 2002, migrant farmworkers in Leamington engaged in an illegal strike, taking sanctuary from growers and government deportation in a local church. This action led them to create the Agricultural Workers Alliance (AWA), a network of migrant farmworkers across Canada who meet regionally and locally to discuss and take action to change their working conditions and quality of life (Dugale, 2009, n.p.). In 1992 AWA opened the first migrant farmworker support centre (United Food and Commercial Workers, 2015). The centre assists workers in dealing with abusive employers, unsafe workplace and housing conditions, medical treatment and accessing parental leave benefits. At the centre, workers engage in education to transform their economic, social and political positions. The pedagogical model enables farmworkers to build on their own knowledge as they share their experiences with other workers and receive new information to meet their needs in understanding labour rights to address their working conditions and access to government services. The information that is provided about laws and services creates an opportunity for farmworkers to discuss their conditions through exploring common histories of colonization, displacement, precarious employment and status. Their resistance begins by creating a shared political analysis that is the basis for economic, social and political transformation—the basis on which they collectively engage in action to challenge the macro-economic and structural barriers that are imposed on them as farmworkers. The case *Dunsmore v. Ontario* (2001) saw mushroom farmers challenge the denial of the right to freedom of association, appealing to the Supreme Court of Canada (Makin, 2011). The Supreme Court ruled in their favour and gave agricultural workers the right to join a union or employee association. Although agricultural workers have still not won the right to collectively bargain, as stated in the 2011 Supreme Court *Fraser* decision, they will continue to lobby for changes in labour legislation until they have the same rights and protections as other Ontario workers (Makin, 2011).

Dei (2015, n.p.) challenges us with this question: "What purpose is a conversation about capitalist structure if it is entangled in other forms of oppression?" An anti-colonial perspective asks us to transform knowledge and practices to oppose colonial power. Therefore, the starting point for a discussion about global capitalism may be better situated in how we move beyond the capitalist system. Moving beyond entails adopting politics for change through action to transform the economic system and power in socioeconomic relationships. To decolonize the global economy, we need to acknowledge—and reject—the relationship between colonialism and capitalism. We need to engage in "border thinking," according to Escobar, and deconstruct whiteness, which I believe includes the knowledge and economic structures that maintain its power (Escobar, 2004, p. 219). In our lifetime we will not see the elimination of capitalism but we are seeing adaptive economic strategies of resistance within it. Loomba reminded us that "colonialism did not inscribe itself on a clean slate" and that there were economic relationships that existed before modern capitalism (Loomba, 1998, p. 78). Awareness of these relationships could help us to design new economies that can create the conditions that respect the humanity of all workers. Cesaire (1972, p. 22) described these economies:

> I am talking about natural economies that have been disrupted—harmonious and viable economies adapted to the indigenous population—about food crops destroyed, malnutrition permanently introduced, agricultural development oriented solely toward the benefit of the metropolitan countries, about the looting of products, the looting of raw materials.

Imperialism destroyed and interrupted the Indigenous economic systems that existed. It prevented us from knowing what was possible. Cesaire (1972, p. 23) references "communal societies," those that were not "ante-capitalist" but rather "anti-capitalist." Not wanting to romanticize these structures, one must recognize that economies thrive beyond capitalism and Indigenous economic resurgences will continue to evolve or be established. This presents a significant challenge to the ability of global capital to accumulate wealth and seize land. If global capitalism does not find ways to address the current social and economic inequalities it creates on bodies, then labour unrest will continue, historically led by those that are most disadvantaged by such capitalism. Robinson (1983, p. 205) recounted this history:

> The list, of course, should not have ended with wage slavery. It properly should also include peonage, sharecropping, tenant farming, forced labor, penal labor, and modern peasantry. Nevertheless, we must also remind ourselves that whatever the forms primitive accumulation assumed, its social harvest would also include acts of resistance, rebellion, and, ultimately, revolution. In the peripheral and semi-peripheral regions of the modern world system, at least, Gramsci's hegemonic class rule was never to be more than a momentary presence.

Dominant bodies in global capitalism also need a new economic system because, as Cesaire (1972, p. 13) explained, "Colonization works to decivilize the colonizer, to brutalize him in the true sense of the word, to degrade him, to awaken him to buried instincts, to covetousness, violence, race hatred, and moral relativism." If owning classes continue to allow for the growing gap in income and wealth, the cost of their greed will impact their human and spiritual development. Anti-colonialism asks those engaged in the anti-capitalist struggle to allow for pluriversal economic knowledges and systems that go beyond, as Grosfuguel (2012, p. 98) observes, "the logics and practices of domination and exploitation characteristic of the Eurocentered world-system" to include global capitalism.

REFERENCES

About AWA. (2015). *Agriculture Workers Alliance*. Retrieved from http://www.ufcw.ca/index. php?option=com_content&view=article&id=2003&Itemid=245&lang=en.

About CIW. (n.d.). *Coalition of Immokalee Workers*. Retrieved from *http://www.ciw-online.org/about/*

Amin, S. (2003). *Obsolescent capitalism*. New York, NY: Zed Books.

Balford, H. (2013). Kellier discusses farmworkers' behavior with Leamington mayor. *Jamaica Observer*. Retrieved from http://www.jamaicaobserver.com

Bhabha, H. K. (1994). *The location of culture*. New York, NY: Routledge.

Boesveld, S. (2013). Mayor of Leamington, Ontario, says sexual harassment from migrant workers a "cancer" on the town. *National Post*. Retrieved from http://news.nationalpost.com

Burkhalter, H. (2012). Fair food program helps end the use of slavery in tomato fields. *The Washington Post*. Retrieved from https://www.washingtonpost.com

Bush, M. (1995). *Zindabad! B.C. Farmworkers' fight for rights*. Retrieved from http://www.vcn.bc.ca/cfu/about.htm

Campbell, H. (1987). *Rasta and resistance: From Marcus Garvey to Walter Rodney*. Trenton, NJ: Africa World Press.

CBC. (2013). Leamington mayor wants "lewd" Jamaican behavior to end: John Paterson says migrant workers have been making life for Leamington women uncomfortable for years. *CBC News*. Retrieved from http://www.cbc.ca

Cesaire, A. (1972). *Discourse on colonialism*. New York, NY: Monthly Review Press.

Cox, B. (2012). Making tomato farming less brutal. *Herald-Tribune*. Retrieved from http://www.heraldtribune.com

Dei, G. J. S. (2006). Introduction: Mapping the terrain—towards a new politics of resistance. In G. J. S. Dei & A. Kempf (Eds.), *Anti-colonialism and education: The politics of resistance* (pp. 1–24). Rotterdam, the Netherlands: Sense.

Dei, G. J. S. (2015). *Unedited lecture notes anti-colonial thought: Pedagogical challenges*. Personal Collection of G. J. S. Dei, Ontario Institute for Studies in Education, Toronto, Canada.

Dei, G. J. S., & Asgharzadeh, A. (2001). The power of social theory: Towards an anti-colonial discursive framework. *Journal of Educational Thought, 35*(3), 297–323.

Dirlik, A. (1997). *The postcolonial aura: Third World criticism in the age of global capitalism*. Oxford, England: Westview Press.

Dugale, V. (2009, June–July). Migrant farmworkers organize. *Our Times: Canada's Independent Labour Magazine, 28*(3).

Escobar, A. (2004). Beyond the Third World: Imperial globality, global coloniality and anti-globalization social movements. *Third World Quarterly, 25*(1), 207–230.

Fanon, F. (1963). *The wretched of the earth*. New York, NY: Grove Press.

Grosfuguel, R. (2007). The epistemic colonial turn: Beyond political economy paradigms. *Cultural Studies, 21*(2), 211–223.

Grosfuguel, R. (2012). Decolonizing Western uni-versalisms: Decolonial pluri-versalism from Aimé Césaire to the Zapatistas. *Transmodernity: Journal of Peripheral, Cultural Production of the Luso-Hispanic World, 1*(3), 88–104.

Hall, S. (1996). When was "the post-colonial"? Thinking at the limit. In I. Chambers & L. Curti (Eds.), *The postcolonial question* (pp. 242–259). London, England: Routledge.

Henry, F., & Tator, C. (2006). *The colour of democracy: Racism in Canadian society* (3rd ed.). Toronto, Canada: Nelson.

hooks, b. (2004). *We real cool: Black men and masculinity*. New York, NY: Routledge.

Justicia for Migrant Workers. (2013, September 3). Open letter to the mayor of Leamington John Patterson over recent comments on 'Jamaican' migrant workers [Tumblr post]. Retrieved from http://j4mw.tumblr.com/post/60232699417/open-letter-to-the-mayor-of-leamington-john

Leamington (municipality of). (2014). About Leamington. Retrieved from http://www.leamington.ca/en/discover/aboutleamington.asp

Loomba, A. (1998). *Colonialism/postcolonialism*. London, England: Routledge.

Makin, K. (2011). Farmworkers have no right to unionize, top court rules. *The Globe and Mail*. Retrieved from http://www.theglobeandmail.com

McIntosh, M. (1989, Winter). White privilege: Unpacking the invisible knapsack. *Independent School, 31–36*.

Movement for the Survival of the Ogoni People Canada (MOSOP Canada). (n.d.). The story of the movement for survival of the Ogoni people. Retrieved from http://www.mosopcanada.org/story.php

Myrie, E. (2013). Myrie: Jamaican workers owed an apology. *The Hamilton Spectator*. Retrieved from http://www.thespec.com

Nicholas, T. (1996). *Rastafari: A way of life*. Chicago, IL: Frontline Distribution International.

Notice of assertion. (2012). *Caldwell First Nation*. Retrieved from http://caldwellfirstnation.ca/notice-of-assertion-2/

Parry, B. (1995). Problems in current theories of colonial discourse. In B. Ashcroft, G. Griffiths, & H. Thiophene (Eds.), *The post-colonial studies reader* (pp. 36–44). New York, NY: Routledge.

Patterson, B. (2015, February 15). Council of Canadians opposes Harper's "four and four" rule for migrant workers [Web blog post]. Retrieved from http://canadians.org/blog/council-canadians-opposes-harpers-four-and-four-rule-migrant-workers

Patwardhan, A., & Munro, J. (Producers), & Patwardhan, A., & Munro, J. (Directors). (1982). *A time to rise* [Motion picture]. Canada: National Film Board of Canada.

Persaud, R. B. (2001). *Counter-hegemony and foreign policy: The dialectics and global forces in Jamaica*. Albany, NY: SUNY Press.

Rios, K. (2011, January 18). After a long fight, farmworkers in Florida win an increase in pay. *The New York Times*. Retrieved from http://www.nytimes.com; see also http://www.nesri.org/news/2011/01/the-new-york-times-after-long-fight-farmworkers-in-florida-win-an-increase-in-pay

Robinson, C. J. (1983). *Black Marxism: The making of the black radical tradition*. Chapel Hill: University of North Carolina Press.

Sahoye, J. (2014). Mayor blasted for insensitive comments about Jamaicans. *The Caribbean Camera*. Retrieved from http://www.thecaribbeancamera.com

Smith, A. (2006). Heteropatriarchy and the three pillars of white supremacy. In INCITE! Women of Color Against Violence (Ed.), *The color of violence: The INCITE! anthology* (pp. 66–73). Boston, MA: South End Press.

United Food and Commercial Workers (UFCW). (2011). *The status of migrant farmworkers in Canada 2010–2011*. Toronto, Canada.

Zeleza, T. (1997). Fictions of the postcolonial: A review article. *CODESRIA Bulletin, 2*, 15–19.

CHAPTER TWELVE

Awanduni (Resistance)

A Process of Indigeneity and Decolonization—(Re)identification and Cultural Revival of the Garifuna in St. Vincent and the Diaspora

REBEKAH TANNIS-JOHNSON

History teaches us that, in certain circumstances, it is quite easy for a stranger to impose his rule on a people. But history equally teaches us that, whatever the material aspects of that rule, it cannot be sustained except by the permanent and organized repression of the cultural life of the people in question. It can only firmly entrench itself if it physically destroys a significant part of the domi- nated people [culture].
  —AMILCAR CABRAL, "NATIONAL LIBERATION AND CULTURE" (1974, P. 12)

The history of the Garifuna is filled with struggles for their survival, land, cul- ture and, ultimately, their rights. Indeed, the Garifuna people have faced a great battle, dating back to their *yurumein* (homeland) of St. Vincent, the largest of the thirty-two islands making up St. Vincent and the Grenadines, in which they faced the imposition of both the British and the French. This ultimately resulted in their forced displacement and exile from St. Vincent and forced migration to Central America—notably, Belize, Honduras and Nicaragua. A third migration occurred from Central America to U.S. coastal regions, including New York City, Los Angeles and other major cities (England, 1999, p. 7). As the chapter's epi- graph captures clearly, the sentiments of resistance, survival and (re)identification are integral to an anti-colonial response. Garifuna Indigeneity is an embodiment of identity and a process of survival and resistance against those that attempted to permanently repress their culture. Not only is culture a significant part of one's life, it also speaks to one's identity. Culture and identity are symbiotic and are par- ticularly important concepts in anti-colonial theorizing. Situating Indigeneity in anti-colonial theorizing is a process that encompasses culture and identity through the politics of reclaiming and resistance. As this chapter's epigraph conveys, a colonial tactic is to go to the very heart of a person or group to directly suppress their identity, their culture. Yet, as the Garifuna peoples demonstrate, resistance comes by fighting against these colonial tactics through a process of Indigeneity.

The forced migration of the Garifuna led to their complex diasporic journeys. Through this migration and resulting diasporic position, their struggle to maintain and preserve Garifuna culture continues to the present day. Garifuna culture is maintained by transnational networks of kinship, economic exchange, grassroots organizations and the movement of Garifuna transmigrants between the United States, Central America and St. Vincent (England, 1999, p. 7). The preservation of Garifuna culture, especially in their diasporic locations of Honduras, New York and Los Angeles, is maintained and nourished through the continuation of Garinagu religion, culture and language even as they fight for their identity in their respective diasporic locations. This discussion takes into account the survival, resurgence, resistance and (re)identification of Garifuna culture in St. Vincent as well as the diasporic locations of New York, Los Angeles, Honduras and Belize. Through the lens of language, culture and the law, this analysis looks at the struggles that still exist to preserve the Indigeneity of Garifuna peoples against colonial forces. Within this discussion, the terms "Garifuna," "Garinagu," "Carib" and "Black Carib" are at times used interchangeably to illustrate the complexity of identity, as these terms, although sometimes contested, signify multiple meanings of identity that are never fixed or static.

It is important to locate myself within this discussion. My ancestral background is rooted in St. Vincent. My parents were born in St. Vincent and the Grenadines, my father in Kingstown and my mother in Bequia, a smaller island that is part of the Grenadines. I identify St. Vincent as my homeland, because for me home is not where I physically reside but where my spirit and heart feel most at peace. Although I was born in Canada, my upbringing was as much as possible a transplanted version of a Vincentian life in all its aspects. Throughout their diasporic journeys, my parents took earnest metaphorical steps never to leave their "home," regardless of where they physically resided. It is not just the land, the water and the air of St. Vincent that makes it home, but the people, the cultural memories, oral histories, traditions and family that live on and are alive wherever we physically reside.

The discussion speaks to a conversation of decolonization and anti-colonial responses that are situated within the Caribbean. The discussion is often tied to North American contexts. The dialogue of anti-colonial and decolonization responses can only be enriched by conversations that are rooted in the Caribbean, thus illustrating the complexities and commonalities that exist when interrogating a variety of worldviews. The discussion starts with a historical overview of what transpired within St. Vincent and the Garifuna people, leading to a discussion of diasporic journeys, resistance, re-identification and revival viewed through the lens of culture, language and the law. A discussion of cultural memory in relation to decolonization to illustrate the continual process of Indigeneity and future possibilities follows.

EXILE, DISPLACEMENT AND MIGRATION— HISTORICAL OVERVIEW

The Treaty of Paris (1763) was a pivotal moment in the history of St. Vincent. As a part of the terms of the treaty, St. Vincent was ceded to the British (Kirby & Martin, 2004, p. 4). The British tried to secure St. Vincent as a sugar colony (Gonzalez, 1988, p. 39). Between 1764 and 1770, the British made attempts to force the removal of Caribs from their land, and it was during this period that the British surveyed and mapped the island of St. Vincent (Gonzalez, 1988, p. 39). The 1795–1796 Carib Wars, a result of the continual advances on Carib land, were a response and illustration of resistance to the cruelties suffered by the Carib peoples of St. Vincent. The ending of the Second Carib War in 1796 occurred when the Caribs of St. Vincent were overpowered by the forces of General Abercrombie (Marshall, 1973), resulting in the Caribs' removal from the island. As historical documents illustrate, as early as 1772 plans for removing Caribs from the island of St. Vincent existed, as indicated by a letter from the Earl of Hillsborough to the governor of St. Vincent:

> If necessity demand the removal of charibbs you do take up such vessels as can be procured, to serve as transports for the conveyance of them to some unfrequented part of the coast of Africa, or to some desert island adjacent thereto, care being taken that they be treated on the voyage with every degree of humanity their situation will admit of, and whatsoever may be judged necessary to subsist them for a reasonable time, and such tools and implements as may enable them to provide for their future subsistence. (cited in Gonzalez, 1988, p. 19)

On April 11, 1797, the Garifuna people were forcibly exiled to the island of Roatan, off the coast of Honduras (Gonzalez, 1988, p. 39). What occurred following their arrival on the island of Roatan is contested, but it is clear that extremely different conditions existed from those of their homeland, St. Vincent. Gonzalez (1988, p. 41) writes that

> the future must have seemed perilous for the survivors at that point. Many were ill, most had lost close relatives and loved ones, they were far from familiar territory, and the supplies left for them are inadequate and in poor condition. The British clearly expected the Caribs to recreate a life style similar to the one they had left behind to be based on agriculture, fishing and mercenary soldering, plus odd bits of trading and wage labour.

The conditions in Roatan made it difficult for the Garifuna to continue their lives after they were forcibly removed from St. Vincent. The conditions that existed were not only different but also rendered survival unattainable. Although the Caribs' life on Roatan was temporary, it was a struggle for survival and an important part of the Carib journey. After Roatan, the Garifuna people would migrate to Mexico, Nicaragua, Belize, other Central American countries and the United States.

GARIFUNA WITHIN THE UNITED STATES, HONDURAS AND BELIZE—ANTI-COLONIAL RESPONSES THROUGH CULTURE, LANGUAGE AND THE LAW

There has been a prolonged discussion and focus in the past regarding the Garinagu culture of Indigenous peoples that has transformed from their homeland of St. Vincent to their present struggles for land and culture in their respective diasporic locations (England, 1999, p. 13). Cultural survival and the continuation of Garifuna culture are important for the Garifuna throughout the diaspora. Garifuna celebrations such as the Jankunu, the ceremonial event of Dugu and the yearly anniversary celebration of their transnational forced migrations demonstrate cultural survival. There is a deep connection to their place of origin without residing there, or even having the possibility of returning. In this sense, the concept of border crossing captures the experiences of the Garifuna, particularly the understanding of Giroux's (1992, p. 18) "individual identity and cultural subjectivity." In this understanding, individual identity is in constant conversation with cultural agency and personhood. There is a "politics that links human suffering with a project of possibility" (Giroux, 1992, p. 18). There is an interconnected relationship in which one informs the other. The border intellectual or border crosser speaks to the idea that one is homeless, in the sense that there is a constant shifting of identity that embodies resistance and allows for the possibility of change and alternatives to hegemonic forces (Giroux, 1992, p. 17). In this understanding, "home" is not simply a location and land, static or fixed; "home" encompasses cultural and social spaces and sites of resistance that go against hegemony. This understanding of "home" can be grounded in cultural, social and political contexts. It is always changing and so its fluidity informs individuals and groups (Giroux, 1992, pp. 17–18). As Giroux states and clearly defines:

> As a border intellectual, he constantly reexamines and raises questions about what kind of borders are being crossed and revisited, what kind of identities are being remade and refigured within new historical, social and political borderlands, and what effects such crossings have for redefining pedagogical practice. (Giroux, 1992, p. 20)

Thinking about this understanding of home and homelessness in the context of the Garifuna and resisting the notion of a static or fixed resistance requires us to understand how their diasporic journeys are shifting and resisting colonial forces. The Garifuna in their respective diasporic locations embody the concepts of home and homelessness, seeing and living the interconnected relationship between identity, culture, politics and space.

The annual Garifuna Bicentennial Celebration in La Ceiba, Honduras, highlights the transnational diaspora of the Garifuna and is an example of how cultural survival has been maintained through grassroots organizations. Organized by the Garifuna organizations in the United States and Central America, and including international participants (England, 1999, p. 13), it is a weeklong event that celebrates the Afro-Indigenous culture, with a focus on issues of racial discrimination, economic exploitation and political marginalization (England, 1999, p. 8). The event highlights the fact that the Garifuna are still dealing with issues that impede their cultural survival and Indigenous rights.

Another example of the preservation of Garifuna culture through the diaspora can be seen in Los Angeles. Linda Miller Matthei and David Smith examined the Garifuna community in Los Angeles on the annual Garifuna Settlement Day, another example of the preservation of culture. On this day, men and women of the community participate in songs, dances and traditions of the Garifuna culture (Matthei & Smith, 2008, p. 219). Beyond Settlement Day, the Garifuna have organized a variety of associations in South Central Los Angeles that focus on instilling pride among Garifuna youth by teaching them the Garifuna history, language, traditional songs, dances and drumming (Matthei & Smith, 2008, p. 220). Cultural preservation in this sense is also generational as it helps the continuation of culture.

As in Los Angeles, transmigration organizations in New York City are created at the grassroots, level and they help fund projects such as the restoration and construction of churches and schools that focus on Garifuna culture (Anderson, 2009, p. 145). The actions of grassroots organizations illustrate that their efforts and resistance will not necessarily be recognized or validated by the state, but instead through the actions of the people for the people. Teaching and encouraging children ensures that the history lives on. The activities in Honduras, Los Angeles and New York City demonstrate the far-ranging importance of Garifuna culture and its preservation. Community is synonymous with "home of origin, dwelling, and return … it is a privileged locus of Garifuna identity, language and culture. Garifuna affirm community as the site for the reproduction of tradition" (Anderson, 2009, p. 45).

Finally, within Belize, struggles of cultural and religious continuity are evident from generation to generation. The fight to preserve culture, language and religious practices is a central issue for Garifuna children, as they are the key to continuing Garifuna culture. Dangriga is a multilingual and multiethnic town in Belize populated by Garinagu, Belizean Creoles and both native-born and for-eign-born Spanish speakers (Bonner, 2001, p. 81). Focusing on the shame that is attached to the Garifuna language, its instruction and use by Garifuna children both in and out of schools, Bonner's case study reveals that discrimination and colonial stereotypes still exist to hinder the preservation of the Garifuna language.

> Colonial-era stereotypes in Belize held the Garinagu to be a "savage" group whose prac-tices and rituals were both foreign and primitive. These negative associations still adhere to Garifuna identities. Perhaps for this reason, Garinagus have tended to live in ethnically homogenous settlements; however, in the case of Dangriga, what was once an ethnically homogenous locale is now a multiethnic town whose population reflects the diversity of Belize as a whole. (Bonner, 2001, p. 81)

Bonner examined the struggles that existed in preserving the Garifuna language in Belize. A member of the local community spoke about this difficulty and wor-ried about the disappearance of the language: "It's sad the children don't speak it because it's a beautiful language. That language is from a long time ago. It's about history. If the language stops, what will happen to the history?" (Bonner, 2001, p. 82). This sentiment illustrates the importance and significance of preserving Garifuna language, part of the history of a people that will continue through gen-erations. Many of the members of the local community identified ties between language and culture for the Garifuna. One individual states:

> 'Speaking a distinct native language offers Garinagu sound power and pride ... the knowl-edge that our people developed a language all our own, just like the English and Span-ish.' Indeed, throughout a history of exclusion from nationalist discourse and positions of power, the uniqueness of Garifuna culture and the Garifuna language has been a source of pride for Garinagu. (Bonner, 2001, p. 82)

Although it is important to acknowledge the initiatives of grassroots organiza-tions, community events and celebrations, struggle and conflict remain. Moreover, it is difficult to qualify and quantify everyday forms of resistance.

These subtle practices speak to the everyday nuances that make up resis-tance—as resistance cannot be solely seen as mainstream. It cannot seek legiti-macy or validation from the dominant forces. In thinking through resistance and the forms of resistance, the questions that arise are: How must we read resistance? What constitutes resistance in anti-colonial responses, and who determines this? The answers are complex, as resistance cannot be validated or determined by oth-ers. Resistance can be read as the "work" done against colonial forces in whatever shape or form it takes. It is a conscious effort to work against colonial forces as an act of an anti-colonial response.

Although this discussion outlines several community events and celebrations, it is difficult to pinpoint other, everyday forms of resistance, which may be subtle or even subversive. Focusing on events and celebrations is problematic as it "avoids any depiction of threatening difference in spiritual practices and beliefs, focusing instead on the now familiar trinity of food, music and which can be seen as consumable culture" (Anderson, 2009, p. 145). This focus on "consumable culture" does not reflect or address the continual, everyday struggles of Indigenous rights and cultural preservation faced by the Garifuna in St. Vincent and throughout the diaspora. Moreover, this focus romanticizes the Garifuna struggle, deflecting from the larger picture of decolonization and the process of Indigeneity. The question is not whether these acts constitute forms of resistance, but how they can transform or be the start of anti-colonial politics against colonial forces. It is clear that these actions speak to a transformation of the past, but more work needs to be done. "[B]y focusing on 'everyday' acts of resurgence, one disrupts the colonial physical, social and political boundaries designed to impede our actions to restore our nationhood" (Corntassel, 2012, p. 88).

ANTI-COLONIAL RESPONSES THROUGH THE LENS OF LAW

Legal contestation of Indigeneity and Indigenous claims is another form of resistance. This is particularly the case for the Garifuna of Honduras and other Latin American Garifuna diasporic locations.

> The politics of Garifuna identity in Honduras disrupts straightforward distinctions between blackness and indigeneity. The Honduran version of multiculturalism represents perhaps the clearest case in Latin America, where indigenous and black populations have become "recognized" ethnic subjects with an equivalent institutional status. (Anderson, 2009, p. 145)

Moreover, Anderson (2009, p. 109) argues that "Honduras is one of the many countries that has taken up the mantle of multiculturalism and redrawn laws to recognize 'ethnic rights.'" During the 1990s, Latin American states attempted to institute constitutional and legal reforms that would establish collective rights for ethnic groups, including, and most prominently, Indigenous peoples (Anderson, 2009, p. 145). This triggered the ever-present questions of who can claim Indigeneity, or who is Indigenous and how is this qualified? Furthermore, how do such steps speak to an understanding of decolonization, if at all? Institutions such as the World Council of Indigenous Peoples and, in the context of the Caribbean, the Caribbean Organization of Indigenous Peoples (COIP), whose members are Belize, Dominica, St. Vincent, Suriname, Puerto Rico and Trinidad and Tobago, have had legal issues regarding these questions. The politics of recognition as discussed by Glen Coulthard (2007) is an integral part of this conversation, particularly in the context of nationhood, land and overall rights of Indigeneity. At times, the latter issues are relegated to legal definitions and understandings framed and recognized by the state. Although discussed within a Canadian context, it is helpful to think of Indigenous and Indigeneity within a global context. Moreover, it is important to read these arguments in conversation with a Caribbean context, as there are parallels that exist.

Coulthard (2007, p. 439) contends the language of recognition forces Indigenous peoples to identify with one-sided forms of recognition that are granted by the colonial forces of the state, thus imposing the very colonial forces they are trying to go beyond.

> The increase in recognition demands made by Indigenous and other marginalized minorities over the last three decades has prompted a surge of intellectual production which has sought to unpack the ethical, political and legal significance of these types of claims. (Coulthard, 2007, p. 438)

Recognition becomes a matter of state acknowledgement, one that can be problematic at times. This is reflected in the historical struggle of the legal definition of the Garinagu as Indigenous by Central American states, as discussed by England (1999, p. 8):

> Garifuna leaders referred to the group as autocthonous to the Americas. They pointed to the long-standing legal definition of the Garinagu as Indigenous by Central American states, and the current alliance of Garifuna grassroots organizations with indigenous organizations struggling for rights to territory, cultural autonomy, and economic development as ethnic nations within nation-states. At these moments, leaders stressed the importance of Garifuna villages in Central America as the homeland, as a territory occupied "ancestrally" that must be defended and maintained as the economic and cultural base of the Garifuna people.

The Garifuna have actively resisted this struggle, implementing strategies to deal with these issues to defend their rights against the colonial forces of the state. The use of United Nations and grassroots organizations to address the state enforcement of international accords, including the United Nations Declaration on the Rights of Indigenous Peoples, whether encompassing issues of legal definition or cultural preservation and land rights, demonstrates the struggle for recognition (England, 1999, p. 8). What the Garifuna peoples are resisting and fighting for is sovereignty, forming a "Garifuna Nation" with their fragmented diasporic locations. Considering the future possibilities for the Garifuna people, the Garifuna organizers of the Bicentennial celebration discuss the forms of resistance at play:

> Garinagu constitute a single ethnic "nation" unified by their common language, culture and origins in St. Vincent—despite their current geographical dispersion and fragmented citizenships. Leaders referred to St. Vincent as the homeland from which the Garinagu have been exiled and as the territorial base of their culture, race and identity. This diasporic

politics emphasizes the historical reality of displacement, exile, mobility and multiple communities but also the possibility that Garifuna Diaspora may be reunited across nation-state borders as the Garifuna Nation, not through literal re-inhabitation of St. Vincent but rather through consciousness of constituting one people and reconnection to an authentic cultural origin. (England, 1999, p. 8)

There is an embracing of their diasporic locations and a call that speaks to decolonization—an anti-colonial response that sees sovereignty and nationhood, as separate from the state. The call of decolonization and Indigeneity sees unification through culture and language and speaks to the possibilities that can be fostered even with their fragmented locations. In this sense, the politics of the diaspora speaks to the possibilities of mobility, unity and nationhood that is a conscious (re) identification with their culture, language, identity and land, both in physical and mental senses. This sentiment illustrates that the starting place of resistance begins with the mind and transforms outwards to a politics of action. Possibilities form by building collectivities, such as the Garifuna Nation, that transform into sites for realizing hopes and dreams. Recalling the "imagined communities" concept proposed by Benedict Anderson (1983), there are possibilities for the Garifuna peoples to reimagine community, nationhood and nation building. Anderson discusses how communities are not necessarily "born" but are imagined into being. Following this logic, for the Garifuna nationhood is a reimagining of community, of a Garifuna nation. It is arguable whether "nation" is used in the same sense as the state, or as a term that signifies unity, solidarity and possibilities for the future. Moreover, an understanding of "nation" can be problematic if there is the involvement of the state, possibly diminishing the call of decolonization. However, this use of "nation" as an organizing construct seems to be only one aspect of decolonization, not the end goal. How, then, do we reconcile, if at all, the modern state with the anti-colonial responses and creations of re-imagined communities and nationhood? It is a loaded question, one that requires an analysis of both previous and future understandings of communities and nationhood.

Decolonization occurred in 1979 when St. Vincent became independent from Britain (Ginio & Schler, 2010, p. 7). Seeing decolonization as mainly the process of building independent nations diminishes and minimizes new possibilities and contemporary possibilities (Ginio & Schler, 2010, p. 9). As history has shown us, the story does not end with an official decolonization date. It is just the beginning. Resistance and resurgence go beyond national borders and reside in the actions, spirits, resilience and hearts of people who are united in solidarity. Decolonization, in this sense, occurs at the sites of change in the political and psychological realms. As Ginio and Schler (2010, p. 10) write, "Decolonization is accomplished not at the moment the colonizer is expelled, but rather when the colonized decide that they can do without their ruler, when they stop their addiction to dependence on the colonizer." The importance of decolonization is not simply a date, but the actions, the transformations and shifts that occur on varying levels. Moreover, as is the case with the Garifuna, decolonization has no end date; it is a continual process, just as Indigeneity is a continual process. The two are intertwined.

The resurgence and (re)identification with the Garinagu language within St. Vincent and throughout the diaspora is an integral element of decolonization. This resurgence and (re)identification can be understood through what is known as cultural memory. Anh Hua, writing in her text "Diaspora and Cultural Memory," discusses the interconnection between diasporic journeys and identity, and how they come to shape one's cultural memory. "Those living in the diaspora have a double perspective: they acknowledge an earlier existence elsewhere and have a critical relationship with the cultural politics of their present home—all embedded within the experience of displacement" (Hua, 2005, p. 195). For the Garifuna, the connection between forced exile and displacement is central to an understanding of one's cultural understandings. Collective memories of what is perceived as the "homeland" are manifested through the experience of diasporic journeys (Hua, 2005). Understanding decolonization in its nuanced forms, as is the case with the Garifuna, requires us to consider that decolonization is shaped by diasporic identities, communities and the identities shaped by their "homeland." Thinking of diasporic communities and their cultural memories requires us to understand that they are not fixed, homogenous or rigid, but evolving, fluid and changing (Hua, 2005, p. 193). Decolonization then in this sense is twofold: comprising the identities of diasporic locations and those of the "home." Similarly, Indigeneity is changing, adapting and fluidly embodying multiple histories and cultural memories. Here, it is important to consider how we can avoid notions of hybridity that minimize and ignore the complexities and multiple situated identities. Hybridity in this sense is the practice that is embedded in universalism and essentialism of identities rather than a sense of hybridity that embraces complexities, contradictions and ambiguities that inform and shape identities. In order to avoid the liminal spaces that can be created and developed within historical and colonial contexts, an anti-colonial response and the call of decolonization should embody difference. Considering the context of the Garifuna, there needs to be an understanding that within collective memories, cultural memories and identity there exist differences, contradictions, complexities and tensions that do not take away from an anti-colonial response; instead, these serve as acknowledgments of differences in power and the materiality of varying existences and identities.

CONCLUSION

The Garifuna language and culture, along with their historical significance, are vital to the Garifuna people, illustrating a sense of pride and ensuring that the history of their people will be continued through generations having come from a history of exclusion and struggle. Language is the foremost way of ensuring the continuation and preservation of culture. Here, Corntassel's (2012, p. 89) "peoplehood model" offers a provocative way to read resistance, resurgence and (re) identification of Garifuna people. This model provides an understanding that the personal informs the collective, and both facets take place where resurgences occur. Moreover, it is important to understand the complexities of resurgence and its interconnection with the spiritual, political, social and linguistic aspects that are deeply tied to the "homeland," oral histories and ceremonies. It is through these practices, what he calls "renewals" of these elements, that the foundations of resurgence are built (Corntassel, 2012, p. 89). "These daily acts of renewal, whether through prayer, speaking your language, honoring your ancestors, etc., are the foundations of resurgence" (Corntassel, 2012, p. 89).

It is clear through these examples that Indigeneity is a reclaiming through resurgence and re-identifying using the facets of culture, language and the law.

> Being Indigenous today means struggling to reclaim and regenerate one's relational, place-based existence by challenging the ongoing, destructive forces of colonization. Whether through ceremony or through other ways that Indigenous peoples (re)connect to the natural world, processes of resurgence are often contentious and reflect the spiritual, cultural, economic, social and political scope of the struggle. (Corntassel, 2012, p. 88)

It is a reclaiming of Indigenous culture that becomes a part of one's life—(re)identification of one's identity that is central to who one is as a human being.

The importance of reframing anti-colonial theory and practice is central to this discussion. The Garifuna exhibit the complexities and nuanced forms of an anti-colonial response through practices of culture, religion, language, identity and other facets. What can be gleaned from this discussion is that there is not one right way to take an anti-colonial and decolonization stance. Multiple, complex and varying practices are required. The Garifuna have gone through (and still are) living a history filled with struggles, exclusion, exile, displacement and migration. Through this journey the Garifuna have made—and continue to make—concerted efforts to create a resurgence, (re)identification and revival of their culture, religion and language within St. Vincent and throughout their diaspora. Their diasporic journey has taken them across nation borders from Central America to the United States and back to St. Vincent. Through this all, there is a deep sense of connection to their *yurumein* (homeland) of St. Vincent. It is because of this that community-building Garifuna events and daily cultural practices continue to foster a connection amongst peoples. The survival and preservation of Garifuna culture, language and religion require the strength of the individuals who fight for their identity and maintain what rightfully belongs to them. The voices of the unheard, the unseen and the colonized create their own histories and a re-envisioning of possibilities for the future. Thinking about the pursuits of resistance and cultural preservation, I am reminded of the following powerful Garifuna proverb:

Luagu lidise wéibugu wasandirei lihürü wanügü.
(It is as we proceed on our journey that we feel the weight of our burdens.)

REFERENCES

Anderson, B. R. O'G. (1983). *Imagined communities: Reflections on the origin and spread of nationalism.* London, England: Verso.

Anderson, M. (2007). *When Afro becomes (like) Indigenous: Garifuna and Afro indigenous politics in Honduras.* Berkeley: University of California Press.

Anderson, M. (2009). *Black and Indigenous: Garifuna activism and consumer culture in Honduras.* Minneapolis: University of Minnesota Press.

Bonner, D. M. (2001). Garifuna children's language shame: Ethnic stereotypes, national affiliation, and transnational immigration as factors in language choice in Southern Belize. *Language in Society, 30*(1), 81–96.

Cabral, A. (1974). National liberation and culture. *Transition, 45,* 12–17.

Corntassel, J. (2003). Who is Indigenous? "Peoplehood" and ethnonationalist approaches to rearticulating Indigenous identity. *Nationalism and Ethnic Politics, 9*(1), 75–100.

Corntassel, J. (2012). Re-envisioning resurgence: Indigenous pathways to decolonization and sustainable self-determination. *Decolonization: Indigeneity, Education & Society, 1*(1), 86–101.

Coulthard, G. S. (2007). Subjects of empire: Indigenous peoples and the "politics of recognition" in Canada. *Contemporary Political Theory, 6*(4), 437–460.

England, S. (1999). Negotiating race and place in the Garifuna diaspora: Identity formation and transnational grassroots in politics in New York City and Honduras. *Identities, 6*(1), 5–53.

Ginio, R., & Schler, L. (2010). Decolonization reconsidered: Rebirths, continuities and erasures. *Hagar, 9*(2), 2–12.

Giroux, H. A. (1992). Paulo Freire and the politics of postcolonialism. *Journal of Advanced Composition, 12*(1), 15–25.

Gonzalez, N. (1988). *Sojourners of the Caribbean: Ethnogenesis and ethnohistory of the Garifuna.* Champaign: University of Illinois Press.

Hua, A. (2005). Diaspora and cultural memory. In V. Agnew (Ed.), *Diaspora, memory and identity: A search for home* (pp. 191–208). Toronto, Canada: University of Toronto Press.

Kirby, I. E., & Martin, C. I. (2004). *The rise and fall of the Black Caribs (Garifuna).* Toronto, Canada: Cybercom.

Marshall B. (1973). The Black Caribs—native resistance to British penetration into the windward side of St. Vincent (1763–1773). *Caribbean Quarterly, 19*(4), 4–17.

Matthei, L., & Smith, D. (2008). Flexible ethnic identity, adaption, survival, resistance: The Garifuna in the world system. *Social Identities, 14*(2), 215–232.

Contributors

Muna-Udbi Abdulkadir Ali is a Ph.D. student in Curriculum Studies and Teacher Development, with a specialization in Comparative International and Development Education, at the Ontario Institute for Studies in Education of the University of Toronto. Her work experience includes working for the Ministry of Justice and Religious Affairs of Puntland and the United Nations Development Programme within the Somali Territories.

Annette Bazira-Okafor is pursuing a doctoral degree in the Department of Social Justice Education and International Development Education, Ontario Institute for Studies in Education, University of Toronto. Her research interests include hip hop and popular culture among African youth, African youth and women in the diaspora, representations of African youth and women in the media and film, anti-racism education, development education and Indigenous knowledges.

Mischa Berlin is currently pursuing a M.Ed. in the Department of Social Justice Education at the Ontario Institute for Studies in Education. Mischa grew up in downtown Toronto, and completed a B.A. degree at McGill University, where he studied Middle Eastern Studies and Philosophy. Mischa is interested in exploring questions of race and power in neo-liberal educational contexts. How knowledge production and colonial epistemologies obscure race and marginality in spaces of institutional learning is a topic of specific interest.

Christopher L. Cully is an Educator in the Greater Toronto Area and an M.A. candidate in the Department of Social Justice Education at the Ontario

Institute for Studies in Education of the University of Toronto. Before studying at the University of Toronto, Christopher earned two B.A. degrees at McMaster University in History and English, respectively, and a B.Ed. from the University of Ontario Institute of Technology. Christopher's research interests include anarchism, anti-colonialism, critical indigenous studies, critical pedagogy and education.

George J. Sefa Dei (Ph.D., University of Toronto) is a tenured Full Professor in the Department of Social Justice Education at the Ontario Institute for Studies in Education of the University of Toronto. He is also the Director for the Centre for Integrative Anti-Racism Studies at OISE, University of Toronto.

Suleyman M. Demi is an environmental activist and educator whose research interests include environmental sustainability, social and environmental justice, food security and Indigenous knowledge and philosophy. He holds a B.Sc. (Agric.) and M.Phil. (Agric. Administration) from the University of Ghana and an M.A. (Social Justice Education and Environment and Health) from the University of Toronto. Most recently, Suleyman was the proud recipient of the Green Saver Alastair Fairweather Memorial Award in the Environment (2014–2015) from the School of the Environment, University of Toronto, where he continues to pursue a Ph.D. in Social Justice Education and Environmental Studies.

Chizoba Imoka is a second-year doctoral student at the Ontario Institute for Studies in Education of the University of Toronto and the founder of Unveiling Africa—a non-profit organization providing a platform for young Africans to become involved in political advocacy, community mobilizing and community service. Chizoba's research interests include educational change in Africa, youth engagement for social change, inclusive education and democratic nation building.

Cristina Jaimungal is a Ph.D. student in the Department of Social Justice Education and Comparative, International, and Development Education (CIDE) at the Ontario Institute for Studies in Education of the University of Toronto. Anchored in anti-colonial research methods, anti-racism studies and critical language theory, her research interests examine the racial politics embedded in the project of English language education. Jaimungal holds a B.A. with Honours in English and Professional Writing from York University and an M.A. in Curriculum, Teaching, and Learning with a specialization in Comparative, International, and Development Education at the Ontario Institute for Studies in Education.

Meredith Lordan (Ph.D., University of Toronto) is an Instructor at the University of Toronto and Ryerson University. As a member of the UN Education Caucus, her research and advocacy efforts support increased access to education.

Emily A. Moorhouse is an M.A. candidate in the Department of Social Justice Education at the Ontario Institute for Studies in Education of the University of Toronto. Her thesis uses anti-colonial and feminist methodologies to examine how minority mixed-race women in Canada understand, negotiate and resist conceptualizations of "mixed race," exoticism, colonialism and anti-blackness.

Stacey Papernick graduated from the Ontario Institute for Studies in Education with an M.Ed. from the Department of Leadership, Higher and Adult Education in June 2015. Her studies focus on union and workplace learning within the labour movement and health care sector. She brings a critique to her work that is rooted in an intersectional analysis of oppression, with a particular focus on race and politics that are committed to social and economic change. Stacey has been a member of a trade union since 1995 and has worked within organized labour since 1997. She is currently working as a union staff representative at the Ontario Nurses' Association. In this role she focuses her efforts on leadership development, education and organizing. Beyond her work within the union she contributes to social movements focused on anti-racism and workers' rights struggles.

Yessica D. Rostan is a Uruguayan-born immigrant to Turtle Island who is inspired by the resilience and creativity of community builders in Toronto, Uruguay and around the world. As a community educator and lifelong learner, she facilitates youth programs in high schools, community centres and social spaces that focus on self and community empowerment, peace building, conflict transformation and collaboratively imagining and creating sustainable futures. She is also a drummer, a pianist and a writer, with a passion for individual and community art as a way to connect, re-imagine and co-create our worlds.

Rebekah L. Tannis-Johnson is a graduate of the Master of Education Program, Ontario Institute for Studies in Education of the University of Toronto, obtaining her degree in Social Justice Education.

umar umangay is a doctoral student at the Ontario Institute for Studies in Education of the University of Toronto. Current research interests involve the decolonization of education research practices in the area of teacher education/training, and the related development of an activity theory of Indigenous-centred education models.